Look Closer

Suburban Narratives and American Values in Film and Television

DAVID R. COON

RUTGERS UNIVERSITY PRESS

NEW BRUNSWICK, NEW JERSEY, AND LONDON

LIBRARY OF CONGRESS CATALOGING-IN-PUBLICATION DATA

Coon, David R., 1974–
    Look closer : suburban narratives and American values in film and television /
David R. Coon.
        p. cm.
    Includes bibliographical references and index.
    ISBN 978–0–8135–6208–7 (hardcover : alk. paper) – ISBN 978–0–8135–6207–0
(pbk. : alk. paper) — ISBN 978–0–8135–6209–4 (e-book)
    1. Suburban life in motion pictures.   2. United States—In motion pictures.
3. Suburban life on television. 4. United States—On television.   I. Title.
    PN1995.9.S74C66 2013
    791.43'62—dc23   2013005971

A British Cataloging-in-Publication record for this book is available from the
British Library.

Copyright © 2014 by David R. Coon

Visit our Web site: http://rutgerspress.rutgers.edu

Manufactured in the United States of America

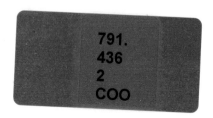

CONTENTS

Acknowledgments　　　　　　vii

Introduction: Welcome to the Neighborhood　　　　　1

1　Traditional Values: Nostalgia and Self-Reflexivity
in Visual Representations of Suburbia　　　　　30

2　Back Yard Fences: The Public, the Private,
and the Family in Suburban Dramas　　　　　69

3　Suburban Citizenship: Defining Community through
the Exclusion of Racial and Sexual Minorities　　　　　103

4　Desperate Husbands: The Crisis of Hegemonic
Masculinity in Post-9/11 Suburbia　　　　　141

5　Protecting the Suburban Lifestyle:
Consumption, Crime, and the American Dream　　　　　179

Conclusion: There Goes the Neighborhood　　　　　212

Notes　　　　　235
Index　　　　　257

ACKNOWLEDGMENTS

I am a product of suburbia. I grew up in Upper Arlington, Ohio, a first-ring suburb just northwest of downtown Columbus. It was here that I first experienced all the benefits and drawbacks of suburbia and ultimately developed a fascination with this strangely complicated aspect of the American landscape. The inspiration for this book is rooted somewhere in my suburban upbringing, and therefore I must thank the entire city of Upper Arlington and all its residents, past and present, for their unintentional contributions to this project.

I would also like to express my gratitude to the colleagues and mentors who inspired and guided me as I worked on this project in its various forms over the last few years. My fellow POPC and CMCL students kept me on my toes and pushed me to work harder. Joe Austin initially suggested that my seminar paper about suburban films might be worth developing into a larger project. Chris Anderson helped me to narrow my ideas into something manageable and graciously shared advice and wisdom about research, writing, and the pitfalls of academia. Barbara Klinger, Yeidy Rivero, and Brenda Weber provided extensive feedback on early drafts, and offered invaluable advice about turning a collection of related essays into a coherent book. Greg Waller, Robert Terrill, Cindy Smith, and Ilana Gershon provided valuable insights along the way, and Jon Cavallero offered advice, optimism, and friendship throughout the process.

During my time at the University of Washington Tacoma, many of my colleagues offered support and advice as I wrote and revised my manuscript while adjusting to my first full-time faculty appointment. In particular, I want to thank Bill Kunz, Chris Demaske, Divya McMillin, Ingrid Walker, Claudia Gorbman, Joanne Clarke Dillman, Riki

Thompson, Ellen Moore, Huatong Sun, Cheryl Greengrove, Larry Knopp, Jenny Quinn, and Anne Taufen Wessells. Thanks also to Paul Lovelady for helping me retrieve illustrations for the book, and to the IAS program for providing funding that made the completion of this project possible.

I am grateful to Jim Leonard, Will Scheffer, and Mark Olsen for taking time to share their thoughts about the suburban narratives that they created (*Close to Home* and *Big Love*), and to Nancy Robinson of the Academy of Television Arts & Sciences Foundation for helping me to connect with these industry professionals.

Portions of chapter 3 were previously published as part of an essay entitled "The Soldier in the Suburbs: *The Pacifier* and Post-9/11 Masculinity," in *September 11 in Popular Culture: A Guide*, ed. Sara Quay and Amy Damica (Santa Barbara, Calif.: Greenwood Press, 2010), 195–197, and are reproduced here by permission of ABC-CLIO.

I thank Leslie Mitchner for seeing value in my work and for providing ideas about how to make it better; Lisa Boyajian for shepherding me through many of the details of the editorial process; and the entire production team at Rutgers University Press for transforming my words and ideas into a finished book. Thanks to Steve Macek for his thoughtful and precise feedback, which helped me to patch the holes and polish the rough edges in my manuscript, and to the anonymous reviewer whose suggestions greatly improved the overall project.

I would never have been able to get this far without the support of my family. I am grateful to my parents, Dale and Judy, and my sister, Julie, as well as my grandparents, aunts, uncles, and cousins. I am also grateful to the many friends who offered support, prayers, advice, or a chance to have fun and forget about work. Thanks in particular to Lisa, Roger, and Mary Marchal, Molly Rule, Pat McCorkle, Rachel Jensen, Emily Buser-Gonzalez, Katie Braun, Rob Ping, Tom Slater, Robert Hasskamp, Jeff Johnson, Mitch Serslev, Shane Morrison, Ron Sebben, Gerda Fletcher, Adrienne Ione, Jason Thrasher, and Rascal.

Finally, I want to thank Ed Chamberlain for supporting and encouraging me through every phase of this project. I dedicate this book to him.

Look Closer

Introduction

Welcome to the Neighborhood

In an early scene from the 1999 film *American Beauty*, the protagonist, Lester Burnham, offers a narration that plays over an aerial shot of a suburban neighborhood. The image reveals rows of large, single-family houses, neatly arranged on tree-lined streets. As the camera slowly moves closer to the street, Lester's narration sets up the film's story.

"My name is Lester Burnham. This is my neighborhood. This is my street. This is my life. I'm forty-two years old. In less than a year, I'll be dead." As the image changes to a shot of Lester in his bed, waking to the sound of his alarm clock, his narration continues. "Of course, I don't know that yet. And in a way, I'm dead already." In the next few scenes, Lester reveals that, despite the pleasant image created by their elegant home and charming neighborhood, the members of the Burnham family are anything but happy.

The pilot episode of *Desperate Housewives* (2004–2012) echoes the opening of *American Beauty*, but exchanges the male narrator for a female. The first image is a crane shot of another typical suburban street. A school bus winds its way down the cul-de-sac as people walk, bike, and jog along the sidewalks. The camera moves down to ground level and along a white picket fence, before pushing into a shot of a woman exiting her front door to stand on her porch. As the woman looks out at her neighborhood, she provides a voiceover narration to set the scene.

"My name is Mary Alice Young. When you read this morning's paper, you may come across an article about the unusual day that I had last week. Normally, there's never anything newsworthy about my life. But that all changed last Thursday." As she continues to narrate, she is shown going about the business of a typical day. She feeds her family breakfast, works on household chores and projects, and runs errands. After all her routine activities, she walks to the closet, pulls out a revolver, and shoots herself in the head.

Although they come from different sources—one a film drama, the other a television comedy—these scenes contain striking similarities. They both open with visual images of seemingly normal, serene, pleasant suburban neighborhoods. And through the voiceovers and actions of their dead narrators, they both reveal that these images are only part of the story. Beneath the charming surface of suburban life lies a darkness that leads to the murder of one narrator and the suicide of the other.

Both *American Beauty* and *Desperate Housewives* draw on previous Hollywood-produced images of suburbia in order to make their first impression. In particular, family sitcoms from the 1950s and 1960s, such as *Leave It to Beaver* (1957–1963) and *The Adventures of Ozzie and Harriet* (1952–1966), helped to develop an onscreen image of suburbia as a utopian space filled with desirable homes, happy families, and trouble-free lives. While *American Beauty* and *Desperate Housewives* both open with a familiar image reminiscent of these earlier images, they waste no time undermining that vision of simple tranquility, offering up a version of suburbia that is loaded with complexity and contradictions.

American Beauty and *Desperate Housewives* are just two examples of a broader trend in recent Hollywood productions that interrogate and subvert conventional images of American suburbia. The 1997 release of the critically acclaimed *The Ice Storm* was followed closely by the commercially successful *Pleasantville* and *The Truman Show* in 1998, and the Oscar-winning *American Beauty* in 1999. These four high-profile films helped kick off a wave of cinematic explorations of the complexities of suburban life.

Films like *Happiness* (1998), *The Virgin Suicides* (1999), *Traffic* (2000), *Far from Heaven* (2002), *The Hours* (2002), *The Incredibles* (2004), *The Stepford Wives* (remake—2004), *The Cookout* (2004), *Garden State* (2004), *The Pacifier* (2005), *Fun with Dick and Jane* (2005), *Mr. & Mrs. Smith* (2005), *Over the Hedge* (2006), *Little Children* (2006), *Disturbia*

(2007), *Lakewood Terrace* (2008), *Revolutionary Road* (2008), *Lymelife* (2008), *The Joneses* (2010), and *The Watch* (2012) have also taken the American suburb as more than just a backdrop. Using suburbia as a space and a way of life that is integral to their thematic and/or narrative development, these films challenge the popular image of suburban bliss cultivated by early sitcoms. While these are not the first films to investigate the darker side of suburban life (see, for example, *No Down Payment* [1957], *The Stepford Wives* [1975], *Over the Edge* [1979], or *Edward Scissorhands* [1990]), it is notable that such a large number of high-profile suburban films (featuring A-list performers or directors, achieving significant critical and/or audience acclaim) have appeared in such a short period of time.

Television has also provided a wealth of suburban images in recent seasons, most of them coming in the wake of ABC's hit series *Desperate Housewives*, which follows the lives of four women living on a seemingly normal suburban cul-de-sac. Taking *Desperate Housewives'* suburban setting and exploring it through different genres are the comedies *Weeds* (2005–2012), *Suburban Shootout* (2006–2007), *Surviving Suburbia* (2009), *Suburgatory* (2011–), and *The Neighbors* (2012–); the dramas *Close to Home* (2005–2007), *Big Love* (2006–2011), *Mad Men* (2007–), *The Riches* (2007–2008), *Breaking Bad* (2008–2013), *Swingtown* (2008), and *The Gates* (2010); and the reality series *The Real Housewives of Orange County* (2006–), *The Real Housewives of Atlanta* (2008–), *The Real Housewives of New Jersey* (2009–), and *There Goes the Neighborhood* (2009). Moving beyond the visions of happiness and tranquility offered by early family sitcoms, these programs find humor and drama in the tensions and conflicts that define contemporary suburban life.

The recent wave of suburban narratives in film and television is more than just a trendy topic or theme for writers, directors, and producers. Suburbia is a concrete spatial arrangement that shapes the everyday lives of the majority of Americans and expresses many of the hopes and fears embedded within American society. Although it may be a far cry from reality, the idea of a perfect suburban life still exists in the collective imagination of millions of Americans. This myth of suburban perfection is built around a variety of social values and ideals, including the importance of tradition, the centrality of the nuclear family, the desire for a community of like-minded neighbors, the need for clearly defined gender roles, and the belief that with hard work and determination anyone can be successful. These values are not limited to suburban fantasies, as they also fuel some of the most intense political and social debates in contemporary America, including those surrounding gay marriage, immigration, and economic reform. Media texts that reinforce the image of suburban utopia, as many postwar sitcoms did, also quietly reinforce the values associated with that image. Conversely, media narratives that challenge the myth of suburban perfection also call into question the values embedded in that myth. This book examines and interprets recent suburban narratives to reveal how directors and producers are mobilizing the spaces of suburbia to tell stories about America. Building on the relationships between suburban life and American identity, the cultural producers behind the films and television series examined in this book use suburbia as a means to explore, celebrate, and critique American values and ideals.

Suburbia in America

According to recent census data, more Americans live in suburban spaces than in central cities and rural areas combined, and suburban growth currently outpaces urban growth in all regions of the country.[1] As the dominant residential pattern in the United States, suburbia has become a part of the everyday lives of the majority of the country's citizens. Offering more than just a place to live, the American suburb stands as an expression of mainstream American values, particularly those held by existing and aspiring members of the middle class. In his historical account of suburbanization, Robert Fishman suggests that suburbia "expresses values so deeply embedded in bourgeois culture that it might also be called the bourgeois utopia."[2] As a significant marker of middle-class status, the detached single-family suburban home is, for many, the ultimate realization of the American Dream.[3] The importance of family, leisure, nature, community, and independence all find expression in the design of American suburbs. Understanding American suburbia is an essential step toward understanding American culture.

The existence of suburbs is not unique to the United States, but the particular forms and patterns of suburbanization that dominate the American landscape are significantly different from those of most other nations. While suburbs in the United States tend to be defined by low-density development and single-family houses inhabited by the more affluent, or at least middle-class, segments of society, this is not the case around the world. The city of Paris, France, for example, looks very different. When Napoleon III decided that he wanted to transform Paris into a grand imperial capital, he charged Eugène-Georges Haussmann with redesigning the city. Haussmann's plan involved bulldozing much of the central city and replacing the existing maze of streets with wide boulevards, flanked by elegant apartment buildings. These buildings became the favored dwellings of wealthy and middle-class Parisians, while the poor and working class were pushed to the periphery of the city.[4] Similarly, cities around the world, including Stockholm, Johannesburg, Mexico City, Cairo, Calcutta, and Rio de Janeiro, feature affluent residential neighborhoods in or near the central city with poorer residents living at the fringes in structures ranging from shanty towns to densely packed high-rises.[5] The unusual forms of suburbia in the United States developed as a result of a combination of factors, including advances in transportation and construction, the availability of cheap yet inhabitable land, and a range of government policies and actions.

One major catalyst for the suburbanization of America was a series of transportation developments, which allowed people to live farther from the central city and which gave distinct shapes to suburban growth. Inhabitants of early cities generally walked to and from work, which meant that they had no choice but to live near their workplace, and that usually meant staying in the city. During the early 1800s, entrepreneurs in various cities introduced numerous forms of mass transit, which operated "along a fixed route, according to an established schedule, for a single fare."[6] Ferries transported commuters across rivers to cities like New York, Cincinnati, Philadelphia, and Pittsburgh. Landlocked cities relied on horse-drawn omnibuses, steam railways, and horse railways. In all cases, these forms of transit allowed those who could afford to build a house and pay the commuting fare to move beyond the bounds of the central city. Around the mid-nineteenth century, wealthy land developers began laying out entire suburban units, imagined as park-like communities with winding lanes and lush landscaping.[7] While the primary residents of these communities were the wealthy elite, they often brought with them servants, who lived in quarters provided on the property or in small houses nearby.

Significant developments during the late 1800s and early 1900s brought suburban life within reach of many middle-class families. As Sam Bass Warner demonstrates in his historical examination of Boston, the introduction of the electric streetcar was a vital part of this process.[8] The low fares and increasingly dense network of tracks built by streetcar entrepreneurs made commuting to and from work much more affordable and practical. With widespread adoption of the automobile in the 1920s, additional spaces were opened up to suburbanization, as people no longer needed to live within walking distance of a streetcar line in order to have a manageable commute. The cost of building a home also dropped during this time with the introduction of the balloon-frame house, which relied on two-by-four-inch studs instead of heavier timber frames, and which could be assembled by two men with a small set of hand tools, making it possible for people to build their own houses if they could not afford to pay someone else to do it.[9] Improved transportation and construction processes combined with relatively cheap land and increasing wages (a result of the United States' prosperous industrialization) began to make suburbs accessible to larger portions of the population.

The federal government also played a significant role in the suburbanization of the United States, by way of policies designed to help the nation survive the Great Depression and later to help people readjust after World War II. In 1933, the Roosevelt administration created the Home Owners Loan Corporation to help protect homeowners from foreclosure and excessive interest payments. The HOLC standardized appraisal procedures and mortgage policies, establishing the government's commitment to supporting single-family homeownership. This was followed by the creation of the Federal Housing Administration in 1934. The FHA encouraged homeownership not by lending money or building houses, but by insuring long-term mortgage loans made by private lenders for the construction or purchase of homes. The backing of the U.S. Treasury decreased the risk for lenders and made them more likely to offer money to those who wanted to move to the suburbs. The efforts of the FHA were later supplemented by the Servicemen's Readjustment Act of 1944 (commonly known as the GI Bill), which helped returning veterans purchase homes after they completed their service during World War II. A decade later, the Interstate Highway Act of 1956 provided for a nationwide network of federally funded roads. Primarily intended to replace worn-out roads and provide quick evacuation routes in case of a military attack, the highway system (along with the tractor-trailers that drove on them) also had the effect of encouraging the outward movement of industrial plants and warehouses, and with them the further suburbanization of residential construction.

While these government acts encouraged and supported suburban development during the mid-twentieth century, innovations in the housing construction industry made large numbers of homes available in a short period of time, which allowed the rate of suburbanization to skyrocket during the latter half of the century. Leading the charge was a development company run by Abraham Levitt and his sons, William and Alfred. While fulfilling a government contract to build over two thousand homes for war workers in Virginia, Levitt and Sons learned and developed more efficient ways to build entire communities of houses, and they eventually applied these methods to the construction of homes for returning World War II veterans. The process employed by the Levitts essentially turned housing construction into an assembly line, with many portions of the nearly identical homes preassembled in shops and then delivered to the home sites, which consisted of concrete slabs placed at sixty-foot intervals on tracts of land that had been bulldozed and cleared of trees. The first Levittown, on Long Island, included more than seventeen thousand homes, and was followed by an equally large development outside Philadelphia, and a third in Willingboro, New Jersey.[10]

The success of Levittown, along with the speed and efficiency with which the Levitts were able to construct new developments, ensured that these processes and designs would be copied by developers across the country. The streamlined mass production of houses coupled with easy access to money by way of FHA and VA loans led to explosive suburban growth, which would continue for the remainder of the century.

According to U.S. census data, the population of metropolitan areas
(including both central cities and their surrounding suburbs) grew
rapidly throughout the entire twentieth century, but from 1940 onward
suburbs accounted for more population growth than central cities. In
1940, the proportion of the nation's population living in suburbs was
15.3 percent—about half the number living in central cities (32.5 percent). In 1960, the proportions were nearly even, with almost 31 percent
living in the suburbs, and just over 32 percent living in central cities.
By the 2000 census, 50 percent of the nation's population lived in the
suburbs, with just over 30 percent in central cities.[11]

As widespread as the growth of suburbia was in the twentieth century, not all groups had equal access to this new life. Although people
of all races and ethnic backgrounds did move to the suburbs during
this period, the rapid growth of suburbia was driven primarily by white
families, while black Americans faced many obstacles that limited
their access to suburbia. In some cases, restrictive covenants written
into deeds prevented blacks from buying particular properties. William Levitt (along with other developers) stated publicly that he would
not sell his homes to black customers. The HOLC and FHA engaged in
discriminatory practices that made qualifying for a loan more difficult
for blacks than for whites. During much of the twentieth century, the
federal government's attempts at urban renewal (intended to improve
life for the urban poor) often had the unintentional effect of increasing
ghettoization and racial tensions in urban areas, thus fueling additional
middle class "white flight" from central cities out to the suburbs. The
racial makeup of suburbia would eventually begin to balance itself, but
the predominance of white families remains a defining feature of the
growth of suburban America.[12]

Throughout its history, American suburbia has been a space
of conflict, contestation, and debate. One of the most fundamental
debates has been over the nature of suburbs as either "utopian models
of community or dystopian landscapes of dispiriting homogeneity."[13] In
the early decades of the twentieth century, citizens, popular magazines,
and, of course, developers promoted the benefits of suburban living,
including an escape from big-city problems like pollution, overcrowding, and crime. The pastoral view of the suburbs stressed a return to

nature and tapped into the Jeffersonian ideal of property ownership as a marker of citizenship.[14]

When, as Dolores Hayden points out, the suburban trend of the 1920s became "a suburban tide in the 1950s," a chorus of critics rose up to decry the negative impact of suburban culture.[15] During the 1950s and early 1960s, journalists, sociologists, and other cultural observers wrote a number of critical accounts of suburbia, many of which became commercially successful books. David Riesman's *The Lonely Crowd* (1950) presented suburbia as a breeding ground for conformity, where individuals were expected to blend in as a way of demonstrating their social status. William H. Whyte's *The Organization Man* (1956) suggested that the supposed security of corporate work and suburban life was making people complacent and unwilling to follow their true passions. Paul Goodman's *Growing Up Absurd* (1960) presented suburbia as an incubator of delinquent youths, while Betty Friedan's *The Feminine Mystique* (1963) depicted it as an oppressive, psychological prison for women, who were expected to take joy in their roles as mothers and housewives. Herbert Gans's *The Levittowners* (1967) painted a more benign picture of the suburbs (specifically Levittown), suggesting that the move to the suburbs did not, in fact, turn everyone into automatons. He did, however, note that many of the women of Levittown faced unhappiness after moving there, usually as a result of isolation. The social concerns identified by these authors have continued to fuel attacks on suburbia as a homogenizing and oppressive phenomenon, but, as the census data demonstrate, increasing numbers of families continue to choose the suburbs as their home.

With critics and supporters engaged in an ongoing debate, suburbia has become a site of political and cultural struggle that literally hits American society where it lives. And the struggle is not just on the outside, in the form of debates about the benefits and drawbacks of suburban development. As Roger Silverstone points out, suburbia itself is defined by a number of paradoxes and contradictions. It is "instantly recognizable though never entirely familiar. Ubiquitous but invisible. Secure but fragile. Desired but reviled."[16] It is both the product of and an escape from urban expansion. Suburban spaces exhibit traces of both urban and rural areas but are technically a part of neither.

Fishman notes that although suburbs seem to be about community, they are often built on principles of exclusion (based on race, class, sexual orientation, etc.).[17] Lynn Spigel argues that suburban spaces produce a constant tension between public and private, as residents establish their place in the public sphere by owning private property.[18]

Although most of these debates have focused on the nature of suburban life itself, this book examines narrative representations of suburbia, which have made their own contributions to the suburban debates. Suburbia exists in our cultural imagination as much as in our landscapes, leading some critics to argue that it should be analyzed less as a physical space and more as an idea, a way of life, or a state of mind.[19] While the space of suburbia may have been constructed by builders, developers, and government agencies, the cultural meanings of suburbia have been heavily influenced by artists, filmmakers, television producers, songwriters, and advertisers who have repeatedly chosen suburbia as the setting and often the subject of their work. These cultural texts reflect, dramatize, explore, and often shape society's views of the landscapes in which they and their neighbors live.

As Catherine Jurca argues, the study of cultural representations of suburbia allows us to explore "the suburb as created in and through various discourses, rather than the suburb itself."[20] Viewing suburbia as a cultural construct helps to reveal the individual ideals and values that define it, and which are less apparent when suburbs are viewed as merely physical spaces. Jeff Hopkins emphasizes the importance of distinguishing between actual spaces and representations of those spaces. He notes that the cinematic landscape is not "a neutral place of entertainment or an objective documentation or mirror of the 'real,' but an ideologically charged cultural creation whereby meanings of place and society are made, legitimized, contested, and obscured."[21] While the space of the diegesis may in many ways resemble spaces in the real world, we must recognize diegetic suburbs as more than a simple re-creation of reality. They are spaces created by cultural producers in order to tell particular stories and convey particular ideas. Given their ubiquity in the American landscape coupled with their frequent use over the years as a rather nondescript and benign backdrop, suburbs, as well as those who populate them, are often seen as typical

. . . average . . . normal. The films and television series that I examine in this book move in the opposite direction. These texts, along with my readings of them, aim to defamiliarize a seemingly quotidian aspect of American life. By making the familiar strange and the strange all too familiar, these texts encourage a reexamination of suburban life. A central goal of this book is to demonstrate how cultural producers mobilize the image of suburbia to reveal and then challenge ideas and values traditionally associated with suburban life in America.

A successful analysis of cultural representations of suburbia must be grounded in an understanding of the history, geography, politics, and economics of such spaces. Scholars from the fields of history, sociology, anthropology, political science, geography, architecture, urban planning and design, literature, and media and cultural studies have all helped to advance our collective understanding of American suburbia, with each discipline offering a slightly different approach to this multifaceted phenomenon.[22] The different viewpoints, methodologies, and theoretical frameworks contributed by each discipline help to clarify the complex web of physical and architectural spaces, behaviors, attitudes, identities, and images that define suburbia as we know it. Incorporating ideas from these disciplines into my analysis of cultural representations, I connect the images offered in suburban texts with societal debates including those about gender, sexuality, family, marriage, race, privacy, and surveillance, to show how the values we associate with suburbia are intertwined with broader cultural concerns.

Suburbia in Popular Culture

The films and television programs explored here are only the most recent in a long line of suburban narratives, and they build on the various images that have come before them. Suburban representations over the years have frequently tended toward one of two extremes: utopian and dystopian. The utopian visions have presented suburbia as the ideal place to escape the crime and congestion of the city, interact with friendly neighbors, raise children, and have a family. The dystopian visions have imagined suburbs as spaces of conformity, oppression, and isolation.

The early utopian images came primarily from advertisements and television sitcoms. As suburban developments expanded, manufacturers quickly realized that new homes could be filled with new appliances, furnishings, and other consumer goods. As a result, the advertisements for these types of goods frequently featured suburban homes as the backdrop for the items being sold. For example, an advertisement for Kelvinator kitchen appliances that ran in a 1944 issue of *American Home* features a young soldier and his wife standing in front of a Christmas tree and holding a small-scale model of a typical suburban house. In the text that accompanies the image, the young couple fantasizes about purchasing a real house after the war is over and filling it with Kelvinator appliances, like the "wonderful electric range with its magical trick of cooking dinners even while we're away."[23] This particular ad connects suburban life with not only time-saving appliances and happy family life, but also American victory in World War II.

Family sitcoms of the 1950s and 1960s supported the idealized, utopian vision of suburbia by emphasizing harmonious family and community relationships in a world where even the biggest problems were always solved within a half-hour. In addition to the previously mentioned *Leave It to Beaver* and *The Adventures of Ozzie and Harriet*, programs like *Father Knows Best* (1954–1963), *The Donna Reed Show* (1958–1966), and *Dennis the Menace* (1959–1963) continued to present suburbia as a space that was miraculously free from the serious problems of the rest of the world. While a handful of programs like *Bewitched* (1964–1972), *The Addams Family* (1964–1966), and *The Munsters* (1964–1966) complicated matters by raising questions about what was or was not "normal" in suburban neighborhoods, they still presented the suburbs as a pleasant place that most people would like to call home.[24]

These sitcoms, despite projecting a utopian image, conveyed some rather problematic messages. Mary Beth Haralovich, Nina Liebman, William Douglas, and Gerard Jones have all shown how postwar sitcoms set in the suburbs generally reflected and reinforced the dominant ideologies of the period. These authors argue that 1950s sitcoms "naturalize[d] the privilege of the middle class,"[25] excluded or marginalized racial and ethnic minorities,[26] and reinforced traditional, patriarchal versions of gender relations,[27] strengthening the associations between these ideologies and suburban spaces. The utopian image projected by these sitcoms was created by repressing or eliminating voices, identities, and beliefs that might disrupt the suburban harmony. Contemporary suburban narratives frequently return to these repressed ideas, mining them for dramatic or comedic conflict and thematic development.

With advertisements and sitcoms emphasizing a utopian view, the early dystopian vision of suburbia frequently came from filmmakers and novelists. In the comedy film *Mr. Blandings Builds His Dream House* (1948), Manhattan advertising executive Jim Blandings decides to move his growing family from New York City to suburban Connecticut, but he faces great economic and emotional stresses when his dream house ends up being more trouble than it is worth. Other films, including *All That Heaven Allows* (1955), *Rebel without a Cause* (1955), and *Bachelor in Paradise* (1961), depicted suburbanites struggling with repressive social mores, generational conflict, and boredom. Novels such as John Keats's *The Crack in the Picture Window* (1956), John McPartland's *No Down Payment* (1957), Sloan Wilson's *The Man in the Gray Flannel Suit* (1955), Richard Yates's *Revolutionary Road* (1961), and various novels and short stories by John Cheever and John Updike all depicted suburbia as a place that destroyed souls, families, individuality, masculinity, and anything else that got caught in its grasp. Some of these novels were made into films during this era, including *No Down Payment* (1957) and *The Man in the Gray Flannel Suit* (1956), while *Revolutionary Road* would eventually return as a film in 2008. These fictional treatments saw very little of the sunny happiness that pervaded the sitcoms of the era, drawing instead on the sociological and quasi-sociological critiques from writers like David Riesman, William H. Whyte, and Betty Friedan.

It is not surprising that both the utopian and dystopian visions of suburbia emerged strongly in popular culture during the postwar suburban boom that was spurred by the GI Bill and mass production in the housing industry. But not everyone was moving to the suburbs in the 1950s, and many films and television series during this era presented a contrast to the suburban imaginary by exploring the complexities of urban life. In her book *The Apartment Plot*, Pamela Robertson Wojcik discusses a range of mid-century films and series that adopt urban

FIGURE 1. *No Down Payment* was one of the first films to explore the darker aspects of suburban life, including alcoholism, adultery, and domestic violence. Frame enlargement.

apartments as crucial elements of their narrative and thematic development. Examining films such as *Rear Window* (1954), *The Seven Year Itch* (1955), and *Pillow Talk* (1959), along with television programs like *I Love Lucy* (1951–1957), *The Honeymooners* (1955–1956), and *Make Room for Daddy* (1953–1965), Wojcik argues that such apartment plots offer an alternative to dominant domestic discourses of the era. She notes that they provide "a vision of home—centered on values of community, visibility, contact, density, friendship, mobility, impermanence, and porousness—in sharp contrast to the more traditional views of home as private, stable, and family based."[28] These stories often examined the lives of those left out of the suburban ideal, including single and divorced people, working-class whites, and racial and ethnic minorities.

In addition to stories that focus on urban domesticity, there are those that emphasize white-collar urban employment. In her book *Skyscraper Cinema*, Merrill Schleier examines representations of the highrise office buildings that define urban skylines, noting that such images often carry ideological significance in that they express certain values, economic philosophies, and gender positions.[29] She discusses films such as *Executive Suite* (1954), *Woman's World* (1954), *Patterns* (1956), and *Desk Set* (1957), arguing that skyscraper films during the postwar era explore the inner dynamics of office buildings, paying particular attention to "interpersonal relationships and power struggles, and the breadwinner's attempt to reconcile professional identity with family life in both ideological and spatial terms."[30] These films, therefore, explored many of the same concerns as those set in urban apartments and suburban homes, but did so by emphasizing the lives of characters at work rather than at home.

Although the apartment- and skyscraper-centered stories discussed by Wojcik and Schleier rarely reference suburban life directly, they do help to define postwar suburbia by way of contrast. As Wojcik points out, the suburban "requires the urban for its definition."[31] The specifics of suburban architecture, spatial design, family structures, and social values become clearer when compared to their urban counterparts. Thus urban narratives have always played a crucial role in defining the suburban imaginary.[32]

These three approaches—suburbia as utopia, dystopia, or the city's default "other"—have remained a part of our cultural imagination since they were established in the mid-twentieth century, with the dystopian views occasionally reappearing in films like *The Stepford Wives* and *Over the Edge*. The utopian version continued to provide a pleasant, uncomplicated backdrop for domestic comedies like *Happy Days* (1974–1984), *Family Ties* (1982–1989), *Growing Pains* (1985–1992), and *Who's the Boss?* (1984–1992), the opening titles of which featured a single father leaving Brooklyn to give his daughter a "brand new life" in suburban Connecticut. I do not want to suggest that there is always a clear-cut distinction between utopian and dystopian, with every treatment of suburbia falling on either one side or the other. In fact, many texts over the years have featured both positive and negative views at least to some degree. Narratives with predominantly dystopian approaches often still find some glimmer of hope for characters willing to change their ways. And the utopian images are only utopian for those privileged individuals who are included within them (i.e., white, middle-class, heterosexual families). This tension between utopian and dystopian views of suburbia can yield both dramatic and comedic results, and it is a defining feature of all the narratives analyzed in this book.

While the utopian and dystopian visions have provided the dominant framework for most onscreen constructions of suburbia, urban stories have also continued to develop suburban imagery over the years, often using suburbia as a point of contrast to help define a particular image of the city. Whether the suburb is portrayed positively or negatively depends on the desired portrayal of the city. On one hand there are the stories that depict urban spaces as filthy, violent, and depressing. This depiction of the city has long been associated with film noir, but, as Steve Macek points out, it became a common trend in a wide variety of films during the 1980s and 1990s, including horror films, detective dramas, comic book adaptations, science fiction, and social problem films.[33] For example, the thriller *Judgment Night* (1993) features a group of suburban men who take a wrong turn into a bad neighborhood of Chicago, witness a murder, and then wind up being chased by the killers as they try to escape back to the safety of their suburban homes. The musical comedy *Little Shop of Horrors* (1985) features a character fantasizing about life in the suburbs as the best possible escape from the poverty and violence that dominate her urban existence. Other films, such as *New Jack City* (1991), *Boys N the Hood* (1991), and *Dangerous Minds* (1996), locate social problems like violence, drugs, and poverty so firmly in the city that the suburb—without being directly depicted—is left as the implied opposite.

On the other hand, narratives that celebrate the joy and excitement of urban existence sometimes present suburbia as a bland and boring alternative to life in the city. This can be seen in an episode from the fourth season of the sitcom *How I Met Your Mother* (2005–) entitled "I Heart NJ." The series features a group of young adults who live in New York City, and in this particular episode, the main character, Ted (Josh Radnor), learns that the woman he plans to marry wants him to move to suburban New Jersey to settle down after they tie the knot. Throughout the episode, Ted debates whether or not he could stand to leave the excitement of New York for what he sees as a more boring life in New Jersey, and he endures endless jokes from his friends about how pathetic his suburban life would be. Similarly, the "Valentine's Day" episode of *Mad about You* (1992–1999) features the main couple, Paul and Jamie (Paul Reiser and Helen Hunt), considering a move from their high-rise Manhattan apartment out to the suburbs. They drive out of the city to look at a house, but after a long, painfully boring conversation with the couple who owns the property, they quickly decide to stick with the sophistication and excitement of urban life. And in an *Ugly Betty* (2006–2010) episode entitled "Sisters on the Verge of a Nervous Breakdown," Betty (America Ferrera) uncovers career-threatening secrets about the hip, stylish, and supposedly gay host of a New York–based fashion channel. Not only is he straight and married, but he lives in the suburbs, suggesting that he could not possibly be as sophisticated or hip as he seems on TV. In these and other similar examples, suburbia becomes the butt of a joke, equated with a lack of culture, sophistication, and excitement.

These three overarching trends form the context for considering any contemporary suburban narrative. The films and television series that I analyze in this book incorporate elements of both the utopian and dystopian visions to create suburban spaces and lives that are anything but boring. The two-dimensional suburban image used as the butt of urban-centric humor is replaced by a more complicated landscape that becomes the stage for a wide range of human dramas.

In the media texts that I examine, suburbia is far more than a setting or backdrop. For some films and television series, suburban space is emphasized so much that it becomes the subject of the story. In this way, these narratives have much in common with landscape painting. As Martin Lefebvre notes, the rise of this genre of painting emancipated landscape "from its supporting role as background or setting" and established it as "a completely distinct aesthetic object."[34] Similarly, films and television series like *American Beauty, Desperate Housewives*, and *Pleasantville* are not just set in suburbia—they are *about* suburbia and suburban life. In other texts, the suburban space is not as clearly foregrounded, but it is still a driving force in terms of how the story plays out. For example, the stories told in *Mr. & Mrs. Smith, Big Love*, and *The Truman Show* could have taken place in other spaces—and in fact, the initial concept for *The Truman Show* placed it in an urban space— but the way that the stories unfold would be drastically different without the suburban surroundings. In all the texts examined in this book, suburbia is not just a static background. Whether utopian, dystopian, or somewhere in between, the suburban landscape is a dynamic force that in many ways defines the narratives contained within it.

The Suburban Façade

Cultural producers use a variety of storytelling techniques to explore the complexities of suburban life. To emphasize the relationship between the positive and negative aspects of suburbia, producers frequently draw on the concept of the suburban façade. On the outside, suburban life seems harmonious and fulfilling, as it always did in the family sitcoms of the 1950s. But dig a little deeper and you'll find hidden desires, secrets, and problems that threaten to disrupt the tranquil suburban existence. The act of peeling away the veneer of suburban harmony to reveal something hidden underneath has become so common that it would almost seem to be a prerequisite for any film or series that adopts suburbia as its setting. The theme—used extensively throughout *Desperate Housewives*—is clearly articulated in the sixth season's episode "You Gotta Get a Gimmick." At the end of the episode, the narrator, Mary Alice, is pulling together various storylines by relating them to one couple's argument about watching a stripper. Over images of the various characters, Mary Alice says, "The act itself is quite simple. You strip away the outer layer and reveal what's underneath. Of course, sometimes the results can be quite surprising. If you strip away the veneer of happy domesticity, you may find grief. If you strip away that façade of wealth, you may find self-loathing. If you strip away the veil of helplessness, you may find cruelty. Yes, stripping can be a dangerous pastime."

The concept of façade is so prominent among suburban narratives that it is built into some of their ad campaigns. For example, the promotional campaign for *American Beauty*, including the movie poster and trailers, is based on the tag line "Look Closer." The original trailer features a series of images from the film broken up by intertitles that read, "You see a street . . . like any other street . . . look closer. You see a man . . . who's hardly there . . . look closer." The trailer for *Far from Heaven* takes a similar approach. Amid shots of the main characters, their picturesque neighborhood, and their seemingly happy life are screens of text that ask the questions: "What lies under the surface? What hides behind the walls? What imprisons the desires . . . of the heart?" As with *American Beauty*, this trailer makes it clear that a primary goal of *Far from Heaven* is to shatter the illusion of idealized suburban family life by exposing what is hidden underneath.

In his review of *Revolutionary Road*, movie critic Owen Gleiberman alludes to the familiar story of suburbanites repressing their true feelings in order to fit in, only to have those feelings revealed during a heated argument or drunken stupor. Gleiberman's comment that this is part of the suburban mythology "we all know in our bones" suggests that viewers have come to expect suburban stories to deal with the conflicts between outward appearances and inner truths.[35] Given that breaking through the façade has become a central preoccupation of suburban narratives, we should pay attention to what each text reveals when the façade is removed. The chapters of this book examine the ways in which each film and television series negotiates the suburban façade. In some cases a façade is depicted as a visual or physical surface, while in other cases characters create a behavioral or emotional façade through their performance and interactions with others. I am particularly interested in what the façades conceal and what each narrative eventually reveals about the specific characters involved and about American culture at large, including its most cherished values and ideals.

The Suburban Intertext

The study of onscreen landscapes and social spaces has frequently focused on spaces that are common to particular genres, like the frontier in westerns or the city in film noir. For example, in his book *The Invention of the Western Film*, Scott Simmon examines the discrepancies between the West on screen and the West as it actually developed in history.[36] The West of the screen is an imagined space, created and refined through repetition and reimagination by writers, directors, and producers over the years. As the genre solidified, so too did particular images of the West, and the iconography of saloons, main streets, canyons, and prairies became more important to the genre than the actualities of the lived American West, especially when it came to expressing the western's themes of rugged individuality, law and order, and civilizing the wilderness.

Similarly, the film noir city is a stylized, amplified version of real cities. As Edward Dimendberg points out, the rise of the modern city in the early decades of the twentieth century led to fears and anxieties about urban life, urban spaces, and modernity in general. By the 1940s and 1950s, these fears were reflected in the darkened moods and themes of film noir, and the city was often portrayed as a contributor to feelings of isolation, anomie, and despair. As Dimendberg notes, the film noir cycle "hyperbolically presents the contrasts and rhythms of the city (including music and sound) as elements of a highly rationalized and alienating system of exploitative drudgery permitting few possibilities of escape."[37]

These and other studies imagine particular spaces as iconic elements that have become familiar building blocks within the genres of which they are a part. Exploring the frontier and the city enables a better understanding of the western and film noir genres. This book, however, is not a genre study, and I am not advocating the identification of a new genre that incorporates every suburban narrative. The films and television series explored in this book cover a wide range of established genres, including situation comedy, procedural drama, domestic melodrama, action-adventure, fantasy, and horror, to name just a few. They may share a preoccupation with suburban life, but the narrative structures and styles that they employ are far too varied to consider gathering them all under a single generic umbrella. However, as with most genre studies, this book is concerned with both the meanings generated by individual texts and the aggregate meanings generated across all the texts. In this way, the approach will be somewhat similar to that of most genre studies. But rather than lobbying for a generic identity, I would argue that the films and television series examined in this book (as well as the advertisements, pop songs, and other cultural texts that play a secondary role in the study) all draw on and contribute to an ever-increasing suburban intertext.

The theory of intertextuality proposes that any single text is always read in relation to other texts.[38] Therefore, the meanings of an individual text are not generated solely by the text itself, but also through the knowledge of other texts that viewers bring with them as they interpret the new text. Genres function intertextually because the repetition of recognizable storylines, narrative structures, character types, and visual images across a genre will shape the creation and reception of any new additions to that genre. What I am calling the suburban intertext has a similar effect. *Desperate Housewives* did not introduce the concept of suburbia to the television landscape when the series premiered in 2004. Rather, it drew upon and contributed to a vast bank of images that together shape our cultural understanding of suburbia, its residents, and their lives. *Desperate Housewives* was, is, and always will be shaped by *Leave It to Beaver* and *The Stepford Wives*, just as it shapes the meanings of *Weeds* and *Little Children*. And this influence is not simply chronological, with new texts being influenced by those that came before them, and then influencing those that follow. Because all these texts continue to circulate in the media landscape (some more than others, depending on popularity and continued relevance), a new episode of *Suburgatory* can breathe new meanings into *American Beauty* and *Father Knows Best.*

As the preceding examples suggest, the suburban intertext cuts across not only genres but also media formats. Film, television, and advertising differ in a number of ways, including their methods of production, modes of reception, and a variety of formal characteristics. For this reason, many scholarly projects focus solely on one media form, rather than juxtaposing heterogeneous source materials. The differences between media should not be discounted, as they do influence the images generated by a given text. For example, a serial television drama returns to its suburban setting week after week and season after season, allowing far more depth and character development than a two-hour feature film or thirty-second commercial. However, given that this book deals with images and themes that circulate freely across media formats, I would argue that in this case the commonalities in content outweigh the differences created by varying formats. The discussions in this book, therefore, follow the intertextual exchanges of ideas to move between different visual media—primarily film and television, but also advertising—leading to an intermedial examination of contemporaneous suburban narratives. Recent books by Catherine Jurca, Robert Beuka, and Martin Dines demonstrate that literary treatments also contribute significantly to the intertextual meanings of suburbia, but the

FIGURE 2. This ad for *Suburgatory* draws on and contributes to the ever-evolving bank of images and stories that make up the suburban intertext. Author's personal collection.

emphasis here is on visual media, and I therefore leave a more detailed discussion of suburbs in literature to others working on the subject.

There are many common themes that run through the suburban intertext, including tradition and nostalgia, family, community, gender identity, and the American Dream. These themes, which form the basis of the chapters that follow, are rooted in the values that are closely associated with the utopian myth of suburban perfection. The themes also resonate on a higher level, as they tap into debates about the whole of American identity. For example, liberals and conservatives have been at each other's throats arguing about how to define a family, and what kinds of values a family should embody. Changing expectations about appropriate gender roles have been a source of anxiety for decades, and the recent presidential and vice presidential bids of Hillary Clinton, Sarah Palin, and Michele Bachmann served as a reminder that not everyone agrees on what is appropriate for each gender. Debates about border control highlight questions about who should be included from and excluded from American citizenship. The nationwide mortgage crisis has forced everyone to realize that the dream of suburban homeownership may not, in fact, be available to everyone willing to work hard. And the tension between looking nostalgically to the past and moving forward to the future shades countless debates on a variety of topics important to all Americans.

Because so many of the values and ideals being debated on the national stage are also central to discussions of suburban life, the suburbs provide the ideal location in which to explore these themes. These ideas are embedded in our collective understanding of suburbia, and cultural producers activate them when they set a text in a suburban space. Producers balance the various themes by bringing some to the foreground and nudging others to the background, but they are all present to some extent in any suburban narrative.

A 2009 television commercial for Lowe's home improvement stores provides an example of the intersection of these themes. In this commercial, a Lowe's worker stands outside a small suburban house and says, "Sixty years ago, a soldier just back from the war moved into this house with his young family." As she talks, big band music plays in the background, and the present-day image is replaced by black-and-white shots of the young family moving in to the house and then the father throwing a football with his son in the front yard while the mother watches from the porch. The announcer goes on to say, "Just about that time, a new store opened—a store with a commitment to keep prices low, so returning GIs could afford the American Dream. That store was Lowe's." The music then changes to a more contemporary pop style, and the black-and-white image is replaced by a full-color image of a new father and son throwing a football while the mother tends the flowerbed. The announcer says, "There's a different family living here now, but Lowe's is still just down the street, and Lowe's is still committed to offering low prices, guaranteed."

This ad is significant for two reasons. First, it shows that the meaning of suburbia is still being contested. As the opening examples from *American Beauty* and *Desperate Housewives* demonstrate, many contemporary media texts present a vision of suburbia that is far from flattering. This commercial, on the other hand, builds on many of the early images that depict suburban life as the realization of a widely shared dream. The image presented here is very similar to those appearing at the beginnings of the texts examined throughout this book, but while those texts reveal that image as a façade that hides deeper conflicts and secrets, this ad presents the image as reality and uses it to sell a store and its products. Instead of critiquing suburban life, this commercial celebrates it, demonstrating that the films and series examined here are responding not only to utopian visions from the past, but also to similar visions being generated today.

This commercial is also significant because it encapsulates most of the themes explored in the rest of this book, even though it does not examine them in depth. For instance, the use of black-and-white images and big band music helps to create a nostalgic view of the past, which is then connected to the suburban present. The commercial also reinforces the image of the privately owned suburban home as the ideal location for families in both the past and the present. Both of the families in the commercial are white, while the announcer, who maintains a position outside the family's yard, is a woman of color, thus quietly reinforcing notions of who lives in the suburbs and who provides labor to support the suburban lifestyle. Both eras in the commercial demonstrate clear gender roles, and the returning soldier easily makes the transition from the battlefield to the domicile. The advertisement overall suggests that suburban homeownership is the ultimate marker of middle-class success, and that the purchase of consumer goods from a local retailer is the best way to cement that success. While these themes and images are visible only briefly in the Lowe's commercial, they are explored in more depth by many contemporary films and television series, and they form the basis of my analysis in the chapters that follow. To explore each theme, I have selected two or three exemplary texts that highlight or crystallize ideas running throughout the body of suburban narratives.

Chapter 1 takes up the concepts of tradition and nostalgia as they are presented in both advertising images and Hollywood narratives, paying particular attention to the problems created by a nostalgic view of the world. While film and television creators are producing images of fictionalized suburbia, real estate developers are producing images of actual suburbs. Through promotional brochures, videos, newspapers, websites, and other visual formats, suburban developers and residents generate images of their communities that are not completely fictional but are certainly constructed. This chapter examines promotional materials from communities like the Village of West Clay in Indiana and the Springfield development of Fort Mill, South Carolina, alongside two related Hollywood narratives, identifying the similarities and differences between these texts. To reinforce the image of suburbia as an idyllic place to live, many of these communities aim to create a sense of nostalgia, which specifically asks people to remember the past in a way that may never have existed in reality. I compare these promotional images to the communities created in *The Truman Show* and *Pleasantville.* These films also rely on nostalgic visions of suburban life to create a fantasy world that is somehow better than the real world. Unlike the promotional materials, the images in the films break down, suggesting that nostalgic versions of suburban communities are not feasible in contemporary society. By comparing the images created by residents and developers in suburban communities with those created by Hollywood producers and filmmakers, I show how various cultural producers compete to define contemporary American suburbia, and how relying too heavily on the past can make it difficult to move toward the future.

The second chapter investigates a social unit that is frequently included in debates about traditional values: the family. In particular, this chapter is concerned with the relationship between the family unit and privacy, a concept that has also been central to historical and contemporary discussions of suburbia. The film *American Beauty* and the series *Big Love* serve as case studies here because they demonstrate how social norms regarding privacy are often intertwined with the protective boundaries we draw around families. In an era when politicians are building entire campaigns around notions of "family values," these texts present images of families in crisis and raise questions about whether the traditional family is really an institution worth protecting. Because suburban life has generally been marked by tensions between the simultaneous desires to isolate the nuclear family and to participate in a community, my analysis looks beyond internal family relationships to explore connections that families have with their neighbors and the community, considering how this interaction articulates contemporary concerns about privacy in our culture.

Chapter 3 examines the concept of community, specifically considering the ways that communities are defined based on who they include and who they exclude. The historical exclusion of certain groups based on race, class, and sexual orientation has led to a suburban landscape that is dominated by those who are white, middle class, and heterosexual. Continued racial tensions, homophobia, and talk of a shrinking middle class have increased anxiety about who is or is not included in the suburban American Dream. This chapter focuses on Todd Haynes's film *Far from Heaven*, the ABC series *Desperate Housewives*, and the politics of suburban exclusion. Although *Far from Heaven* revolves around a white female protagonist, the stories of her collapsing marriage to a gay husband and her romance with a black gardener overtly confront suburban patterns of exclusion as both men are effectively run out of the neighborhood. *Desperate Housewives* takes up similar concerns as they pertain not only to gay men and African Americans, but also to Latinos, Asian Americans, and immigrants living in the United States. Through stories of individuals struggling for acceptance in suburban communities, both these texts raise broader questions about the challenges faced by minority groups struggling for full and equal status as citizens of the United States. While the plots of both texts expose the mechanisms frequently used to exclude minorities from communities of all kinds, the visual and narrative styles employed by the creators reveal the artificiality and construction of any definition of normal and suggest that difference can never be eliminated.

The fourth chapter examines the performance of masculinity in the domestic realm. Despite the fact that suburbia and the home are often viewed as feminine spaces, the suburban ideal is partially structured around the image of a male head of household/breadwinner. As if to demonstrate the difficulty of living up to this ideal, a large number of suburban films focus on men and their struggles to prove their masculinity in the face of family crises, financial hardships, and marital struggles. *The Pacifier* and *Mr. & Mrs. Smith* take an exaggerated form of masculinity—the violent, heroic kind that is usually reserved for intense action films—and place it in the domestic sphere of suburbia. This chapter examines these films in the context of ongoing discussions of masculinity in both popular and scholarly circles, paying particular attention to gendered responses to the 9/11 terrorist attacks. While both films outwardly celebrate a heroic form of hegemonic masculinity, they also raise questions about the compatibility of this image with the domestic lives of most American men.

Chapter 5 focuses on the hard work involved in achieving and maintaining the American Dream. The television programs *Close to Home* and *Weeds* feature two women who are on opposite sides of the law but working toward the same goal. Using very different methods, each woman is doing everything she can to protect her own piece of the American Dream. *Close to Home* follows a prosecutor who specializes in crimes committed in suburban Indianapolis. Although the young mother is employed outside the home, her job keeps her in the realm of suburban domesticity, enabling an intersection of home and work rarely seen in suburban narratives. By relocating the police/courtroom procedural from its typical urban setting to the suburbs, *Close to Home* also challenges the image of suburbia as quiet, peaceful, and safe. Handling the relationship between work and crime in a more comedic fashion is the Showtime series *Weeds*. In direct contrast to the stereo-typical images of black, male drug dealers in poverty-stricken urban slums, this series features a white, middle-class, suburban widow who starts dealing drugs in order to maintain the middle-class lifestyle that she and her family have grown accustomed to. The series is an inter-esting contrast to *Close to Home*, since the work being done to protect the suburban way of life in *Weeds* would be a punishable offense in the world of the procedural drama. While the texts discussed in pre-vious chapters tend to assume an affluent, crime-free environment, these programs emphasize the tenuous nature of such privilege. Taken together, these two series suggest that maintaining the ideals of the suburban American Dream can be even more difficult than achieving the dream in the first place.

Like storytellers working in a particular genre, those who mobilize the narrative space of suburbia draw on a bank of images and ideas that connect their stories to a larger body of work and position them within an ongoing cultural conversation about suburban life and the people who live it. The media texts examined in this book draw on and respond to earlier depictions not only of idyllic suburbs but also of deteriorating cities.

Macek demonstrates that urban-set films of the 1980s and 1990s presented the city as a space dominated by violence, drugs, crime, and poverty. He argues that these portrayals amplified "alarmist, anti-urban tropes and stereotypes" which tended to blame the urban crisis on those who were actually its victims—generally poor people of color.[39] This, in turn, legitimated the ideologically conservative views employed in dominant political and journalistic discourses of the time, which depicted cities as problem areas in need of stricter policing. In this framework, the suburbs stood as the antidote to the ills of the city.

I noted at the beginning of this chapter that the utopian myth of suburban perfection is based on a set of widely shared values. To be more precise, the values embodied by the suburban ideal—includ-ing a celebration of the traditional nuclear family and clearly defined gender roles—tend to be ideologically conservative in nature. Thus stories that reinforce the suburban ideal, like postwar family sitcoms or the Lowe's advertisement described above, also reinforce generally conservative views.

The films and series that I examine in this book provide a counterpoint to the images of collapsing cities and idealized suburbs that circulate in popular culture, showing that problems are not limited to the city and that the suburbs are not flawless. But these stories go beyond simply dismissing suburbia as a failed utopia. Using the narrative motif of the suburban façade, storytellers explore the tensions and contradictions that are inherent to the conservative values embodied by the suburban myth. For example, breaking through the façade of a unified community reveals patterns of discriminatory exclusion, while removing the façade of easy middle-class status exposes the unsavory behavior that is sometimes necessary to achieve such status. These contradictions are never fully resolved, but each suburban narrative that works through them in dramatic or comedic fashion exposes their complexities and invites further inspection. These stories suggest that conservative ideals, often naturalized as universal or normal, are not as simple and clear-cut as they might appear. By questioning the suburban myth and its associated values, these texts are thus challenging conservative ideologies with respect to discussions of tradition, family, community, gender roles, and the American Dream. By setting their stories in the seemingly typical world of suburbia, cultural producers use American life at its most mundane to explore American values at their most complex. Building on Chris Healy's idea that suburbia is "a way of talking about other things," this book analyzes recent suburban narratives to figure out what they are talking about, what they have to say, and why we should be listening.[40]

1

Traditional Values

Nostalgia and Self-Reflexivity in
Visual Representations of Suburbia

A promotional video for the Village of West Clay, a suburban development outside Indianapolis, Indiana, opens with a title card reminiscent
of those found in silent films. The image shakes a bit, and the sound
track features a solo piano along with the sound of a film projector.
The title card says, "Mother has some errands that need to be run."
This is followed by a shot of a neighborhood street. The image is black
and white with scratches and other imperfections, suggesting the look
of old film stock. The camera pans past two cars that appear to be from
the 1920s or 1930s and eventually settles on one house on the street.
Two children play in the yard, and their parents watch from the front
porch. As the mother waves to the children and then gives them a piece
of paper with some instructions, a voiceover narrator says, "There was
once a time when a mother could send her children to the corner store
on a simple errand." As the kids leave the front yard and walk down
the street, a circular wipe replaces the original image with a new one.
The street and the children are the same, but now the image is in color,
and old cars and clothing are replaced with contemporary styles. The
voiceover goes on to say, "Times have changed, the pace of our lives has
quickened. But the yearning for safe, lively neighborhoods, filled with
the good things in life, has not. Welcome to the Village of West Clay, a
new neighborhood founded on traditional values."

Drawing on positive associations with aspects of the past as a way of
selling itself to potential residents, the Village of West Clay represents

FIGURE 3. Although shot recently, some of the footage in the promotional video for the Village of West Clay is degraded to make it look older than it is. Frame enlargement.

a common trend in the marketing of suburban developments across the country. New developments in Orlando and Jacksonville, Florida; Fort Mill, South Carolina; Las Vegas, Nevada; Charlotte, North Carolina; and Orange County, California, are just a few of the many communities whose promotions follow an approach similar to that of the Village of West Clay. In an attempt to create their own identity and distance themselves from the generic subdivisions emblematic of suburban sprawl, promoters of these communities often appeal to buyer's nostalgic sensibilities, asking them to look to the past as they buy homes for the future.

Fictional suburban narratives regularly draw on nostalgic imagery as well, but for different purposes. In a scene from the 1998 film *The Truman Show*, the title character leafs nostalgically through an album of old family photos while watching the beginning of his favorite television program. To introduce the show, an onscreen host announces that it is time for "golden oldies," as he presents "the enduring much-loved classic *Show Me the Way to Go Home*," a series that revolves around the fictional Abbot family of Camden Village. In his introduction, the announcer previews some of the episode, telling viewers that the "scene with the bowl of cherries is going to have you splitting your sides with laughter all over again," suggesting that this is an old program that viewers have seen many times before and are happy to watch again.

Similarly, the 1998 film *Pleasantville* opens with a close-up of a television screen as an unseen viewer surfs through a variety of channels before settling on TV Time!, which an announcer's voice introduces as "the only network playing lots of old stuff in nothing but black and white." The voice then announces that this nostalgia-inducing network will be running a marathon of episodes of the postwar suburban family sitcom "Pleasantville,"[1] which focuses on the Parker family and their life in the town of Pleasantville. The announcer encourages viewers to "flash back to kinder, gentler times" by spending the evening immersed in this old television show.

These scenes highlight two themes that are central to *The Truman Show* and *Pleasantville*: the power of nostalgia and the influential role that media play in creating and recycling nostalgic images. In both films, nostalgic versions of the past—or, more accurately, televisual constructions of the past—are presented as initially appealing, but ultimately unsustainable, as the limitations introduced by nostalgia clash with human desires for freedom, knowledge, and growth. As the lead characters in these stories struggle with the constrictive nature of a nostalgic worldview, they enable the films to fully work through ideas that are raised more subtly by many contemporary suburban narratives. The 2002 film *Far from Heaven*, for example, is set in the 1950s and draws on popular filmmaking styles of that period. By dealing openly with conflicts caused by sexual repression, adultery, and racial tension, and by setting them in this earlier era and style, the film suggests that the 1950s were not as fabulous as some people would like to believe. Similarly, films and series such as *The Ice Storm* (1997), *The Virgin Suicides* (1999), *The Hours* (2002), *Revolutionary Road* (2008), *Mad Men* (2007–), and *Swingtown* (2008) use stories set in the past to develop critiques of suburban American life both past and present. Even stories set in the present, like *American Beauty* (1999) or *Desperate Housewives*

(2004–2012), borrow imagery from earlier media texts to create the illusion of harmonious suburban life, which they then seek to undermine.

For most contemporary suburban narratives, a nostalgic view of the suburban American past is an important element of the critiques that they present, but it generally remains in the background. In both *The Truman Show* and *Pleasantville*, this relationship between the present and an imagined past is brought to the foreground and examined in great detail. *The Truman Show* tells the story of Truman Burbank (Jim Carrey), a young man who is the star of a twenty-four-hour-a-day television program called "The Truman Show," but who has no idea that his entire life exists in a giant studio and is watched by millions of people around the world. Adopted at birth by a media corporation and raised in front of hundreds of cameras planted throughout the community in which he lives, Truman has lived his entire life on television without ever knowing it. A series of events leads him to become suspicious of his surroundings, and his search for an explanation eventually results in his departure from the artificial world in which he lives.

Pleasantville features two teens, David and Jennifer (Tobey Maguire and Reese Witherspoon), who live in a drab contemporary Southern California suburb with monotonous neighborhood designs and private security vehicles patrolling the treeless cul-de-sacs. In school, the kids are subjected to endlessly discouraging lectures about declining job prospects, increasing disease rates, and global warming, and at home they have to listen to their divorced parents argue about weekend custody. David's primary escape is watching his favorite sitcom, "Pleasantville," which is built on the model of classic suburban family sitcoms from the 1950s, like *The Adventures of Ozzie and Harriet* (1952–1966) and *Father Knows Best* (1954–1963). After receiving an unusual television remote from a mysterious TV repairman, David and Jennifer are magically transported into the diegetic world of "Pleasantville," where they begin to alter the community's existence by bringing outside knowledge and a contemporary sensibility to the people who live in an imagined past. The film follows their attempts to get back home and to deal with the changes that they have caused within the world of "Pleasantville."

By emphasizing the role of media in the creation, circulation, and recycling of nostalgic suburban imagery, *The Truman Show* and

Pleasantville highlight the intertextual processes that have left specific views of suburbia embedded in the American psyche. Additionally, each film takes as its primary setting a suburban community that is specifically constructed for consumption by an audience. In order to appeal to the desired audience, producers have created picture-perfect images of inviting neighborhoods filled with friendly people. By emphasizing this careful construction and maintenance of suburban harmony, *The Truman Show* and *Pleasantville* call attention to the aforementioned promotional campaigns of suburban developers, which use language and images to generate feelings of nostalgia in an attempt to attract potential residents.

Nostalgia has often been discussed as a key component of postmodernity. Fredric Jameson argues that in postmodern culture, we have experienced a willful disconnection from lived history and now tend to favor a pastiche of historical signifiers. The past has become "a vast collection of images, a multitudinous photographic simulacrum." Cultural productions functioning in the nostalgia mode approach the past "through stylistic connotation, conveying 'pastness' by the glossy qualities of the image."[2] Many of the promotional materials for contemporary suburban developments follow this model, making vague references to indeterminate times and events from the past in their attempt to make the present more appealing.

The Truman Show and *Pleasantville* may initially seem to emulate the nostalgia mode that Jameson describes, but they actually work to undermine it. Jameson argues that many nostalgia films draw on the styles of older films to evoke certain eras of the past, rather than drawing on history itself. While both of these films do, in fact, draw on the styles of earlier media texts, they do so not in order to evoke a certain time period, but to openly reference an *artificial construction* of a particular period. The self-reflexive way in which these films play with nostalgia reveals rather than conceals the process of manipulating the past. By examining these two films side by side with promotional images from new suburban developments, we can see how each of them simultaneously draws on and contributes to the ever-evolving suburban intertext. While many promotional materials use nostalgia to make suburban life seem appealing, *The Truman Show* and *Pleasantville* reveal the dangers and complications of turning a nostalgic view of the past into a seemingly utopian version of the present.

New Urbanism—The Solution to Sprawl?

In order to grasp the significance of the critiques offered by these films, one must understand the characteristics and history of the design movement that is generally credited with inspiring neo-traditional suburban planning—New Urbanism. The New Urbanist movement first gained national attention with the mid-1980s unveiling of the coastal Florida resort town of Seaside—the town that would eventually serve as the shooting location for *The Truman Show*.[3] Seaside was designed by the Florida firm Duany Plater-Zyberk (DPZ), which has gone on to become the most outspoken and best-known designer of the New Urbanist movement. The design of Seaside and other New Urbanist developments share a number of characteristics, including mixed land use, pedestrian scaling, open public spaces, distinctive architectural character, and a sense of community.[4] A characteristic that was not an explicit part of the original movement but which has become closely associated with it is the revival of architectural and design styles from the past, along with the nostalgic sensibilities that such designs evoke.

The New Urbanist movement and its design characteristics were a direct response to the problems brought on by suburban sprawl, including strain on resources, the destruction of green space, and the isolation and anomie experienced by many suburban residents. The problems associated with sprawl began during the postwar suburban boom of the 1950s, which set the stage for continued growth in the areas surrounding cities in the United States. As more and more families moved away from inner cities, more homes appeared on the outskirts of those cities, accompanied by shopping malls, movie theaters, gas stations, and office parks. As this development drifted farther from the urban cores, and the boundaries of metropolitan areas continued to blur, critics began to refer to this phenomenon as suburban sprawl. In her book *A Field Guide to Sprawl*, Dolores Hayden describes sprawl as "unregulated growth expressed as careless new use of land and other resources as well as abandonment of older built areas."[5] The unchecked growth associated with suburban sprawl has been connected to a variety of social, economic, and environmental problems. As New Urbanist designers Duany, Plater-Zyberk, and Speck argue, "Even at relatively low population densities, sprawl tends not to pay for itself financially and consumes land at an alarming rate, while producing insurmountable traffic problems and exacerbating social inequity and isolation."[6] Creating solutions to these problems is the driving force behind the New Urbanist movement.

In 1996, a group of designers known as the Congress for the New Urbanism set forth a list of principles that they said should "guide public policy, development, practice, urban planning and design."[7] These principles established guidelines for development at all levels, from the individual house and street to the neighborhood and to the metropolitan region, suggesting that urban designs must take all levels into account to be sure that they function together as an efficient whole. The Congress participants argued that metropolitan regions should have definable boundaries, and that the countryside should be protected and treated as an important counterpart of the metropolis. They suggested that rather than continuing to spill out into the countryside, metropolitan regions should focus their energies on infill development, incorporating newly developed (or redeveloped) communities into the existing social and economic fabric of the area. Affordable housing should be distributed evenly throughout the region, allowing workers in all kinds of jobs to live near their place of employment and preventing the concentration of poverty in certain areas.

The Congress for the New Urbanism had some lofty goals, believing that design practices could have an impact on social, cultural, economic, and environmental concerns. Their ideas were driven largely by the desire to correct what they perceived as the mistakes that had been made by planners and suburban developers in the 1950s, 1960s, and 1970s. While the charter does include a desire to bring people together to form communities, the bulk of the principles of New Urbanism are driven by concerns about sustainability, both economic and environmental. These designers wanted to establish practices in the present that would help preserve and protect natural and financial resources for future generations.

Despite good intentions and many admirable characteristics, New Urbanism has faced criticism over the years, as many have pointed out that the movement falls far short of providing a coherent plan for reforming urban and suburban development. One of the most vocal critics, Alex Krieger of the Harvard Graduate School of Design, has argued that New Urbanism has generally failed to incorporate serious, long-term environmental strategies, and that it relies too heavily on private management of communities, at the expense of locally elected governance.[8] Julie Campoli and Alex MacLean demonstrate that while New Urbanism may be an improvement over earlier modes of suburban development, building at even higher density has significant benefits with respect to use of resources, pollution, and efficiency of infrastructure.[9] Recent studies of specific New Urban developments have shown that even if such communities encourage walking within the neighborhood, they do little to decrease the dependence on automobiles or increase mass transit use for longer trips.[10]

Some critics have focused specifically on the role of New Urbanism in the U.S. Government's Hope VI initiative. This program, which began in 1992, was intended to replace the failing system of oversized, blighted, urban housing projects, most of which had become isolated centers of concentrated poverty, riddled with crime and drug use. When the Department of Housing and Urban Development (HUD) decided to replace the old public housing projects, they turned to New Urbanism, seeking mixed-income communities that would support economic mobility for their residents. While the new Hope VI developments did provide visually appealing enclaves that were connected to the surrounding neighborhoods, the lower density of these projects meant that there was not enough room for all of the people who had lived in the housing units that were demolished in the process. As a result, a large proportion of public housing's most economically vulnerable population was displaced or left homeless.[11] In this case, the appealing façade of New Urbanism obscured a deeper, harmful social cost of the Hope VI program.

The most publicly debated and criticized New Urbanist development of all is certainly the Disney-designed town of Celebration, Florida, located just outside the gates of the Walt Disney World theme parks near Orlando. Like other examples of New Urbanism, Celebration was imagined and promoted as a small community defined by walkable streets and friendly neighbors, but in this case with the added value of a close association with the ultimate family-friendly company, Disney. For potential residents, this was a dream come true, but many were uncomfortable with the idea of a planned community designed and manipulated by the same Imagineers who were responsible for bringing fantasies to life in the nearby theme parks. Not long after the town's 1994 groundbreaking, journalists, scholars, and other social commentators began to offer their critiques of the new development, questioning such details as the corporate control over civic life, and the experimental approaches taken by the town's schools.[12] In a book written after living in Celebration for a year, Andrew Ross shares stories of families spending so much of their life savings to live in Celebration that they were left with empty rooms that they could not afford to furnish. He also describes the many problems early residents faced as a result of sometimes-shoddy construction.[13] Keally McBride points to the town's lack of economic diversity and a dearth of public transportation as characteristics that prevent it from living up to its own hype.[14] The spotlight on Celebration may have been extra bright because of its association with Disney, but as an iconic example of New Urbanism it demonstrated that even the best intentions might not lead to perfect housing solutions. Despite these critiques, Celebration has provided a model that countless developments continue to follow as they try to create family-friendly communities that look like something other than sprawl.

Although early New Urbanist designers were not driven by a desire to re-create the past, the concept was embedded in their plans. As real estate development consultant Lloyd Bookout notes, the New Urbanists felt that communities designed before the suburban boom of the 1950s already possessed many of the qualities that they were advocating, and they turned to these established communities for inspiration. This revival of past designs is what led to New Urbanist developments being referred to as neotraditional communities or Traditional Neighborhood Developments (TNDs). According to Bookout, "Neotraditional designers believe there is great value in studying these successful models and recreating their most enduring qualities."[15] In this way, there is a sense of history built into any New Urbanist development, and while it may not be the driving force for the designers, this connection to the past and a nostalgic vision of days gone by has become a key component in the marketing of such communities. In some cases, developers have gotten away from many of the design principles of New Urbanism, but continue to draw on its neotraditional elements as a way of attracting new residents. The use of nostalgia has therefore become a critical strategic element in the selling of many new suburban developments.[16]

Nostalgia

Nostalgia is often seen as simply a longing for the past. However, the use of nostalgia to sell homes suggests that it is also tied somehow to ideas about the present and the future. The concept of nostalgia was first introduced in 1678 by a Swiss doctor named Johannes Hofer, who identified and treated it as a medical condition that primarily afflicted students and mercenaries spending time away from home.[17] Eventually doctors and scientists rejected the medical explanation, and the concept of nostalgia was expelled from medical discourse around 1900. No longer a diagnosable medical condition, nostalgia came to be regarded as a normal and generally harmless emotion, consisting of a wistful recollection of the past.

Although nostalgia is no longer discussed in pathological terms, sociologists, psychologists, and cultural critics have argued that it still plays a significant role in our society. Some contend that changes in our culture over the past century have led to increased feelings of nostalgia in our society as a whole. For example, Svetlana Boym points to "the rapid pace of industrialization and modernization" as a cause for people's nostalgic feelings.[18] David Lowenthal argues that the constant parade of newer and better ideas (in technology, fashion, mass culture, etc.) has meant faster cultural turnover. "Obsolescence," he suggests, "confers instant bygone status."[19] In other words, with change occurring at a more rapid pace, we are given more to be nostalgic about, and instead of reminiscing about styles, behaviors, and customs a hundred years in the past, we nostalgically remember cultural icons, catch phrases, and electronic gadgets from less than five years ago.

While nostalgia as we understand it began as a private affliction that doctors hoped to cure, it can also be seen as a mindset that is shared by large groups and even entire cultures. Fred Davis makes a helpful distinction between private and collective nostalgia. In his discussion, private nostalgia refers to "those symbolic images and allusions from the past which by virtue of their resource in a particular person's biography tend to be more idiosyncratic, individuated, and particularistic in their reference; e.g., the memory of a parent's smile."[20] In contrast, collective nostalgia refers to "that condition in which the symbolic objects are of a highly public, widely shared and familiar character, those symbolic resources from the past that under proper conditions can trigger wave upon wave of nostalgic feeling in millions of persons at the same time."[21] Collective nostalgia plays a large role in our media landscape. Old television reruns, like those in the examples that opened this chapter, not only count on this type of nostalgia for their success, but also help to reinforce it. It is primarily this collective nostalgia that developers of neotraditional towns tap into as they conceptualize and promote their communities.

Nostalgia must be distinguished from two related concepts—memory and history. At a basic level, memory is composed of individual and collective recollections of past events, while history is a consensual recorded account of past events. In their own ways, both memory and history help us to understand the past, and they are essentially the raw materials of nostalgia. We selectively choose details from each in our own nostalgic imaginations, highlighting the positive and minimizing the negative, which is what has led some to define nostalgia as "history without guilt"[22] and "memory with the pain removed."[23] History, memory, and nostalgia all work to construct and reconstruct the past in a way that helps us make meaning in the present. The marketers of neotraditional communities use this to their advantage by manipulating various positive interpretations of the past in an effort to sell homes in the present and expand their developments in the future. *The Truman Show* and *Pleasantville*, on the other hand, explore the manipulative potential of nostalgia in television and other media, and in the process raise questions about its power in all aspects of American culture.

Selling the New Urbanist / Neotraditional Community

One of the goals of neotraditional town planners is to create a sense of community and a sense of place in the neighborhoods that they develop, since critics have complained that these attributes are lacking in many suburban developments. But unlike some of the principles of New Urbanism like pedestrian scale and mixed-use development, a sense of place and a sense of community are not easily created on the drafting table. They take time. As Bookout points out, "The prototypes for most neotraditional plans are places that have been allowed to form and evolve over decades,"[24] and I would argue even longer in many cases. Because planners do not have the luxury of waiting for their developments to age and establish a sense of character and past, they turn to more creative means to accomplish this. The challenge, therefore, is to produce images that signify historical depth and continuity even when such characteristics do not truly exist.

By drawing on the past in their promotional materials, developers aim to create the image of a unique and desirable community, which is important for reaching not only potential buyers, but also politicians, concerned neighbors, and local business owners. After all, developers rarely build a new community that is a freestanding political entity. They are more commonly inserting their development into an existing township, city, or other municipality. The local mayor, city council, or zoning board must be courted in order to gain approval for the development, and concerned residents and businesses in the surrounding area must be convinced that the new development will be beneficial rather than detrimental. A small but vocal minority of NIMBYs (Not In My Back Yard) can often sway politicians and block the progress of developments for months or years, or even permanently.[25] Therefore, the marketing and PR strategies must create and present a desirable image of a completed community before it actually exists. This is accomplished in part by creating for the new development a nostalgic sense of history and continuity with the past so that neighbors will not see it as a drastic and unwanted change.

Nostalgia can be a powerful selling tool in part because of what Boym refers to as the phenomenon's "utopian dimension,"[26] which allows individuals to see past times and other places as somehow better than the here and now. There are three basic ways that the marketers of these communities attempt to use the past as a selling tool. One way is to convey a sense of age through the look and feel of the promotional materials, using surface appearances to convey messages that enhance the written or spoken word. A second way that marketers draw on ideas about the past is through the use of language that invites potential buyers to remember, reflect, and reminisce about days gone by. The third way is to make direct references to actual history, whether it is the history of the development itself or of the surrounding area.

These three approaches raise questions that parallel significant narrative concerns within both *The Truman Show* and *Pleasantville*. For example, while the promotional materials use surface images to convey a sense of the past, both films show that a carefully constructed surface image often hides a very different underlying truth. Both films also emphasize the dangerous relationship between knowledge and control, while the tactics employed within the promotional materials aim to filter knowledge through memory and tradition and to carefully control the past to make it serve the needs of the real estate developers. I am not suggesting that *The Truman Show* and *Pleasantville* are meant as direct critiques of real estate promotions, nor would I advocate reading them in this way. They do, however, deal with themes and images that are prominent in the promotional materials. When examined side by side, the films shed light on the mechanics of the promotional materials, illuminating significant aspects of nostalgia that the promotions work hard to conceal.[27]

Visualizing the Past

Many of the promotional materials for neotraditional communities attempt to evoke the past through their visual presentation. The style of presentation and the basic look and feel of the materials often emphasize a rather vague sense of "pastness." The promotions for the central Florida community The Villages offer the most extensive and elaborate use of visual signifiers of the past, memory, and nostalgia.

The promotional packet for The Villages is labeled as a "Lifestyle Portfolio." Designed to visually represent an actual portfolio, the packet is printed to look as though it were made of leather, complete with a handle at the top, a zipper on the back, and brass clasps on the front. The outside of the portfolio features eight photographs. The edge of each photograph is marked by a tight scalloped pattern, like the perforated edges of a stamp. The photos are placed at odd angles, as though slapped onto the portfolio by someone checking luggage as it travels the world. Like the baggage check stickers that commemorate a traveler's adventures, these images suggest the adventures that await visitors to (and residents of) The Villages, while simultaneously encouraging new residents to bring their memories of the past with them as they move to their new home.

The full-color glossy brochure included in the lifestyle portfolio is designed to look like a scrapbook. Scrapbooks contain memories in the form of photographs, artifacts, and written text. Like nostalgia, which involves selectively remembering high points from the past while conveniently forgetting the low points, scrapbooks are containers for the past as we would like to remember it. The first and last pages of the brochure are printed to look like a leather cover. Brass decorations mark the corners of the leather cover, and the book is held together with a hand-tied piece of yarn that runs through two brass eyelets near the spine. The title "The Villages—Our Hometown," is made to look as though it were stamped onto a piece of cloth or parchment, and then stitched onto the thick leather front cover.

The inside pages are printed to look like heavy-stock manila paper, complete with tiny bits of wood pulp on each page, creating the impression of a slightly rough texture. The photos in the brochure display the ornately decorative edges of old snapshots, as if pulled from someone's personal collection, rather than taken by a professional photographer to be used in a sales brochure. The photographs are arranged so that some of them overlap with one another, and all the photographs seem to cast a slight shadow on the page, giving them a three-dimensional appearance. This makes them look as though they were not printed as part of the page but instead placed on the page by hand, one at a time. In addition to the pictures on each page, there are a number of artifacts such as theater tickets (next to a photo of a musical stage performance) and Mardi Gras beads (near a photo of Mardi Gras revelers). Captions for individual photos are printed in a font that looks like cursive handwriting written directly on the manila pages with a fine-tipped marker or pen. Additional boxes of text appear on many of the pages, offering broader information than the individual captions. Even these boxes appear to have been printed separately and then affixed to the pages of the book. The rough edges and slight shadows around these boxes of text give the impression that they were printed on another piece of paper (one of higher quality than the visibly pulpy stock used for the book itself), torn or cut out, and then placed in the book alongside the photographs.

The various elements of this booklet come together to make it look like something other than a marketing tool. The booklet does not project the image of a corporate-produced package designed by executives in a distant office and then printed by the thousands in a warehouse printing facility. Instead, it projects the image of a hand-crafted keepsake. It is as though someone started with an empty book and then began filling it with materials and memories collected from their own life—photographs, small artifacts, bits of printed text. Captions were written in by hand to provide personal descriptions of the images displayed. This is not the work of a salesman trying to unload property in the community, but a carefully assembled collection of fond memories, gathered together by a resident who is happy with their Villages life. Even the title "The Villages—Our Hometown" reflects this, suggesting that the creator of this scrapbook is, in fact, a resident of the community. Presented in this way, the scrapbook-like brochure establishes The Villages as a welcoming community of friends where good memories are created and kept, rather than as a commercial development that wants to fill its vacant lots or as an institutionalized space where older adults live out their final years alone.

The scrapbook approach does more than simply present an appealing vision of The Villages. It goes so far as to establish an imagined relationship between the creator of the book and the reader of the book. The handmade scrapbook is traditionally an item shared with intimate acquaintances—members of the family or close personal friends. It is not a mass-produced item intended for consumption by strangers or the general public. By being invited to view the collection of memories from "our hometown," the reader has already been included within the

Shop the day away in all our unique boutiques and specialty shops!

Catch all the latest movies on our silver screens!

There's always a musical presentation you will want to see & hear.

We love a Parade!

...and enjoy the celebrations all year long, from Mardi Gras to Oktoberfest!

Stroll down memory lane every month at our classic car Cruise-Ins!

FIGURE 4. The scrapbook-like appearance of the brochure for The Villages imagines a connection to memories made with family and friends. Author's personal collection.

close circle of family and friends being addressed by the contents of the scrapbook.

Other materials in The Villages' promotional packet also use visual style to evoke a sense of the past. The DVD that includes a video tour of the community is printed with a silk-screen design that mimics the look of a 45 RPM vinyl record. The floor-plan samples offer sepia-toned images of each home style, surrounded by elaborate matting and framing in muted colors, making them resemble cherished images of childhood homes rather than an artist's rendering of a home yet to be built.

While The Villages presents the most extensive and elaborate use of surface level references to the past, many other communities make similar use of these techniques. For example, the Springfield development in Fort Mill, South Carolina, also borrows the scrapbook style for its brochure. Videos for Amelia Park (outside Jacksonville, Florida), Mountain's Edge (Las Vegas, Nevada), and the Village of West Clay (Indianapolis, Indiana) open with black-and-white or sepia-toned images that eventually give way to full-color video, suggesting that these are old communities that have evolved over time, rather than new communities that are still under construction.

In all these examples, the images use techniques of visual design to suggest history, age, memories, and traditions that do not exist for these communities. The image on the surface obscures the reality that lies beneath it. The tensions between outward appearances and inner truths are a prominent theme for most suburban narratives, and *The Truman Show* and *Pleasantville* take a very literal approach to this idea. Through their focus on constructed fictional spaces that collide with reality, both films emphasize the effort required to create and maintain the suburban façade.

Most Hollywood productions seek to establish a sense of reality within their diegeses. In some cases this is accomplished through a mimetic re-creation of the world in which we live, while in other cases media texts display an internal logic that assists viewers in their suspension of disbelief, allowing them to accept elements as real within the diegesis. Both *The Truman Show* and *Pleasantville* call attention to their unreal status by constantly highlighting the boundaries between reality and artifice within their own diegetic realms. Each film features a real world (the space outside the dome in *The Truman Show* and the world that David and Jennifer inhabit at the start of *Pleasantville*) and an artificial world (Seahaven and the town of Pleasantville). The boundaries between real and artificial are repeatedly highlighted within each film. In *The Truman Show*, for example, the line between onstage and offstage is emphasized by actors who shift in and out of character and by the conversations of the producers and crew members working to shape Truman's environment from the control room. In a key scene midway through the film, as Truman is beginning to sense that his environment is not what it seems, he confronts his wife, Meryl (who is actually an actress, Hannah Gill, played in turn by Laura Linney), and demands to know what is going on. When Hannah becomes frightened by Truman's violent advances, she turns to a camera planted in the ceiling and screams, "Do something!" This slip on Hannah's part raises Truman's suspicions further, as he demands to know who she is talking to, and her attempts to cover the mistake clearly do not satisfy him.

FIGURE 5. Images that appear as though they are captured by tiny cameras planted on the actors call attention to the construction of all images in *The Truman Show.* Frame enlargement.

Hannah's faltering performance is emphasized visually by choices in cinematography. As Truman and Meryl/Hannah argue, their interaction is captured using small "button cameras" planted on their clothing. Unlike typical objective camera work that remains largely invisible to the viewer, the images from these subjective cameras are shaky, slightly blurred at the edges, and circular, thus drawing attention to themselves as images, and emphasizing the construction of the scene. At the moment when Hannah screams for help, the image onscreen is made to look like a display on a television monitor. The monitor's edges are visible in the frame, and the image itself is of noticeably lower quality—suggesting an inferior electronic reproduction or transmission of the actual scene. This could be the image seen by the television audience, but Hannah's direct address suggests that this is what the producers are seeing in the control room. Either way, the image serves as a reminder of the construction of Truman's entire existence.

The boundary between reality and artifice is also emphasized in scenes where the directorial work of the show's creator, Christof (Ed Harris), is shown on screen. For example, when Truman's long-lost father is reintroduced to "The Truman Show," the scene within the film cuts back and forth between Truman's interaction with his father and

Christof's efforts to make the scene more dramatic and emotional. As Truman walks toward his father and embraces him, Christof selects the camera shots that will best capture the scene, tells a crew member to go "easy on the fog," and requests a swell in music to heighten the emotion of the moment. Occasional shots of viewers watching the scene and smiling, applauding, or crying suggest the immediate results of Christof's manipulations. Crew members in the control room also react, though instead of applauding the father/son reunion itself they celebrate the successful construction of the televisual moment, shouting things like "Great television!" and "That will win the ratings period." By exposing the construction and manipulation of performers and emotions in a particular televised moment, this very self-reflexive scene calls attention to the construction of the film and most other images that circulate in popular culture.

Pleasantville emphasizes its unreality largely through the use of black-and-white imagery. The 1950s, after all, did not occur in black and white, but television programs (constructed realities) did play out in monochrome. Viewers watching sitcoms in the 1950s were unlikely to pay much attention to the black-and-white nature of the television image, because this was the norm of the era. Pleasantville's use of black and white in 1998, however, is a little more jarring, particularly as the main characters are suddenly transported from their color-filled world into the black-and-white existence of the sitcom. The unusual nature of a black-and-white world becomes even more pronounced as individual objects and eventually people begin to appear in full color. The contrast of color with black and white in the same frame draws attention to the surface of the film as an image, reminding viewers of its construction.

The superficial nature of color is particularly pronounced in a scene involving Jennifer and David's TV mother, Betty (Joan Allen). After Betty turns from black and white to color, she is upset and worried that her husband and others will reject her. David takes out some of Betty's makeup and carefully conceals her beige and peach skin and red lips with light and dark shades of gray. In a very literal way, this scene uses a false black-and-white surface image to conceal the true colors of what lies beneath. The scene also calls to mind the heavy makeup that is worn by performers in any film or television production. Indeed, both Joan Allen and Tobey Maguire would have gone through similar processes before the filming of the scene. While such makeup is generally used to refine actors' appearances in a way that makes them look natural, this scene undermines that façade by displaying the mechanics of its creation.

Both films also point to their constructed reality by referencing the audience that is watching the respective programs. *The Truman Show* features many shots of audience members in the "real" world, including a huge crowd of people gathered at the Truman Bar, as they watch and cheer for Truman. The crew members in the control room function as a specialized audience, watching Truman on monitors and responding to his actions so that they may shape future behavior. The audience for "Pleasantville" is only shown at the beginning of the film, when David watches the show in his living room. After David has become part of the show, however, the mysterious repairman tells David that he is worried about what he is seeing in the reruns, suggesting that the program continues to run and an audience continues to watch it. In both cases, the references to the audience within the films establish an intermediate space between the artificial worlds of Seahaven (a constructed world) and Pleasantville (an imaginary world), and the real world inhabited by the viewers of the films. This emphasizes the constructed nature of not only the television programs, but also the films of which they are a part, reminding the film audience that what they are watching exists for their entertainment in the same way that the television series exist for the entertainment of the fictional audiences.

The self-reflexive move of calling attention to the construction of their own images allows the films to comment on the constructed nature of everything within their own diegeses. This includes the towns of Seahaven and Pleasantville themselves, as well as the lifestyles they represent. Both of the towns are initially set up to represent a nostalgic vision of the past, as seen through the eyes of Christof and David. But neither of these characters is nostalgic for the past as it actually existed. They are instead longing for a televisual version of the past— an artificial world that has been made to seem real through its endless circulation in reruns.[28] As the films progress, they break down this nostalgic vision, not only by pointing out its flaws, but also by showing the construction of that vision. In other words, the past that people feel so nostalgic about is shown to be a fabrication—a fictional world designed to appeal to a mass audience.

The boundary between reality and artifice that runs through these films parallels the experience of nostalgia in general. While nostalgia is to a certain extent based in reality, it also involves a longing for or desire to return to a past as it may never have existed. For example, Janelle Wilson's sociological study of nostalgia reveals that many blacks who remember being victims of racism in the 1950s still have nostalgic feelings for that era,[29] suggesting that Lowenthal's definition, "memory with the pain removed,"[30] is accurate. Nostalgia helps us to blend reality with the constructions and fantasies of our own mind, thus blurring the lines between them. Many of the promotional materials discussed above rely on these blurred lines to construct the nostalgic façade that is essential to the image they want to project. *The Truman Show* and *Pleasantville* begin to reclarify those lines, showing how nostalgia leads to a deliberate reconstruction of the past, and reminding us how the desirable world we create in our minds often contrasts with the harsh reality of our true existence.

Memory, Tradition, and Knowledge

The promotional materials for most New Urbanist and neotraditional developments go beyond creating a visual façade to connote age. In many cases, they offer vague linguistic references to the past, memory, and tradition, all filtered through a nostalgic lens to make them seem desirable. *The Truman Show* and *Pleasantville* both suggest that because memory is often faulty and tradition is selectively constructed, they can both contribute to a false understanding of the world in which we live.

Memory involves personal recollections of what happened to us in the past. It is based on personal experience, and it accounts for our own interpretations of our life's events. As Lowenthal points out, memory is not fixed. Recollections are instead "malleable and flexible; what seems to have happened undergoes continual change."[31] Collective memory refers to the shared memory of a group of individuals. In this way, one's memory as an individual is expanded beyond those events that he or she personally experienced, and includes events experienced by other members of the group. As George Lipsitz discusses, collective memory is often supported and enhanced by mediated mass culture and can help to establish and maintain a sense of group identity.[32] Memory plays an important role in nostalgia, as the longing associated with nostalgia is dependent upon the memory of that which is longed for. In some cases, the memory is readily available, but in other cases it needs some assistance.

The marketers of neotraditional communities make significant efforts to jog (and in fact shape) the memories of potential buyers. For example, the brochure for the Village of West Clay in Indianapolis, Indiana, reminds potential buyers that "there was a time . . . when you could send your kids on a quick errand to the shop around the corner . . . when the place you lived was more than just a house." The direct address ("you") asks the reader to remember something from his or her own life, which hopefully brings back images of happy times. Of course, many people may never have experienced such a time in their own lives, but the copy insists that such a time did exist, suggesting that one should try to remember it even if one did not experience it.

This example raises two significant issues. The first is a question of audience. When the promotion refers to "you," it is not addressing just anyone. Despite comments about diversity and variety, the Village of West Clay (like other communities of this type) is targeting affluent white families. An interviewee on the video comments about the benefits of having high-income and moderate-income families living side by side, but there are no comments addressing the needs of lower-income families and individuals. This is not a housing project for the poor. And even though carriage houses and small apartments are allowed in the community, the narrator is quick to point out that they are intended for the "returning child or aging parent" who wants to be close to the family, not for a stranger who cannot afford to purchase his own home. The video also addresses a primarily white audience. All the residents interviewed and the vast majority of individuals shown in the video clips are white, suggesting what the desirable neighbor might look like.

Second, the address to a white, middle-class, heterosexual audience relates to the question of memory. When the audience is asked to "remember" certain ideas, they are not being asked to draw solely on their own personal experiences, but rather on collective memory drawn from images of other white, middle-class, heterosexual families. Such images, which the viewer is asked to remember as his or her own, have been circulated for decades in advertising, art and design, and, of course, television, particularly in the suburban family sitcoms like those critiqued by *Pleasantville* and *The Truman Show*. So the "memory" being sparked by the promotions is actually a familiarity with recycled cultural imagery—an intertextual knowledge of the version of suburbia that the developers of West Clay are selling.

Highgrove, a development in Charlotte, North Carolina, also encourages specific memories. A brochure produced by the developer opens with a series of questions. "Remember when neighbors really knew each other? Remember a time when kids walked to the neighborhood park, just knowing there would be other kids playing a game of 'kick the can'?" As with the materials from West Clay, the Highgrove brochure asks its reader to remember a particular set of circumstances as temporally located somewhere in an indefinite past. In this case, however, the copy alludes to the fact that not everyone shares the same experience by saying, "Even if you don't recall such a time, you can experience it now at Highgrove." Interestingly, this phrase suggests that any difference in experience is actually a difference of memory ("Even if you don't recall . . ."), and goes on to offer a remedy for this memory failure by promising to provide the experience in the present. The brochure suggests that even if you do not share it, this memory is one that is worth repeating. This is similar to what Arjun Appadurai defines as ersatz or armchair nostalgia, "Nostalgia without lived experience or collective historical memory."[33] The promotion essentially asks people to feel nostalgia for something that they may never have experienced themselves—a nostalgia for someone else's experience.

Another idea that plays an important role in these materials is tradition. In particular, the words "tradition" and "traditional" are used to describe everything from architecture to community values to the overall town plans. Despite the frequency of their use, the terms are never explored in any of the promotional materials but rather are used as markers of inherent value. For example, the tagline appearing on many of the materials from Habersham, South Carolina, including letterhead from the sales office, is "In the Tradition of Beautiful Coastal Towns."

The materials never explain what the traditions of those towns consist of, or why they might be of interest. The materials seem to assume that anything following in the footsteps of towns like Charleston and Savannah (both of which are mentioned frequently) must be desirable. The Village of West Clay sells itself as "a new neighborhood founded on traditional values." The word "traditional" is again used very vaguely, suggesting something from the past that has been handed down through generations. The phrase implies that traditional values are desirable values, but the materials never explain why that would be the case.

Folklorist Henry Glassie insists that tradition must be understood as "a process of cultural construction,"[34] whereby people use elements from their past in the creation of the future. Traditions do not just happen—they are consciously and willfully kept alive. As historian Eric Hobsbawm argues, traditions "seek to inculcate certain values and norms of behavior by repetition."[35] In this process, certain values are reified while others are rejected or marginalized.

The vague use of the word "tradition" in these promotions would suggest that its connotative meaning might be more telling than its denotative meaning, especially in terms of revealing the values being promoted. In the culture wars of the last few decades, "traditional" has been used by the political right as a marker of white, heteronormative, middle-class, Christian values. Thus, for many people, traditional values equal dominant, conservative values, which would be a selling point for some buyers while conveniently steering others away.

Both memory and tradition act as specialized forms of knowledge. Based on personal and collective memories, we think we "know" what happened to us and to others in the past. When we invest in and continue traditions, we imagine that we are reproducing certain activities and ideas based on what we "know" about how events occurred in the past.

In both *The Truman Show* and *Pleasantville*, the acquisition of knowledge on the part of one or more characters provides the central conflict and drives the development of the narrative. However, each film suggests that what we think of as knowledge (often interpreted as fact or truth) is highly unstable and easily influenced by the world around us. In particular, the films show how our knowledge of the past is actually a carefully constructed interpretation of reality.

The very premise of "The Truman Show" depends on a certain lack of knowledge on the part of its star. While all the actors who inhabit the town of Seahaven know that they are on a television program, Truman has no idea that his entire life is staged. It is this lack of knowledge about the truth of his existence that makes Truman interesting to watch and appealing to the television audience. Truman's knowledge of his existence comes to him in part by way of his memory. Truman keeps a trunk filled with mementos locked in his basement. Early in the film, he unlocks the trunk and goes through some of its contents, reminiscing about the past. In particular, he thinks back to his lost love Lauren, and as he does this, the onscreen audience is shown a highlight reel that encapsulates the brief story of Truman and Lauren. The clips play out as though they were actually Truman's memories, creating a shared memory for the entire viewing audience. In this way the film comments, as Lipsitz does, on the ability of mass media texts to create a "collective memory" for its viewers, establishing a shared heritage that would otherwise not exist.[36] As the audience gets caught up on what Truman is remembering, he tries to bring his memory to the present by creating a picture of Lauren using pieces of photos torn out of fashion magazines. Like the memories we have, the picture Truman creates is composed of many fragments, which he tries to bring together into a coherent image. Memory is an imperfect form of knowledge, and we are often left with gaps that we must fill in with our own imagination.

In some cases, the gaps in our memory are filled in with some outside help, as the film demonstrates when Truman and his wife and mother flip through an old scrapbook. The book is filled with photographs from Truman's past which help to reinforce "memories" of his youth, enhanced by the commentary of Truman's mother. When he sees a picture of his family at Mount Rushmore, he comments that it looks very small. His mother quickly says, "Things always do when you look back, darling," attempting to pass off the obviously faked monument as a trick of Truman's faulty memory. This scene shows how easily our memories can be manipulated. They are, as Lowenthal describes them, "malleable and flexible,"[37] and therefore unreliable.

Like *The Truman Show*, *Pleasantville* also features a lead character whose entire world exists as part of a television show. Unlike *The Truman*

Show, however, *Pleasantville*'s central character, David, is one of the only characters (along with his sister, Jennifer) who knows that his world is a fictional construction. Before David is transported to the world of "Pleasantville," he possesses a wealth of knowledge about the series and its inhabitants. Preparing for the "Pleasantville" trivia contest that TV Time is holding in conjunction with its all-night "Pleasantville" marathon, David and a friend review some of the more minute details of the series, including the occupation of a neighbor and the name of a stray cat the kids found in a gutter. Not only would this knowledge be helpful to David in a trivia contest, but it also helps him find his way around once he and his sister end up inside "Pleasantville," and he is able to interact with neighbors and classmates, explaining details to Jennifer as they go along. However, the usefulness of this knowledge runs out as soon as things begin to change. While David's knowledge of the past is helpful as groundwork, the changes taking place in the present do not allow him to rely on that past knowledge, and he is forced to change and adapt. In other words, now that David's perspective has changed from that of a passive outsider to that of an active insider, the knowledge he had acquired—filtered through the mediation of television—is insufficient, and he must work to gain a more complete understanding of the environment that he now inhabits.

The town soda jerk, Mr. Johnson (Jeff Daniels), demonstrates another way that knowledge can be inhibited. He is accustomed to doing things the same way every day. He has a set routine for opening up the soda fountain, wiping down the counter, and preparing burgers for customers, but he never stops to think about why he does these things, or if there are other ways to do them. When David's unpredictable behavior interrupts the usual routine, Mr. Johnson is unable to function on his own, because he is used to doing things the way they've always been done. While Mr. Johnson's actions would be described more as habit or routine, his behavior has much in common with some traditions, especially those that people keep alive simply because they have never known anything different. Blind, uncritical adherence to routine or tradition can limit one's willingness or ability to change, which, as Mr. Johnson eventually learns, can inhibit social growth and personal fulfillment.

The Truman Show and *Pleasantville* both suggest that knowledge gained from other people, from traditions, or even from our own memories can be faulty, inadequate, or intentionally untrue. In a sense, these are filters that inhibit our ability to achieve a full awareness and understanding of the world in which we live. Nostalgia acts in a similar way, filtering our understanding of both the past and its relationship to the present and future. When we filter out the bad, the negative, and the unpleasant (as we do when we are thinking nostalgically), we are left with an incomplete picture of our existence. This is what the television producers have done in the creation of Seahaven and Pleasantville, and it is also what developers do when they create communities and images of communities based on nostalgic visions of the past. For Truman and David, a nostalgic view of the world (self-imposed by David and forced on Truman by Christof) inhibits the achievement of self-awareness. Both films suggest that we can only find happiness when we achieve self-awareness, and that this can only be accomplished when we break free from an overly nostalgic worldview—the exact worldview that is encouraged by many contemporary real estate developers.

Controlling the Past and the Present

The most direct way that marketers connect their developments to the past is through specific references to history. Using careful constructions of particular aspects of the past, developers are able to present an image over which they have a great deal of control. *The Truman Show* and *Pleasantville* demonstrate how individuals and groups of people evolve over time, making their behavior difficult to predict and nearly impossible to control. While developers often make significant efforts to manipulate communities in the present and future (frequently by way of homeowners' associations), it is much easier for them to sell images of a static, unchanging past, even if that past has little connection to the lived existence of present and future residents.

History, according to Lowenthal, "extends and elaborates memory by interpreting relics and synthesizing reports from past eyewitnesses." In a sense, history is the verified and supported version of memory. That is not to say, however, that history should be seen as an accurate account of the past. As Lowenthal suggests, history is both "less than" and "more than" the past.[38] It is *less than* the past in the sense that, by its very nature, history is consensual and subjective. What gets written down and accepted as history is generally that which is agreed upon by those writing the history. Their account may not be entirely accurate, and it cannot include everyone's interpretation of events. At best, history can be seen as identifiable, recorded traces of the past. History is *more than* the past in the sense that separate, distinct traces of the past are woven together to create narratives that join those traces into a coherent whole.

The use of history in suburban promotions can be broken down into three strategies. Some draw on the natural history of the area, including its land and waterways. Others rely on a history of landownership and family genealogies. The third and most radical strategy is to create a history from scratch. In all cases, the presented history is a fabrication, carefully constructed and thereby controlled by marketers in order to sell a community with very little history of its own.

One common approach is to shift focus away from the actual community to emphasize the history of the land on which the community is built, or the surrounding area of which it is a part. For example, Mountain's Edge, a development outside Las Vegas, Nevada, goes to great lengths to show that the land around the community has played an important role in American history. The development's website contains a page entitled "History of the Land," which claims that "Mountain's Edge is a special place: from here, you can see hundreds of millions of years of mountain building," thus connecting the development not only to human history, but to the natural history of the land itself, long before humans had a chance to alter it. By connecting history and nature, this claim not only draws on the past to help create an identity for the development, but it also taps into the long-held suburban ideal of being in touch with nature. Conveniently, it simultaneously obscures the fact that the area's natural landscape is being encroached upon by expanding suburbs. Under the guise of celebrating nature, the promotion diverts attention away from the fact that green space, farmland, and wetlands across the nation are being replaced by residential developments.

The discussion of Mountain's Edge goes on to describe additional historical events and people, including the "nomadic ancient Indian tribes" who left petroglyphs "in the canyons surrounding our community"; the pioneers who carved out the Old Spanish Trail "which passed right by Mountain's Edge"; and the fact that "in 1905, just a couple of miles away, you could have witnessed the symbolic hammering of the last spike," which signified the completion of the last major railroad built in the United States. While the current development has no real connection to the events described, the website points out the physical proximity of these events to the land that has now become Mountain's Edge, and uses phrases like "you could have witnessed" to imagine a connection between the Mountain's Edge community and the area's history. After referencing the area's unique history, colorful settlers, and dramatic growth, the site suggests that "at Mountain's Edge, you have the best promontory to witness it all." Somehow, the residents of Mountain's Edge, just by living where they do, are able to witness the past in a way that others cannot, thus giving them a sense of permanence and belonging to the land that they inhabit—or so the promotions would have you believe.

The references in the Mountain's Edge promotions are excellent examples of the nostalgic tendency toward selective memory. They draw on historic events and peoples and their connection to this land, but conveniently omit any mention of Native American "relocation," or the abuse suffered by the many Asian (and other) immigrants who toiled to build the railroads and were then left jobless when the last spike was hammered. These events from the past are out of sync with the positive imagery being created by marketers and are therefore erased from the promotional version of history.

Some promotions aim for a more personalized history. Instead of connecting the land with Native American tribes, frontiers, and other wider historical moments, a number of promotional items turn to the history of landownership in a given area. For instance, the promotional brochure and website for the community of Springfield in Fort Mill, South Carolina, offer details about a particular family with deep roots in the area. The brochure features a page with the heading "History is Alive and Well Here." This page recounts the story of the Springs family, identified as "inextricably linked to this community." After describing the various contributions that the family has made to the region over the years (including the establishment of the local textile industry), the brochure mentions that "members of the Springs family still live in Fort Mill and the surrounding area. Springfield is, in fact, being built on what was Springs family land and is named after the family's original home, built in 1804."

This focus on an individual family and their longtime connection with the area is significant for three reasons. First, it establishes Springfield as a family-centered community where genealogy-as-history plays a significant role in the local identity. Second, it establishes continuity in the face of massive changes. According to the brochure, "In an era of constant change, Fort Mill maintains the same charm it had at the turn of the century." Proving the existence of a quality as subjective as charm is, of course, next to impossible. However, the long history of the Springs family (dating back to the mid-1700s) paints a picture of a place that people love enough to stay for many generations, suggesting that the charm has, in fact, remained intact.

Most significant, the focus on the Springs family, their commitment to the land, and their contributions to the area essentially erases the history of another group who likely also lived on this land: African American slaves. A wealthy South Carolina family working in the textile industry in the early 1800s would most certainly have depended on slave labor for their success. While the Springfield land may have been owned by the Springs family, it was cultivated by slaves, whose history is notably erased from the story being told about this community's past.

The continuity of family is also important in the promotion of other communities. As K. Till points out in her study of Rancho Santa Margarita in Orange County, California, the promotional materials for the village state that the current owners of Rancho Santa Margarita are descendents of a family that has owned the land for generations, working as ranchers and farmers. "The legacy of the O'Neill family— described in 'historical newsletters' published by the Santa Margarita Company—is presented as evidence that the development company-family will continue the tradition of 'caring for the land.'" But as Till also points out, the O'Neill "family" history presented in the materials is really the history of the family's patriarch, Richard O'Neill, and his male heirs.[39] It thus presents history from the perspective of the white European land-owning male, erasing the stories of women, migrant workers, Mexican Americans, and others who have contributed to the area's development.

These examples demonstrate some of the political implications of selective memory and a nostalgic take on history. By choosing to emphasize (whether consciously or unconsciously) the past events and persons most likely to resonate with a mainstream audience, these promotions create images of communities that might seem comfortable to white, heteronormative, middle-class families. At the same time, the materials make certain groups (often minorities) invisible not only in the past as represented by the images, but also in the present and future that these promotions imagine.

The promotions for The Villages go a few steps farther than most, taking a great deal of creative license in their representations of the past. As the video host describes her grandfather's vision for The Villages, she notes that he wanted to create a town that was "rich in history." Rather than drawing on the history of the land before it was developed into a community, promotional materials available in The Villages (as well as plaques posted around the town squares) provide an *invented* history for the town. For example, the Lake Sumter Landing Historical District Map, available in the Sales and Information Center, provides descriptions of the history of various landmarks in the town square. Although most of the buildings are just a few years old, the map tells of their construction in the mid-1800s, noting the important role these buildings played in regional transportation, trade, and agriculture. The map makes no pretense to reality, openly announcing that the history it contains is partially invented and partially "borrowed . . . from Florida history, from American history, from local legends and from family stories."

Although The Villages may be unique in its presentation of admittedly fabricated history, these materials can be read as an extension of the techniques used by other communities. While other promotions may not include fictitious events in their historical accounts, their version of history is still manufactured. By choosing to emphasize certain aspects of history while minimizing or eliminating others, the promotional materials reflect a series of creative decisions through which historical 'authenticity' is packaged as a consumable image. In this case, as Till argues, "History becomes a spectacle: it is selectively arranged by neotraditionalists" and given an aura of authenticity and value, which is then passed on to the present community.[40] In the end, this is a question of control, as developers seek to regulate and manage every aspect of the idealized communities that they are creating.

Control is also a significant theme within *The Truman Show* and *Pleasantville*. It becomes very clear early in *The Truman Show* that the success of "The Truman Show" is dependent on the program's creator, Christof, maintaining control over Truman and his surroundings. Regulating Truman's surroundings proves to be the easier of the two tasks. Truman lives in the town of Seahaven, which was constructed by the show's producers solely for the purpose of providing a setting for Truman's life/television program. The town of Seahaven is essentially a giant television studio set, complete with artificial lighting and weather systems run by a computer. All of the town's inhabitants are actors, and they all take direction from Christof. Working on an enclosed set with paid actors allows Christof to manage most of the elements of Truman's existence, which is crucial to maintaining the illusion of reality for Truman. But it also gives Christof complete authority over an idealized town that has been constructed to his specifications. He has created a society that is devoid of any serious problems (at least in his view), and he does everything he can to maintain its status, which includes keeping Truman in the show.

Christof tries to control Truman by manipulating his emotions and his social interactions, usually with the help of actors. When these methods fail, Christof and his cast and crew resort to more physical, sometimes even violent tactics, physically inhibiting Truman's ability to move about as he desires. For example, when Truman tries to drive out of town, the street fills with traffic, halting his progress. When he manages to get around the traffic, and continues his path out of town, producers have to step up their efforts to limit his mobility. They first stage a forest fire, which Truman drives right through, and then a leak at the nuclear power station, which he also tries to get around. When the shift from irritation (traffic) to danger (fires and radiation) fails to persuade Truman to stop, the producers are left with violence as their last resort. Truman is eventually stopped by a group of police officers and men in hazmat uniforms who chase him into the woods, tackle him, and return him home. Later, when Truman decides to use a sailboat to escape Seahaven, Christof commands his crew to create a violent storm that will capsize Truman. While Christof's more subtle manipulations initially go unnoticed, his actions become more obvious when they turn violent. As the obsessive creator of the world in which Truman lives, Christof would rather kill Truman than lose him to the outside world. By exaggerating Christof's manipulative behavior to hyperbolic proportions, *The Truman Show* critiques the subtler influences used by those who design the everyday spaces in which we live, particularly neotraditional communities.

While in *The Truman Show* a single person (Christof) has almost complete authority over everyone and everything, in *Pleasantville* it is much less clear who or what is in charge. Initially, David and Jennifer assume that the mysterious TV repairman responsible for sending them to Pleasantville is the one determining their fates. Eventually, David realizes that his actions have the potential to change the course of events in the town, and he begs Jennifer to play by the rules, saying, "If we don't play along, we could alter their whole existence, and then we may never get home." He decides that maintaining the status quo is the only way to manage the situation and find a way home.

When the presence of David and Jennifer begins to have an effect on the town, the local Chamber of Commerce (composed entirely of middle-aged white men) steps in to assert their authority. Before the changes introduced by David and Jennifer, this authority was unnecessary, because the status quo was always maintained. With change in the air, the Chamber of Commerce, acting as the town government, composes an official code of conduct for the town, emphasizing stasis and continuity, and requiring schools to teach the "non-changeist" view of history. The code also establishes rules about aesthetics, specifying such things as acceptable paint colors. In this way, the Chamber of Commerce's rules begin to mimic those of the homeowner's associations popular in many neotraditional communities, and they emphasize just how frustrating these rules can be.

Whether it is the TV repairman, David, or the Chamber of Commerce, those attempting to gain or maintain control in *Pleasantville* do so by trying to prevent change. As Davis argues, nostalgia is a strategy for establishing continuity between a seemingly static past, a turbulent present, and an unpredictable future.[41] Wilson offers a similar view, arguing that nostalgia helps to ground us in times of uncertainty. She says that "the acts of remembering, recalling, reminiscing, and the corollary emotional experience of nostalgia may facilitate the kind of coherence, consistency, and sense of identity that each of us so desperately needs."[42] As a result, many resort to nostalgia as a way of avoiding or denying change.

In the case of *Pleasantville*, all the characters eventually realize that the prevention of change is impossible. In a typical sitcom world, which "Pleasantville" was before David and Jennifer arrived, events are captured on video and then replayed again and again, and nothing changes. The viewer, in this case David, is able to view a particular scenario repeatedly, knowing exactly what will happen and when it will happen—there are no unexpected developments or surprises. This is part of what makes old television programs so comforting for David, who regularly escapes into "Pleasantville" to avoid the turbulence of his life in the present. This is also part of what makes nostalgia so comforting. Our fond memories of the past (accurate or not) do not seem to change very much in our minds. While our understanding of past events does evolve with time, age, and experience, this evolution is a gradual one without any drastic changes.

In the end, *Pleasantville*'s David has much in common with *The Truman Show*'s Christof. In both cases, they look nostalgically to an idealized and fictionalized time and place, finding a certain comfort in it. Christof imagines a utopian world that is rooted in early family sitcoms, and then assembles the resources needed to create that world for someone else to live in. David's mastery of every detail of "Pleasantville" trivia gives him a different sense of comfort, providing a degree of stability in the changing world that he inhabits. For them, and for us, nostalgia is intimately tied to a fantasy of control. A nostalgic view of

FIGURE 6. After being transported into the world of the sitcom, David (Tobey Maguire) and Jennifer (Reese Witherspoon) realize that they have a lot to learn about their new environment (*Pleasantville*). Frame enlargement.

the past is one that springs from our own mind. It is, of course, helped by other people's recollections, written histories, cultural representations, etc. But our own nostalgic view of the past is just that—our own. We control it, just as Christof controls the Seahaven that he created in his mind and David controls the town of Pleasantville that exists in his imagination. But when Christof physically re-creates an idyllic past in a studio, or when David travels to the fictional past of his favorite TV show, those past worlds become the present, which is something Christof and David can no longer control. While the promotions for many new communities seem to promise a lifestyle rooted in unchanging traditional values, *The Truman Show* and *Pleasantville* suggest that these are promises that cannot be kept, because change is inevitable. The films also suggest that while there is a sense of comfort provided by a nostalgic view of the world, any attempt to re-create or reinhabit a nostalgic past is likely to lead to frustration and disappointment. This is, of course, exactly what the promotional materials described above tend to do, with their present identity so heavily dependent upon a carefully constructed past. As both David and Truman figure out by the end of their respective stories, the present may be complicated, but it beats the repression and repetition of a life stuck in a nostalgic past.

Rerun, Reuse, Recycle

The emphasis on a desirable, nostalgic vision of the past is clearly a common strategic element in the promotions of new communities throughout the United States. While a few prominent design firms like Duany Plater-Zyberk (DPZ) and Calthorpe Associates have made their marks nationwide, most communities are planned and designed by local and regional companies. However, the similarities between their marketing approaches point to the high degree of centralization that structures this industry, especially in terms of idea generation. This is, in part, due to the enduring success of DPZ. As previously mentioned, this is the design firm behind Seaside, Florida, the development credited with kicking off the wave of New Urbanism and Traditional Neighborhood Development. DPZ and its projects continue to serve as models for smaller companies and designers nationwide.

DPZ's Seaside not only serves as a model of New Urbanism, but also as the home of the Seaside Institute, which, according to its website, offers forums and conferences that "provide the information and the tools to drive and inspire the successful communities of the future."[43] Building on the principles established by the Congress for the New Urbanism, the Seaside Institute helps developers with ideas for design, financing, political negotiating, and marketing. For example, the institute's seminar entitled "Marketing New Urban and Smart Growth Communities" provided developers, builders, and realtors with the tools necessary to maximize sales in their communities, and recommended that new developers work with marketing firms who had experience with other similar communities.[44] One such company is Milesbrand, a firm whose clients include the Seaside Institute, the Congress for the New Urbanism, various builders, developers, and over thirty TNDs and Master Planned Communities across the country. As TND marketer Scott Doyon notes, "The challenge for developers is the relative dearth of such providers."[45] With a limited number of marketing firms catering to developments across the country, it is not surprising that so many of the promotional materials follow similar strategies.

The promotional materials examined for this project go to great lengths to draw on the past, history, memory, and nostalgia in their attempts to sell their communities to potential residents, investors, and politicians. The promotions draw elements of the past into their sales pitch in three key ways: by visually referencing the past through the surface appearance of brochures, videos, and other materials, by verbally evoking a vague sense of "pastness," and by making direct references to actual history. These strategies all depend on one thing for their success. The audiences to which they are appealing must have a nostalgic view of the past. In other words, they must long for a return to the past that is imagined within these promotions—even when such a past never existed. The materials work very hard to assist that longing by painting an appealing picture of the past, suggesting that things really were better in days gone by.

If nostalgia is an act of selective memory used to make meaning in the present, then the carefully designed nostalgic images in these materials may tell us something about the communities that the developers are creating. By choosing to emphasize certain aspects of history while removing any negative images associated with the land (such as slavery or Native American relocation), these materials present a "new and improved" version of history, where conflict and oppression are forgotten. In the process, the histories of many groups and individuals are conveniently erased from the communities' imaginations. What is left is a safe and comfortable version of the past, used to create a safe and comfortable new community that subtly reinforces the ideologies of a white, heteronormative, middle-class society.

This nostalgic approach to the world is not limited to promotional materials for suburban communities. Many social debates in America involve an argument based on nostalgic versions of the past. For example, the Tea Party movement became a visible political force during the 2010 midterm election cycle. This conservative grassroots movement built its platform on the belief that the American people need to return to the Constitution for guidance, and that the original intent of the document and its authors should continue to guide the nation's policy decisions. While this return to our origins may sound patriotic to some, others have pointed out that the Constitution was written in a very different time, and adopting the attitudes of that time would mean negating the advances of women, people of color, gays and lesbians, and other minorities. Similarly, prominent conservative politicians and pundits, including Sarah Palin, Michele Bachmann, Rick Santorum, and Glenn Beck have espoused the need to return to "traditional values" centered on God and family. While this approach has openly endorsed the preservation of heteronormative definitions of marriage at the expense of gay rights, critics have suggested that it also includes more subtle overtones of racism and sexism.

Some of the debates explored in the following chapters also point to the problems caused by a nostalgic worldview. For example, when people label the nuclear family structure as "traditional" and present it as a key characteristic of the "good old days," it becomes easier to demonize those whose families do not fit this mold. When people "remember" a version of American history with fewer minorities and immigrants, it becomes easier to exclude them in the present. As the films examined here demonstrate, clinging too tightly to nostalgic visions of the past can have negative consequences for individuals and society in the present and future.

Clearly there is a relationship between *The Truman Show* and *Pleasantville* and the neotraditional communities represented by the promotions examined in this chapter. One might suggest that the towns of Seahaven and Pleasantville are based on the types of communities that I have described. On the other hand, many of the existing communities project images that reflect the idealized suburbia created by 1950s sitcoms—the very communities targeted by both films. It is difficult to say which image was the inspiration for the other, or if there is even any identifiable original. As Jean Baudrillard has argued, the breakdown of the distinction between representation and reality has led to "the generation by models of a real without origin or reality: a hyperreal."[46] This hyperreal image of a particular suburban way of life is bounced around from film to television to community promotions, seemingly disconnected from any historical reality. As Nezar AlSayyad suggests, today's neotraditional community may in fact be a copy without an original, "a simulacrum once removed from the object it tries to reproduce."[47]

In this circulation of suburban images, all the texts examined in this chapter draw from and contribute to the ever-expanding bank of meanings that make up the suburban intertext. While the films rely on existing suburban images as the foundation of their critique, the promotional materials rely on flattering suburban imagery to help generate the positive feelings that they are trying to sell. Through a filter of nostalgia, each text creates new images of its own—some of them critical, others celebratory—which then circulate and shape the meanings of other suburban narratives and images.

In the end, the self-reflexivity of *The Truman Show* and *Pleasantville* is a crucial element in the distinction between their use of nostalgia and the promotional materials' use of nostalgia. Robert Stam differentiates reflexivity from illusionism, which he says "presents its characters as real people, its sequence of words or images as real time, and its representations as substantiated fact."[48] The promotional materials examined above fall into this category. They offer images of communities, families, individuals, streetscapes, and homes, asking the viewer to read them as realistic representations of the developments they promote. Even when all the images come from stock photo collections (as is the case with communities that have not broken ground or are currently under construction), they generally do not seek to draw attention to themselves as created images.

An image that is self-reflexive, on the other hand, "points to its own mask and invites the public to examine its design and texture."[49] When read in conjunction with the images of neotraditional community developments, *The Truman Show* and *Pleasantville*, through their self-reflexive presentation, invite us to examine not only the films themselves, but all manufactured images of suburban spaces. They reveal the complex process whereby nostalgia is used to create suburban imagery, which is in turn used to create a sense of nostalgia, binding the two together in a simulacral relationship that suggests that American suburbia exists as little more than a set of intertwined images, incessantly replayed for our consumption.

2

Back Yard Fences

The Public, the Private, and the Family in Suburban Dramas

In a revealing sequence from *American Beauty* (1999), suburban father Lester Burnham (Kevin Spacey) is eavesdropping outside his teenage daughter's bedroom door. Inside the room, Lester's daughter, Jane (Thora Birch), is trying to ignore the comments of her friend, Angela (Mena Suvari), who is talking about how attractive Lester is, and how she would willingly have sex with him if he worked out a little. Although Lester is outside the door listening and cannot see into the room, the sense that he is inappropriately crossing certain boundaries is enhanced by the fact that Angela (and potentially Jane, though the framing makes it unclear) is dressed only in her underwear.

When the girls hear a noise at the window and go to investigate (and Lester runs off, worried that he has been caught), the girls discover that the boy next door, Ricky Fitts (Wes Bentley), has left a message for Jane, written in fire on the ground outside her house. As the girls stand near the open window contemplating Ricky's intentions, Ricky is in his own bedroom with his video camera pointed toward them. When Jane suggests that Ricky is probably taping them, Angela pulls the curtains open all the way and begins posing for the unseen voyeur. Ricky, however, ignores the exhibitionist Angela, and zooms in his camera to a reflection of Jane's face as she sits in front of a mirror, away from the window. Ricky hears a noise from the garage of the Burnham home, and then points his camera at Lester, who, after hearing Angela's comments, has decided to begin lifting weights (naked) in the garage.

Ricky continues shooting through the Burnhams' windows (muttering "Welcome to *America's Weirdest Home Videos*") until he is interrupted by a knock at his door. As Ricky closes his blinds and puts his camera away, his father, Frank (Chris Cooper), reminds Ricky that he does not like locked doors in his house. When Ricky finally opens the door, Frank hands him a small plastic cup and says that he needs to collect a urine sample from Ricky (Frank's attempt to keep Ricky off drugs).

This sequence highlights the complex and shifting boundaries between public and private that exist within and between families in the suburban domestic sphere. It raises questions about how the boundaries used to determine privacy in our culture match up with the boundaries we draw around families. It also shows how accepted privacy norms often privilege certain groups (in this case men and heads of households) over others. Various characters within this sequence violate the privacy of others, only to have their own privacy violated moments later. Each privacy breach differs from the others based on factors such as physical boundaries, familial relationships, and social expectations. Lester and Frank cross boundaries within their own homes, and in the process breach the privacy of their own children, while Ricky crosses a line between his parents' home and the neighbors' home. Lester breaches Jane and Angela's privacy aurally, while Ricky intrudes upon the Burnham home visually, and Frank demands physical access to the contents of Ricky's body. By videotaping what he sees in the neighbor's home and referencing a long-running network television program, Ricky's actions serve as a reminder of the ability of mass media to turn people's private activities into a public spectacle served up for a mass audience.[1] The overall sequence demonstrates how complicated the management of privacy has become in our daily lives.

The suburban setting of these scenes highlights the tensions between public and private that have been a part of suburban life since the earliest developments. On one hand, suburban neighborhoods provided an opportunity for nuclear families to find privacy and intimacy in a detached home. On the other hand, families moving into the suburbs were expected to be active participants in newly formed communities. This tension was emphasized by the basic design of most suburban tracts, which featured single-family houses connected to neighbors by way of yards, sidewalks, and shared streets. Although the physical designs and demographics of suburbs have changed over the years, the image of nuclear families balancing private family life with public community engagement has remained central to the suburban imagination.

With its longstanding connection to the family and its inherent tension between public and private, suburbia provides the ideal narrative setting to explore the intersections and contradictions between family structures and privacy boundaries. As a result, questions of privacy and the family play a significant role in many suburban narratives. For example, in *The Ice Storm* (1997), parents Ben and Elena Hood (Kevin Kline and Joan Allen) attempt to be good parents by asking about their children's activities and relationships, but the kids (Tobey Maguire and Christina Ricci) seem to see such questions as awkward and irritating encroachments upon their private lives. *Happiness* (1998) features a psychiatrist who is the father of two young boys and who is also a pedophile (Dylan Baker). Realizing that even his own home does not provide the privacy he requires, he resorts to drugging his entire family in order to hide his activities from them. In *The Truman Show* (1998), Truman's friends and family are actually actors who help to enable Truman's private life to be broadcast to an audience of millions of viewers around the world. In *Disturbia* (2007), a murderer relies on the privacy of his suburban home to conceal his illegal activities, but his crimes are uncovered by a teenaged neighbor (Shia Lebouf) who witnesses suspicious behavior from next door. Much of the salacious drama of *Desperate Housewives* (2004–2012) comes from revealing the private secrets that individual families on Wisteria Lane hide from the other families living around them.

While concerns about family and privacy play at least a small role in most suburban narratives, two texts in particular foreground the intersection of privacy and family boundaries as they play out in the American suburb: *American Beauty* and *Big Love* (2006–2011). Both these texts emphasize how much is at stake for individuals and families when it comes to demarcating their own privacy boundaries, and the development of both stories depends largely on characters' abilities to negotiate those boundaries. Additionally, because these stories emphasize relationships both within families and between families and their neighbors, they illuminate the complex and shifting nature of privacy boundaries in the domestic sphere. Most important, *American Beauty* and *Big Love* demonstrate how the rights to define one's own family or to determine one's own privacy boundaries are not granted equally to all groups in our society.

American Beauty is the story of the last year in the life of Lester Burnham, a suburban family man who has found his existence to be far less satisfying than he had hoped. His job has become tedious and meaningless, his marriage is more of a chore than a relationship, and his teenage daughter wants nothing to do with him. His wife, Carolyn (Annette Bening), and daughter, Jane, are equally unhappy with their own lives, as are the Burnhams' neighbors—Frank, Barbara (Allison Janney), and Ricky Fitts—as well as Jane's best friend, Angela. The film, with its tagline "Look Closer," tries to see beyond the superficial tranquility associated with suburban life, revealing a sense of dread and despair that eventually manifests itself in drug use, adultery, and murder.

The HBO series *Big Love* focuses on the unusual life of Bill Henrickson (Bill Paxton), a seemingly typical Utah man who happens to be a polygamist. He lives in the suburbs of Salt Lake City with his three wives—Barb (Jeanne Tripplehorn), Nicki (Chloë Sevigny), and Margene (Ginnifer Goodwin)—and their seven children. In order to blend in more effectively with the neighborhood, the Henricksons live in three neighboring houses, with each wife residing in her own house, and Bill rotating among all three. As described on the series' website, the Henricksons are "just another suburban family trying to live the American Dream, struggling to balance the needs of seven kids, three wives, three separate houses, and one husband-in-chief."[2] While concerns about privacy are a part of the entire series, much of the drama in the first season is especially focused on protecting the family's secrets by guarding their privacy. Therefore, my analysis in this chapter focuses on the series' first season, though I occasionally comment on pertinent developments in later seasons.

Both *American Beauty* and *Big Love* draw on an intertextual bank of suburban images to create an initial impression of the families involved in their stories. In fact, the streets and houses presented in the opening sequences of each text are reminiscent of the images offered by the sales brochures discussed in chapter I. The houses borrow from popular and tasteful architectural styles like Craftsman, Victorian, and Colonial Revival. They feature carefully manicured lawns and gardens, as emphasized by Carolyn pruning her roses in the opening of *American Beauty* and Bill dodging his automatic sprinklers in the opening of *Big Love*. The neighborhood in *Big Love* looks like many of those displayed in contemporary ads, with its brand-new houses and recently planted trees that sit well below second-story windows. The neighborhood in *American Beauty*, with its mature vegetation and lived-in yet well-maintained homes, looks more like what the new developments aspire to be. While these images initially suggest the happy suburban nuclear family life imagined by postwar sitcoms and recycled in contemporary promotions, both texts ultimately undermine such images by showing that there is more here than meets the eye.

American Beauty and *Big Love* make use of their suburban settings to comment on the intertwining of privacy and families not only in the space of the suburban home, but in American culture at large. By exaggerating privacy breaches and family crises to hyperbolic proportions, they point to the ways that laws, policies, and social norms governing privacy often reinforce the social hierarchies that exist in our society. My investigation of these texts is situated within ongoing conversations about the nature of privacy and the family not only in suburbia, but also in American culture as a whole. Using these conversations as a starting point, this chapter offers an in-depth look at *American Beauty* and *Big Love* to show how the producers of these texts use the narrative space of suburbia to reveal ways in which discourses of privacy and the family protect mainstream, conservative values at the expense of those who do not fit social norms.

Privacy and the Family in Suburbia and America

The tensions between public and private in suburban life are in some ways tied to the relationship between *Gemeinschaft* and *Gesellschaft*. These concepts, introduced by German philosopher and sociologist Ferdinand Tönnies and usually translated as "community" and "society," represent an idealized dichotomy of human relationships. Gemeinschaft-like relationships are characterized by strong identification with the community and its traditions, as well as emotional bonds with and interdependence on other members of the community.[3] Gesellschaft-like relationships are more impersonal, emotionally disconnected, temporary, and often the means to an end, as people engage in these relationships as a way of achieving other goals.[4] Writing in the late 1800s, Tönnies associated Gemeinschaft-like relationships with extended families and rural villages, and suggested that Gesellschaft was more common in larger, industrializing cities.[5] Early champions of suburbia presented it as a Gemeinschaft-like antidote to the alienation of urban life.[6] Frederick Law Olmsted, a landscape architect and prominent figure in the early development of American suburbs, noted that a successful suburb must engender "the harmonious association and cooperation of men in a community, and the intimate relationship and constant intercourse, and inter-dependence between families."[7] As suburbs grew in popularity, participation in the community and friendly engagement with neighbors came to be seen as important ways of fitting in, and as crucial components of suburban life.

Embracing suburban community life often meant giving up a certain amount of privacy. One aspect of Gesellschaft-like urban life that some see as an advantage is the fact that the more fleeting, impersonal relationships allow for a measure of anonymity, which functions as a kind of privacy, and thus allows for more personal freedom. In her classic analysis of urban life, Jane Jacobs notes that this urban privacy still allows for a good deal of public contact in places like streets and sidewalks, which "bring together people who do not know each other in an intimate, private social fashion and in most cases do not care to know each other in that fashion."[8] People are therefore not isolated by urban privacy, but are essentially left to their own devices and free from unwanted personal intrusions.

Suburban life, on the other hand, often reduced personal privacy. In addition to the emphasis on public interaction in the community, certain residential design elements like the picture window and the sliding glass door became popular in postwar suburbs. Combined with the tightly packed arrangement of many developments, these elements created what became known as a "goldfish bowl" effect, and actually opened the house up to visual inspection by neighbors and passersby.[9] Since part of the appeal of suburban living has always been the opportunity to own a detached house that could serve as a family's retreat from the outside world, efforts to protect privacy became a priority. In her analysis of postwar homes, Dianne Harris points out that books and magazine articles about housing design during the era "repeatedly emphasized the need to exclude the outsider's gaze and to reduce interior familial frictions through proper design for privacy."[10] This desire for privacy continued to influence subsequent suburban designs, which carefully managed sightlines through the placement of walls, windows, and landscaping.

Promotional materials for contemporary suburban developments like those discussed in chapter 1 demonstrate the continuation of this public/private tension with repeated references to the privacy of the home and public life in the community. For example, the promotional website for Brenwick homes, a suburban developer in Indianapolis, says that "Brenwick's approach to community building has focused on shaping the land to create the spaces that evoke emotion, and *encourage social interaction while protecting privacy.*"[11] The social expectations of suburban life dictate that residents will balance their private life inside the home with a public face in the community.[12]

In addition to being seen as a private retreat within a community of neighbors, the suburban home has long been imagined as the ideal space to raise a family. Robert Fishman notes that increasing life expectancies and changes in economic structures during the eighteenth century led to the development of what we now commonly call the nuclear family: "closed in around itself, separated from its environment, focused especially on mutual intimacy and on child raising."[13] Many began to feel that the goals of this new type of family were at odds with the lifestyle available in urban areas. Writing in the mid-1800s, social reformer Catharine Beecher, horticulturalist/landscape architect Andrew Jackson Downing, and other champions of suburban life celebrated the importance of the family, and argued that the suburbs were the best place for domestic happiness.[14] The privacy offered by the house and lawn encouraged home-centered recreation and supposedly offered better opportunities for family bonding.[15] Over the years, developers, advertisers, magazine publishers, and other media producers have solidified the connection between the nuclear family and the suburban home, presenting them as almost inseparable.[16]

Debates about privacy and the nature of families are certainly not limited to suburbia. Legal historian Lawrence Friedman argues that "perhaps the most serious legal, political, and cultural struggle of the next generation will be the struggle over privacy—the struggle to contain and control technology and preserve our sacred, individual space."[17] Whether or not it ultimately becomes the next generation's most serious struggle, it is fair to say that concerns about privacy in its multitude of forms have worked their way into the nation's consciousness, playing a role in numerous contemporary debates.

In recent decades, science and technology have produced significant advances that have made privacy more difficult to protect. Microchips and magnetic strips allow government and commercial institutions to track the purchases and behaviors of citizens and consumers. Surveillance cameras, internet tracking software, satellite imaging, facial recognition software, and even advanced consumer electronics allow for the easy capture, storage, and transmission of personal images and information.

As technological advances have made privacy more difficult to protect, debates about the rights of AIDS patients, abortion and contraception, medically assisted suicide, and gay marriage have all raised questions about the boundaries of privacy in our culture. But no single event has contributed to privacy-related anxieties more than the terrorist attacks of September 11, 2001. More specifically, privacy fears have been fueled by the government's response to the attacks, in the form of the Patriot Act, which amended several federal laws pertaining to communications, banking, and immigration, ultimately expanding the government's surveillance activities in the name of national security.[18] Although some have agreed that giving up some privacy is an acceptable sacrifice in our attempts to combat terrorists, others have suggested that the War on Terror has led to a war on privacy.

As with the anxieties about privacy, public concerns about the family have been very visible in recent years. While the importance of familial relationships has been a concern of many people for many years, the so-called "family values" debate took on a life of its own in 1992, when Vice President Dan Quayle launched his infamous attack on the television character Murphy Brown. Arguing that the character's choice to have a baby out of wedlock was a threat to American family values, Quayle kicked off a debate that would become a significant talking point in the 1992 presidential campaign and continue to inflect political discussions for years to follow.

Michael Shapiro argues that the aim of the family values discourse is "to install a commitment to the moral and political importance of the traditional family, a regulative ideal that is represented as both contractual and natural."[19] At the heart of the debate has been the very definition of what constitutes a family. Conservative politicians have sought to maintain an idealized image of the family in its nuclear form. Often celebrated as the "traditional" structure for a family, this image tends to be rooted in nostalgic—and frequently inaccurate—views of the past. Others have pushed for more flexible models of the family that allow for extended families, blended families, single-parent households, and so forth. This argument has played out most visibly in the debates about same-sex marriage. Since the married couple is held up as the appropriate core of the ideal family, the definition of marriage is a key component of the definition of family.

The struggle over the family is certainly not new, nor is it limited to political platforms. As Robert Wuthnow notes, "The family has become a topic that pundits, public officials, social scientists, lawyers, clergy, and community leaders seem unable to leave alone. Diagnosing its ills has become a cultural industry."[20] In her study of onscreen families in the 1980s, Sarah Harwood notes the difference between the ideal of "the family" (an ideological construct based on stasis and tradition) and material "families," which are more likely to exist in real life. She argues that it is the gap between real families and the nearly impossible ideology of "the family" that leads people to see the family as being in crisis.[21] For some, the family is in crisis. For others, it is merely in transition, as it always has been and always will be.

With questions about privacy and the family playing such a significant role in political debates, news coverage, and legal arenas, it is not surprising that cultural producers would engage with these issues in their work. With its detached, single-family homes connected to neighbors by yards, sidewalks, and public streets, the spaces of suburbia provide an ideal setting for the exploration of privacy and the family in American culture. *American Beauty* and *Big Love* present very different families and situations, but they reach very similar conclusions about the effects of privacy on mainstream and alternative families.

The Onion of Privacy

As evidenced by the sequence from *American Beauty* described above, identifying the boundaries of privacy is not a simple task, in part because not everyone defines public and private in the same way. For example, there is the liberal-economistic model, which is common in most public policy discussions. In this model, the distinction between public and private is seen as the difference between state administration and the market economy.[22] Jürgen Habermas, Hannah Arendt, and others theorizing the public sphere see the public as the space of political citizenship, distinct from both the state and the market.[23] Others define the private as that which is beyond the reach of law and government. A fourth view defines the public as a space of sociability and visibility, with the private offering the chance to be away from such interaction and scrutiny. Of these various public/private models, the model that plays the biggest role in *American Beauty* and *Big Love* is that which defines public and private based on social relationships and activities, rather than legal or economic parameters.

Philippe Ariès offers a helpful account of the social relationship between public and private in his examination of the history of family life.[24] Ariès's approach seeks to situate the family in its social context, which leads him to discuss the relationship between private family life in the home and the social life that exists outside the home—in public. The importance of public space for Ariès is not the potential it offers for democratic participation and citizenship, as it is for Habermas and Arendt, but rather its potential for social interaction. In particular, Ariès's work is significant because he identifies a shift over time from a world based on public, social interaction to one centered on the private home. As Jeff Weintraub notes, "The decay of the older public world and the emergence of the modern family (along with other relationships committed to creating islands of privacy and intense intimacy) form a mutually reinforcing process."[25] Ariès sees the public and the private as mutually constitutive, with changes in one bringing about changes in the other.

Within this model, there is still a complexity that makes simple definitions of public and private impossible. The sequence from *American Beauty* that opened this chapter demonstrates a range of privacies, and their juxtaposition highlights the similarities and differences between them. As Beate Rössler suggests, the onion offers a helpful model here, in that it allows us to distinguish between different layers of privacy.[26] In this case, the outer layer is the boundary drawn around each family's home. Ricky visually invades the Burnham home not only by looking into their windows, but also by recording images with his video camera. Within the Burnham home, Jane's bedroom creates another layer, which Lester invades aurally by placing his ear to the door to listen to the girls' conversation. At the center of the onion is the realm of personal or bodily intimacy, in this case exemplified by Ricky's body and personal autonomy, which his father invades by demanding a urine sample. While the second and third examples demonstrate the breaching of personal privacy boundaries within a given family and their home, the first example shows a breach of the boundary between two families, or between a family and the outside world.

Each of the examples is slightly different based on how the privacy boundary is breached and the relationship between the individuals on either side of the boundary. What they all have in common is the fact that they all fall primarily within the realm of social privacy, rather than legal privacy. As Ferdinand Schoeman suggests, "Understanding how privacy works in the social context is more complicated than understanding how privacy works in the governmental context."[27] While legal definitions of privacy are anything but simple, and are often open to interpretation by the courts, there is at least a written basis for establishing guidelines. Privacy that is granted to individuals based on social norms is far more complex. Norms shift and change over time, they vary from person to person and family to family, and the failure to negotiate them can have unpredictable consequences.

Of the above examples, Ricky's act of peeping is the closest to crossing legal boundaries. However, he is not trespassing or physically entering his neighbors' home, but rather viewing them from his own bedroom, which just happens to be positioned in such a way that its windows afford a view of the Burnhams' house. The Burnhams have voluntarily left their windows uncovered, and if a next-door neighbor happens to see in those windows, there is little room to argue for a legal invasion of privacy. It may be socially frowned upon, but it is not illegal. And while some employees have contested the privacy invasion involved with employer-ordered drug testing, a court is very unlikely to step in to protect the legal rights of a teenager whose father orders a drug test, choosing instead to protect the privacy of the family unit by allowing the parent to make decisions about raising his child. Lester's eavesdropping is a similar case. Tapping someone's phone line may be against the law, but a father secretly listening to his daughter's conversation in the family home is unlikely to draw any legal attention. The homeowner's privacy from outside intervention is protected over the daughter's privacy from her father.

These examples show the fine line between legal privacy and social privacy, demonstrating how acts that occur *within* the domestic sphere (whether within a family, or between a family and their neighbors) are handled differently from those that cross from the fully public realm into the legally recognized privacy of domestic space. While Colonel Fitts's behavior may be extreme and Lester's behavior may be creepy, neither is illegal. And because they both occur within the homes that these men own, the behaviors are shielded from outside scrutiny by laws that protect the privacy of property owners. As such, the scenes highlight one of the ways that American privacy laws benefit certain groups (in this case, adult male homeowners) to the detriment of others (their wives and children.) Feminists have long argued that domestic privacy laws have been misused in ways that perpetuate rape, incest, and domestic violence.[28] While the behaviors displayed in this sequence do not fall into these categories, in a later scene Colonel

Fitts's behavior does escalate to violence as he kicks and beats Ricky in his bedroom. In addition to demonstrating the unequal application of privacy in our culture, the above sequence also shows the ease with which boundaries of privacy are breached within the domestic sphere.

Big Love also highlights the layered complexity of privacy for the suburban family, but unlike the characters in *American Beauty*, whose primary concern is for their personal privacy and the protection of individual secrets, the Henrickson family of *Big Love* must deal with one big secret that includes them all. Given that polygamy is not accepted in our society, the mere fact that they *are* one big family is something that they try to conceal from all but the most trusted of friends, and their attempts to keep this secret provide much of the dramatic tension within the series, particularly in its first season. In addition to this inside/outside boundary, conflicts related to privacy frequently surface within the family itself.

The physical arrangement of the Henrickson family makes their situation more complicated than most families. While they consider themselves one large family, they live in three neighboring houses as a way of hiding their status. Thus the boundary that is most commonly relied upon to separate the private family from the public world—the perimeter of the single-family home—in this case marks boundaries between three segments of one family. Though the characters repeatedly talk about the fact that they are one family, and that there should not be any secrets between them, they also try to rely on the boundaries of their individual houses to provide the privacy afforded to most "normal" families.

As an example, one story arc in the first season deals with Nicki's excessive spending habits and her attempts to hide the extreme credit card debt that she has accrued. Living in her own house, away from Bill and his other wives, gives Nicki the privacy necessary to make purchases over the phone, receive packages, and field calls from creditors without anyone's knowing. However, the privacy afforded by the house is, in this case, especially tenuous, because family members are constantly coming and going. In the episode "Eclipse," as Nicki begins to feel overwhelmed by the rising debt, she locks herself in the bathroom, later telling Barb and Margene that she did it because it was the

FIGURE 7. The Henricksons live in three neighboring but separate houses as a way of blending into the community (*Big Love*). Frame enlargement.

only way she could have any privacy. And in the episode "Eviction," when Barb discovers the boxes of credit card bills that Nicki has been hiding under her bed, Nicki explodes in anger, accusing Barb of invading her privacy.

Another example from the first season comes from a story arc involving Barb and Bill having an affair. Although the two are married, Bill has certain nights scheduled with each of his wives, and Bill and Barb repeatedly meet for sex on days not designated as "Barb's night." They soon realize that Barb's house does not provide the privacy they require, and they resort to meeting at a hotel in order to avoid the watchful eyes of the rest of the family.

These examples demonstrate the conflicts that arise when individuals within a family have different ideas about where privacy boundaries should be drawn. They also highlight the fact that the distinction between public and private is often contextual, and can change based on where a person is, who they are with, and who is making the distinction. For example, in Nicki's case, the privacy of the home (defined in contrast with the public street outside) is not private enough. In order to get away from members of her family, she retreats to a specific room within the house, the bathroom, which then becomes private in contrast with the more public nature of the rest of the house. Nicki's actions and comments thus act to carve newly defined public and private spaces out of what was previously an entirely private space. Similarly, when Barb and Bill cannot find the privacy they desire in Barb's house, they move their activities to a building that is generally public, but which allows them to pay for access to a room which becomes, temporarily, their own private retreat inside the larger public building. The relative and contextual nature of public and private that these scenes highlight is part of what makes policing and protecting privacy so tricky. It is also what allows privacy boundaries to be manipulated and interpreted in ways that benefit those already in power.

While the individuals within the Henrickson family seek privacy as a way of keeping secrets from one another, they are all united in their attempt to keep secrets from those outside the family. As Schoeman suggests, "Associations of people, like the individuals who compose the associations, require privacy. . . . Privacy functions in the context of enabling and facilitating associative features of life."[29] In other words, privacy is not limited to individuals, as groups require intimate zones that allow them to nurture relationships without the interference of outsiders. In the Henricksons' case, privacy is essential for the protection of the family, as public knowledge of their polygamist arrangement would open them up to criticism, hatred, and ostracism from the community (as it does in later seasons). Therefore, even more important than the privacy boundaries that exist within the family are the boundaries that exist between the family and the outside world. As with *American Beauty*, the privacy concerns raised by *Big Love* show how different layers and types of privacy interact in ways that both threaten and protect the family, demonstrating the complex nature of privacy in our culture.

Privacy and Visibility

Visibility is a crucial component of any debate that seeks to determine what counts as public and what counts as private. In the broadest and most simplified sense, the public is defined by visibility, while the private is defined by invisibility. Varying definitions of what constitutes visibility make the relationship more complicated than a clear-cut pairing of two binary oppositions, but it is fair to say that some version of visibility plays a part in any discussion of public and private.

Hannah Arendt, for example, builds her definition of the public realm in part on the fact that "everything that appears in public can be seen and heard by everybody and has the widest publicity." She goes on to note that the distinction between public and private "equals the distinction between things that should be shown and things that should be hidden."[30] Interestingly, this comment places the burden on the individual (or perhaps a family or other group) to make something either public or private by showing or hiding it. At the same time, it suggests that the individual must follow certain socially determined norms, given that there are some things that Arendt suggests *should* be either public or private. Shapiro goes so far as to connect the family to these ideas of privacy and visibility, noting that "much of bourgeois family life has been organized around a designed control of visibility." In other words, a family's identity is often shaped by a careful regulation of privacy, an "economy of exposure and concealment" that determines how much of the family's business is to be known by others.[31] Families that keep their private lives invisible have a much better chance of controlling the image they present in public.

The spaces of suburbia are often designed to assist in the creation of an invisible private life. The single-family homes and spacious yards that dominate suburbia minimize the problem of neighbors overhearing conversations—a more common concern in tightly packed urban spaces with thin walls. The privacy concern in suburban spaces thus shifts to visibility, leading designers and homeowners to focus on fences, walls, and strategic landscaping in order to decrease visibility and increase privacy.[32] While these techniques may block visibility in the real world, they are ineffective in the narrative spaces of cinema and television, given that the camera has access to the homes of most characters. Setting a story inside the suburban home essentially takes a private space and puts it on public display. The audience is given access to activities and conversations that are usually off-limits to outsiders. While granting an audience visual access to the private lives of fictional families may seem inconsequential, the process is not that different from what occurs on reality TV programs like *The Real*

Housewives of Orange County (2006–) or *Extreme Makeover: Home Edition* (2003–2012), where real people invite the cameras into their homes. Whether the families on screen are real or fictional, cameras that enter the space of the home provide access to that which is usually off-limits to spectators. By crossing the usual boundaries of visibility, these narratives draw attention to the importance of managing such boundaries in our daily lives.

Concerns about visibility run throughout both *American Beauty* and *Big Love*, and nowhere are they more apparent than in the relationships between the central families and their neighbors. Neighbors often breach the standard boundaries of privacy simply by virtue of their physical proximity, which often allows for increased visual access to activities of those living near them. While they may not be as close as family, they are certainly closer (both physically and socially) than the community at large. As Constance Perin notes, "Of all the relationships we have, those with neighbors are likely to be the most ambiguous. . . . Outside our closest circle of kin and the friends we share our houses with, only neighbors might see us offstage in our bathrobes taking in the paper, wearing our shabbiest clothes to paint the trim."[33] The neighbors in *American Beauty* and *Big Love* also see things that most people would not, often leading to complications for those involved.

Ricky breaches the privacy boundary of the neighboring Burnham home when he videotapes Jane, Angela, and Lester through the windows of their house. While the presence of the camera raises the stakes a bit (permanently recording images rather than just catching fleeting glimpses), Ricky's behavior is generally facilitated by the standards of suburban design. That is to say, the proximity of the two houses and the placement of their windows (not unusual for a suburban community) make it very easy for the neighbors to see into each other's homes. Ricky's father also crosses the boundary into the Burnham home when he looks out the window to see his son interacting with Lester in the Burnhams' garage. Misinterpreting what he sees, Colonel Fitts thinks that he is witnessing his son performing oral sex on Lester.

The visual privacy breaches between neighbors in the film are multidirectional, as evidenced by a scene in which Jane witnesses Colonel Fitts beating Ricky as punishment for entering his locked study. At the beginning of the scene, Jane and Ricky are looking at each other through their respective windows. Ricky is videotaping Jane, and she responds by removing her shirt and bra. At this point, they have each invited the other (at least visually if not physically) into their private bedrooms. When Colonel Fitts bursts in unannounced and attacks Ricky, Jane witnesses what Colonel Fitts most likely assumed was a private moment. Treating Ricky's room as private space, Colonel Fitts clearly thinks that his abusive actions will be hidden from view rather than being put on display. He is initially unaware that Ricky has opened his room to Jane's gaze, thereby making the space semi-public and exposing the physical attack. And when Colonel Fitts looks out Ricky's window and into Jane's, she quickly closes her curtains as a way of shutting Ricky's father out of the private space that she had recently invited Ricky to (visually) enter.

These scenes serve as a reminder of how easily the bounds of privacy are breached by nearby neighbors, and how difficult it is to maintain control over exactly who has visual access to one's private space. The scene involving Ricky's beating also points to the dangers of protecting one person's privacy at the expense of another person's safety—a concern commonly voiced in discussions of domestic violence.

Visibility is also a significant concern in *Big Love*. In this case, the Henricksons are especially worried about concealing the fact that they are polygamists, and visual concealment is a significant component of this. The Henricksons' biggest threat comes from their neighbors Pam and Carl Martin (Audrey Wasilewski and Carlos Jacott), who live across the street. The Martins frequently serve as a reminder of the tenuous nature of the Henricksons' privacy, as they constantly appear, standing outside their home, silently witnessing the goings-on of the Henrickson houses. As Nicki's conspicuously large family leaves at the end of her son's birthday party to return to their polygamist compound, Carl watches from his front porch. When Barb's sister, who disapproves of polygamy, storms out of the house and speeds off in her car, Pam is watching from her front yard. And when the family returns from the disastrous Mother of the Year ceremony, where the revelation of Barb's involvement with polygamy leads to her disqualification, Carl is again watching from the porch. Rössler describes privacy as freedom from "the look of the Other."[34] She argues that even if someone is unable to take actions to physically alter your behavior, the social pressures embodied in their look can inhibit your sense of freedom. Privacy as invisibility offers an escape from this look and the accompanying pressure. The proximity of neighbors can make it difficult to completely escape their gaze and become invisible. The Martins' proximity allows them to see and hear things that the Henricksons would rather keep hidden, demonstrating the fragile boundaries that exist between individuals and their neighbors when it comes to privacy.[35] Even when they are witnessing seemingly inconsequential moments, Carl and Pam, by physically seeing snapshots of the Henricksons' life, stand in for the metaphorical eyes of society, constantly watching anyone who deviates from the norm.

The relationships between neighbors in *American Beauty* and *Big Love* also point to the differences between what Laud Humphreys, in his discussion of public sex, refers to as "physical visibility" and "social visibility." Physical visibility, as the term suggests, refers to the degree to which something can actually be seen. On the other hand, Humphreys says that spaces are *socially* visible "in the degree to which they preclude the initial consent to copresence of those who may be involved as witnesses or participants in the act."[36] In other words, the social visibility of a space is increased if strangers or other uninvited individuals are likely to enter that space without notice. The family home, therefore, is characterized by low social visibility because of the fact that we generally regulate who is in the house, inviting guests to a position within the household layer of privacy. Social mores, and most laws, dictate that those outside the home will essentially avert their gaze from the activities taking place within the private home, giving it a certain socially sanctioned invisibility. But as the previous examples have shown, neighbors complicate the matter. The physical visibility afforded by their proximity overrides the social invisibility granted to the private home, leading to conflicts between neighbors, and reminding viewers that social norms are not effective when it comes to protecting the bounds of family privacy.

Both *American Beauty* and *Big Love* use neighbors as stand-ins for the eyes of society. They build on the physical visibility afforded by suburban spaces to draw attention to broader notions of visibility in

our society. The individual characters who physically see and judge
the activities of their neighbors remind us of the ways that the "eyes
of the mainstream" are always on the lookout for non-normative
behavior. Marginalized groups rarely have control over their own visibility, and are made visible or invisible depending on the needs of the
mainstream. In this way, privacy by way of visibility is manipulated to
maintain social hierarchies in favor of mainstream values and to the
detriment of more subordinate groups within our culture.

Performance and the Value of Privacy

The distinction between public and private is not entirely determined
by visibility or invisibility. Individuals and families can strengthen
and manage their own public/private boundaries in part through their
behavior. It is not uncommon for people to behave a particular way in
the workplace and social settings so as to carefully manage their public
persona while allowing very different behaviors to define their private
identities. Erving Goffman's ideas about the performances people enact
in their daily lives are helpful in understanding these shifts in behavior. In Goffman's framework, performance is not limited to the theater
and silver screen. Instead, he suggests that we are all performing all
the time. We perform the role of husband, wife, boss, student, and any
others that suit our needs, modifying our behavior to fit expected social
norms. A central component of Goffman's ideas about performance is
the concept of the stage. Coinciding with the different roles that we
perform are different stages, such as work, school, and church. Goffman
elaborates further by suggesting that we can identify front and backstage regions of our lives. "A back region or backstage may be defined as
a place, relative to a given performance, where the impression fostered
by the performance is knowingly contradicted as a matter of course. . . .
Here the performer can relax; he can drop his front, forgo speaking
his lines, and step out of character."[37] While Goffman does not directly
equate front and backstage with public and private, his description of
backstage spaces correlates in many ways with the descriptions other
scholars give for private spaces. In particular, the space of the home,
seen by most as private (despite the complications discussed above),

is also seen as a kind of backstage, where people let down their guard, step out of their public personas, and become their "real" selves.

While we each have access to our own onstage and backstage personas, we are not often privy to backstage views of other people. This is, after all, what distinguishes them as "backstage," and it is closely related to the previously discussed concept of visibility. We generally try to make our backstage selves and lives invisible to all but our closest family and friends. By their very nature, film and television narratives give viewers access to both the onstage and backstage performances of the characters on which they focus, allowing viewers a glimpse of how people shift back and forth between various versions of their personas. The contrast between onstage performances and backstage realities is of special significance to suburban narratives because it is frequently a crucial element in the construction of the suburban façade. Characters' onstage personas typically blend in with their neighbors so as to maintain an image of suburban harmony, while backstage identities frequently undermine this carefully constructed exterior by expressing frustration, rage, or deviations from social norms. Storytellers thus use the split between onstage and backstage in suburban narratives to pry open the contradictions between hard-to-reach ideals and the realities of most people's lives.

In *American Beauty*, the difference between onstage and backstage is demonstrated most significantly by the Burnhams. On the outside, they appear to be a relatively happy, functional suburban family. Inside the home, however, their lives are filled with arguments and tension, leading to resentment, betrayal, and adultery. Although the distinction between onstage and backstage roughly follows the boundaries of the home, the line is drawn differently by different characters. For instance, Carolyn is the character most concerned with keeping up appearances whenever possible. When she and Lester attend a business reception, she says to him, "My business is selling an image, and part of my job is to live that image. . . . Just do me a favor—act happy tonight." As her comment suggests, the appropriate image is an integral part of her life, leading Carolyn to extend her onstage performance inward. She is concerned not only with growing flawless roses to make the outside of her house look beautiful, but also with keeping up a similar appearance on the inside. She does everything she can to create the ideal family tableau, as evidenced by an early scene involving a family dinner. The immaculate dining room is tastefully decorated with elegant furniture, drapes, and art on the walls. The table is set with wine glasses, candles, and a vase full of roses. Music plays softly in the background, and Carolyn attempts to lead the family in pleasant conversation. The symmetrical framing of the scene, with Carolyn and Lester at opposite ends of the table and Jane in the middle, enhances the forced appearance of harmony in the scene. Even when tensions arise, Carolyn tries to maintain the façade of the in-control wife and mother. Despite her best efforts, Carolyn's performance as the model wife and mother is not always convincing, and her true feelings often surface through sarcasm and back-handed compliments.

Lester, on the other hand, puts less effort into his performance, allowing his unhappiness and resentment to show and revealing the truth behind the façade. As the narrator of the film, he makes comments to the audience about how miserable his life has become. He even tells Colonel Fitts that his marriage to Carolyn is "just for show. A commercial for how normal [they] are." As Carolyn's and Lester's performances show, the boundary between on- and offstage will vary from person to person, even in the same family.

Big Love offers a clear physical manifestation of the concept of the stage and backstage by way of the homes in which the Henricksons live. Before moving to their current location, the family all lived in a single house, each wife having her own room. The novelty of the new arrangement is that from the street, their houses look like any other houses in the suburban neighborhood in which the Henricksons live. Each is a single-family home, and, based on the appearance of the front yards, they seem to belong to separate families. Their back yards, however, tell a different story. The family has removed the fences between the houses, creating one giant back yard that connects the three homes, physically joining the three households into one family. This joint back yard is a physical manifestation of the true structure of the Henrickson family— their backstage selves. The fronts of the houses represent the stage on which they perform their public personas, a visual façade to match the behavioral façade they must construct through their daily activities.

FIGURE 8. The Henricksons' joint back yard connects the occupants of the three houses as one large family (*Big Love*). Frame enlargement.

To strengthen this façade, Bill makes it a habit to enter and exit only through the front door of Barb's house, entering Nicki and Margene's houses through back doors that are out of sight of the neighbors. Again, the relative invisibility of the back yards creates a private backstage for the Henrickson family. To polish the image, Barb has a cover story prepared for any potentially curious new neighbors. When Carl and Pam first move in, she marches to Pam's front door with a cake, and proceeds to explain how she and Bill live in one house, rent a second house to Nicki, and have taken young Margene under their wing out of kindness. The actions and words of Bill and Barb help to set the stage that so carefully masks the truth of their backstage lives. The Henricksons' situation is, of course, unusual, and therefore requires a very elaborate performance to construct a façade that will pass as normal. But their exaggerated behavior points to what most of us do every day. We put on a show of normalcy so that people will leave us alone and stay out of our business. While most of us have elements of our backstage lives that we know would meet with disapproval from the general public, we conceal them with our carefully performed public persona. Those who cannot or will not perform normalcy on the public stage are the ones most likely to be targeted as deviants, freaks, and outsiders. We construct our stage by making sure that the exteriors of our homes and lawns will meet with the approval of neighbors. This sets up our behavior, which must also conform to public norms by keeping certain activities, like fighting or sexual contact, confined to the backstage areas of our lives.

In life, as in theater, a successful onstage performance depends on a private backstage that is shielded from the audience to allow for physical and emotional preparation. Rössler notes the importance of taking a break from performing: "Whereas on the stage itself particular forms of behavior, particular performances, are intentionally and consciously acted out or put on, behind the scenes, in the private spaces, roles are rehearsed, invented, practiced, rewritten, and put to one side for a break." In this way, Rössler notes, "privacy becomes a condition for self-definition and self-invention."[38] In *American Beauty*, instead of just showing Carolyn's onstage performance of suburban success, the filmmakers emphasize the amount of effort she puts in backstage to prepare that performance. One significant scene depicts Carolyn, who works as a realtor, preparing for an open house in one of the homes that she has listed. As she walks into the home, she announces, "I will sell this house today," a phrase that she repeats to herself as she washes countertops, vacuums carpets, and polishes mirrors. She is using the private, backstage time not only to prepare the house for prospective buyers, but also to prepare herself for the performance she must put on as a realtor. Before entering the home, and during her cleaning process, she exhibits frustration and self-doubt, but she takes time backstage to rehearse the role of a confident, polished sales agent. When she finishes prepping the house and herself, she opens the front doors dramatically and with a broad smile says, "Welcome! I'm Carolyn Burnham," displaying the public, onstage persona that she has worked so hard to prepare.

The backstage, private spaces of life are important to protect, as they are where we have the chance to be who we want to be, even as we prepare ourselves to be what others want us to be. Offstage, in our private lives, we have more autonomy than when we are onstage, because we set our own rules and follow our own guidelines. This sense of autonomy is of particular importance to *Big Love*'s Henrickson family, as they are choosing to live a lifestyle that is not sanctioned by society at large. Their daily performance and the strict separation of onstage

FIGURE 9. Carolyn (Annette Bening) puts a great deal of effort into preparing herself and the house before displaying her polished public persona (*American Beauty*). Frame enlargement.

and backstage are crucial to the protection of their family. Without the backstage life to retreat to, the Henricksons would not be able to have a family life at all.

While theirs may be an exceptional case, the Henricksons' situation stands as a reminder of the important role that privacy can play in encouraging family unity. As Schoeman suggests, privacy allows for vulnerability.[39] By offering a sense of protection, privacy allows us to let down our guard and stop performing. When individuals can be honest and sincere with one another, they make themselves vulnerable and enhance the sense of intimacy that exists between them, thus strengthening their emotional bonds. While this certainly does not happen within all families, Schoeman's argument suggests that a private, backstage life is a prerequisite for even the possibility of intimate family relationships. The Henricksons' successful cultivation of a backstage life contributes significantly to their strength and happiness as a family. The Burnhams, on the other hand, do not have a healthy backstage life, in large part because of Carolyn's reluctance to stop performing and truly engage with her family. Her only backstage time is when she is alone, and the home that she shares with Lester and Jane is treated as public space, with Carolyn performing accordingly. As a result, the vulnerability and intimacy made possible by the privacy of the home are hampered by the failure to align the private home with the concept of the backstage realm.

By providing us with a backstage area where we can prepare ourselves for our public performances, lead a more autonomous life, and
nurture vulnerability and intimacy in relationships, privacy allows us to
escape from the "everyday pressures of normalization."[40] Unfortunately,
as the texts examined here demonstrate, this escape is only temporary because inevitably one has to return to the stage to be judged,
rewarded, and/or punished according to dominant social norms. In
the cases of *American Beauty* and *Big Love*, the most significant stage on
which the families play is the suburban stage. They attempt to adjust
their public performances to coincide with the expectations of their
respective communities. Like so many others both onscreen and off, the
Burnhams and Henricksons play the role of the happy, traditional family on the stage of suburbia, but their private backstage lives reveal the
amount of effort that goes into rehearsing that performance. The fact
that they have to restrict any non-normative behavior to the backstage
portions of their lives indicates the degree to which acceptable public
behavior is determined by mainstream values. In this way, both texts
reveal how the public/private boundary can be used to police certain
social norms and thereby strengthen existing social hierarchies.

Negotiating the Boundary

The boundary between public and private is significant to the families
in *American Beauty* and *Big Love* for a number of reasons. It draws a line
between the families and the outside world, and sometimes between
individual members of the families. It identifies spaces as either visible
or invisible, suggesting the types of performances appropriate for those
spaces. And in both texts, negotiations of the tenuous boundary between
public and private serve as a reminder of what is at stake here. By dramatizing the effects of small privacy breaches within and between families,
American Beauty and *Big Love* show that privacy is not a given and must be
actively and carefully managed in order to avoid serious consequences.

Some of *American Beauty*'s most important plot developments are
tied to the public/private boundary and individuals' success or failure at negotiating and manipulating that boundary. For example, the
Burnhams' marriage takes a nosedive when Carolyn gets tripped up by

the ambiguous nature of an icon of mobile suburban culture—the automobile. While the automobile may create a feeling of privacy, people generally operate their cars in public spaces. Carolyn misjudges the privacy afforded by her car when she and Buddy, the man with whom she is having an affair, go through the drive-thru lane of the fast-food joint where Lester has taken a job. Thinking that they are alone, or at least out of sight of anyone who would care, Buddy and Carolyn canoodle in the front seat of her car while waiting for their food at the pickup window. When Lester delivers their food and catches them in the act, they realize their mistake. Though Lester and Carolyn have been having marital problems for some time, this particular event brings those problems to a head and confirms the collapse of their relationship. This all happens as the result of Carolyn and Buddy's failure to appropriately distinguish between public and private, onstage and backstage, allowing what should have been kept private to be seen in public.

Lester's death in the film's climax also has roots in the negotiation of public and private. On multiple occasions, Lester and Ricky talk about drugs, exchange drugs for money, and even use drugs together. Though they attempt to keep this behavior private, they are not successful. Colonel Fitts witnesses some of their interaction—in one case peering through the windows of the Burnhams' home—and misinterprets what he sees. Based on his misinformation, he concludes that Lester is gay, and, apparently in response to some latent homosexual tendencies of his own, he eventually kisses Lester. After Lester rejects him, Colonel Fitts shoots Lester, seemingly the result of a combination of embarrassment, rage, and shame. This dramatic turn of events is set in motion by the combination of Lester and Ricky's failure to guard the privacy of their activities and Colonel Fitts's failure to fully recognize and respect that privacy.

The difficult negotiation of public and private also leads to significant complications in *Big Love*, including a string of tense moments throughout the series as well as the climactic ending of the first season. In the early episodes of the series, Barb is portrayed as the most responsible and level-headed of the three wives. Nicki, with her credit card debts and fiery temper, is portrayed as somewhat impulsive, while Margene's inexperience and naïveté cast her as the immature wife.

Barb is the oldest of the women and is Bill's first wife, and she takes her leadership role very seriously. Barb is also usually the one who most carefully directs the public performance of the family, making sure that they project an appropriate, acceptable image to the world and keep their family secrets to themselves. Along the way, both Nicki and Margene engage in behavior that threatens to expose the family's private life. Margene's friendship with her neighbor Pam repeatedly threatens the security of the family's secrets, and Nicki's short temper and lack of discretion often get her in hot water and draw attention to the family's situation.

Although Bill and Barb are constantly worried about Nicki and Margene exposing the family's secrets, their indiscretions in front of the neighbors pale in comparison to the mistake that Barb makes. Toward the end of the first season, Barb finds out that her daughter Teenie has nominated her for a mother of the year award. Initially she dismisses it as a silly award, but when she finds out that the winner will be announced at a ceremony at the governor's mansion, she begins to take it more seriously. Bill, Nicki, Margene, and Barb all express concerns over the public nature of the event and the attention that it could draw to the family, but Barb eventually decides to go through with it. The final episode of the first season focuses primarily on the awards ceremony, which comes with significant consequences. Just before the winner is to be announced, the contest officials confront Barb and directly ask her if she is a polygamist, which she is unable to deny. She is immediately disqualified from the contest and escorted out of the building. As the season reaches its finale, the family is left wondering what will happen to them with their secret having been exposed in such a public forum.

Because of the contest's focus on Barb's role as a mother, it draws her family out of its private home and places it on display in a very public spotlight. While Nicki's and Margene's behavior threatened to reveal the family's private life to a few neighbors, Barb's failure to appropriately manage the boundary between public and private has risked exposing them to the entire community. This, in turn, threatens the family not only in social ways but in financial ways as well, given the potential impact on their livelihood, Bill's home improvement stores.

In both *American Beauty* and *Big Love*, the main characters face serious consequences for their failure to appropriately negotiate the boundaries between public and private. Whether that leads to the exposure of secrets, the collapse of a marriage, or death, both texts suggest that improper maintenance of these boundaries can have dire consequences. Specifically, and of particular relevance to this discussion, *American Beauty* and *Big Love* warn that the failure to protect privacy can potentially lead to the destruction of the family.

Hierarchies of Familial Privacy

Through the dramatization of the delicate negotiations surrounding the boundaries between public and private, *American Beauty* and *Big Love* raise questions about power as it relates to those boundaries, particularly by drawing attention to the existence of hierarchies of privacy. Numerous feminist critics have warned that the protection of the private sphere (with its boundary often drawn around the borders of the family home) is in many ways dangerous for women. Catharine MacKinnon argues that by keeping the home free from government intervention, privacy laws can and often have "shielded the place of battery, marital rape, and women's exploited labor."[41] This, in turn, has allowed for the continuation of social inequalities between men and women. For the sake of protecting women's rights, MacKinnnon argues, the protection of privacy must be balanced with the protection of individual autonomy. As a genre, family melodramas (including the texts analyzed here) regularly dramatize the damaging relationships that exist within the privacy of the home, helping to emphasize MacKinnon's point. Consider, for example, Colonel Fitts's abuse of his son or Lester's near seduction of the underage Angela. While abuse and statutory rape are not protected by law, these behaviors are somewhat shielded from outside scrutiny because of the privacy granted to the homeowners involved.

Harper makes a similar argument, suggesting that different individuals and groups within society seem to have different access to privacy. He points out, for example, that homosexuals are in a particularly complicated situation.[42] On one hand, they fight against government actions that seek to make private sexual behavior a matter of public debate and legislation. On the other hand, many social norms seek to force homosexuality into privacy by arguing that gays and lesbians should not flaunt their sexuality in public (by doing such scandalous things as holding hands) but should keep it out of sight. *American Beauty*'s Colonel Fitts represents this viewpoint. After meeting his gay neighbors, Jim and Jim (Scott Bakula and Sam Robards), he asks his son, "How come these fucking faggots always have to rub it in your face?" And when he sees Jim and Jim out for a run in the neighborhood, he asks, "What is this? A fucking gay pride parade?" His comments reflect the belief that homosexuality should be kept hidden, secret, and private.

Moving in the other direction, *Big Love* demonstrates people's desires to drag polygamists (or any other non-normative families) into the public realm, where they can be scrutinized and socially punished. For example, when the Henricksons' neighbor Pam concludes that Nicki is a polygamist, she says that she is going to alert the local neighborhood watch association, so that everyone will be aware of her presence. When one of Bill's employees suspects that Bill's business partner is a polygamist, she tries to convince Bill to expose him. After learning that Bill is also a polygamist, she feels that it is her duty to expose him as well, and it is her tip that eventually leads the Mother of the Year committee to disqualify Barb.

American Beauty and *Big Love* demonstrate how social privacy norms are applied differently to various segments of the population. While people feel the need to force privacy on some, they want to deny it to others. Either way, it often comes down to social norms, with those who fall outside the norms having less of a say in where to draw their own privacy boundaries. By highlighting this differential access to privacy, *American Beauty* and *Big Love* reveal the hierarchies of privacy at work in our society. And by stripping main characters of the ability to determine their own privacy boundaries, these texts remind us of how much individuals stand to lose when privacy is determined by the norms of mainstream society.

Both texts also make use of the tenuous nature of suburban privacy to comment on the state of American families. At the core of most "family values" debates is an idealized version of the family based on particular structures and behaviors. For most, this version consists of a nuclear family with a mother, father, and one to three children, all living under the same roof. The father is the primary breadwinner, and the mother is a homemaker or may work outside the home once the children are grown. To protect them from maturing too soon, children are shielded from full-time participation in the workforce while being encouraged to focus on school and recreation.

In her books *The Way We Never Were* and *The Way We Really Are*, historian Stephanie Coontz takes aim at this vision of the ideal family. She argues that the "traditional family" that people often imagine is actually "an ahistorical amalgam of structures, values, and behaviors that never coexisted in the same time and place."[43] Defining elements of family life from the colonial period through the postwar era get jumbled together in the creation of a mythical vision of the ideal family.[44]

Although the 1950s is frequently identified as a "golden age" of traditional families, Coontz demonstrates that this period was actually a radical departure from what had come before. She notes, "For the first time in more than one hundred years, the age of marriage and motherhood fell, fertility increased, divorce rates declined, and women's degree of educational parity with men dropped sharply."[45] Also during this period, as families flocked to the suburbs, they often left behind extended families and extrafamilial networks of friends in the city, breaking traditions to shift their focus to the nuclear family.[46] Coontz also points out that not everyone was happy during this era. Many women were pushed out of the workforce and into the home when large numbers of male soldiers returned from their service during World War II. Both men and women were pressured into accepting family roles, so as to avoid being labeled gay or lesbian, and although it was rarely reported at the time, many women later revealed that they had been victims of domestic violence.[47] Not only was 1950s family life far from traditional, it was also far from perfect.

Coontz goes on to argue that alternative family arrangements have the potential to function just as well as any "traditional" nuclear family. She cites a variety of recent studies that have shown that children who are raised by gay or lesbian couples, single parents, divorced couples, or step-parents are as likely to be well adjusted and successful as those raised by two opposite-sex biological parents living together.[48] Overall,

Coontz demonstrates that there is no one stable version of the family, because the family has always been and will always be in a state of flux. Additionally, she posits that "how a family functions is more important than its structure or its formal roles."[49] By featuring "traditional" families breaking down and nontraditional families thriving, both *American Beauty* and *Big Love* offer dramatic support for Coontz's challenge to the image of the ideal family.

In *American Beauty*, the seemingly perfect family is revealed to be nothing more than a shallow performance. The nuclear Burnham family initially presents a front of normalcy as their public façade. By its very nature, filmmaking essentially invades the privacy of its main characters, and *American Beauty* takes the viewer inside the family to reveal the dysfunction that defines their lives. During the course of the film, the true state of this family is made public to neighbors and colleagues, and they are held up as a model of what has become of the ideal nuclear family. The Fitts family, also following the traditional nuclear structure, does not fare much better, with a drug-dealing son, nearly catatonic wife, and sexually confused and murderous husband.

The only family that seems to be happy and functional is the one that least resembles a traditional nuclear family—the gay couple, Jim and Jim. While the filmmakers narratively invade the privacy of the Burnhams and Fittses by revealing their secrets to the viewer and other characters within the film, they essentially protect the privacy of Jim and Jim by only showing them out in public spaces. In this way, the film exposes the failure of the traditional nuclear family while simultaneously giving the nontraditional family the privacy they need to protect and develop familial intimacy. This is not to say that Jim and Jim are without faults. In fact, when it comes to the film's critique of suburban conformity and materialism, they seem to be just as guilty as everyone else. And as far as the audience knows, Jim and Jim's public persona might be just as much a façade as Carolyn's. But by taking the approach that it does, the film reverses the usual treatment of families in American culture, which involves scrutinizing the private lives of non-normative families while leaving "traditional" families alone. In this way *American Beauty* calls attention to a damaging double standard that pervades our society.

Big Love takes a different approach but offers a similar point of view. Although the series invades the privacy of the Henricksons by taking viewers inside their lives, the result is not the exposure of a failed nuclear family, but rather the celebration of the success of a nontraditional family. The Henricksons regularly deal with internal conflicts, but they are generally a loving, caring family. While the threat to the Burnham family comes from within (the family essentially collapses on itself), the biggest threat to the Henrickson family comes from the outside. They successfully deal with and move on from the conflicts that arise within the family, but in the first season finale and at other points in the series, it is the exposure of their lifestyle that threatens to destroy them. The story takes a rather dramatic turn in the fourth season, when Bill decides to run for a seat in the state senate, driven by the belief that once he is in a position of political power it will be safe for him to go public about his family and his beliefs. When he introduces his wives at an election night victory party, he is immediately met with anger and disapproval from many of the people who campaigned and voted for him. Much of the fifth season features the family struggling with the backlash that results from making their lives so public. *Big Love* suggests that a nontraditional family is capable of succeeding if it is shielded from public scrutiny and granted the privacy necessary to nurture family bonds.

The series does, however, avoid suggesting that *every* nontraditional family is automatically worthy of protection and acceptance, and it cautions against taking privacy to an extreme. To emphasize this point, the series presents a stark contrast to the suburban Henricksons by way of the residents of Juniper Creek, an isolated mountain compound inhabited entirely by polygamists. Both Bill and Nicki are originally from this compound, and they both still have family there, which allows for multiple story arcs that bring the Henricksons in contact with Juniper Creek. While the Henricksons are presented as a loving, caring family that treats everyone with respect, life in Juniper Creek constantly provides examples of what can go wrong with polygamy. Men rule their wives and children with verbal and physical abuse. Underage girls are forced to marry older men. Teenage boys are kicked out of the compound and left to fend for themselves. Those who threaten to make waves are often murdered by the men who control the compound. In the case of Juniper Creek, the compound's isolation provides too much privacy from the outside world, making their crimes very easy to hide and blocking the victims from getting help. Showing this darker side of plural marriage keeps *Big Love* from being an uncritical celebration of polygamy. Instead, the series shows that alternative family arrangements have the same potential for success or failure as nuclear families. The results depend on the individuals involved, because a family's structure does not determine its ability to provide for and nurture its members.

American Beauty and *Big Love* use their suburban setting to foreground questions about privacy and the family. They each build on cultural anxieties connected to both these concepts, showing how they play out at the level of individual families and their neighbors. The Burnhams and the Fittses stand in for the imagined ideal nuclear family, while Jim and Jim and the Henricksons stand in for all kinds of family arrangements that do not fit the nuclear norm. By focusing on the ways that immediate privacy breaches (being seen by neighbors, for example) can hurt a family, these texts hint at the ways that laws and policies with a basis in privacy can have a similar impact on larger social groups. After all, the means that individuals use to police the privacy of their neighbors in these texts are not all that different from broader efforts to control the privacy rights of marginalized groups in our society. Privacy tends to be encouraged and supported when it favors the reification of conservative ideologies and so-called family values, but it is less secure when it places those same values in danger. *American Beauty* and *Big Love* demonstrate how important the right to privacy and the institution of family are in American society, and how the ability to define privacy and family are not granted equally to all people. In a culture that seems obsessed with rooting out the evils caused by families that do not fit the norm, *American Beauty* and *Big Love* suggest that it is precisely these non-normative families and the segments of our population that they represent that are most in need of being nurtured, protected, and granted privacy.

3

Suburban Citizenship

Defining Community through the
Exclusion of Racial and Sexual Minorities

In the promotional video for the town of Mount Laurel, a new suburb of Birmingham, Alabama, one resident speaks of her family's decision to move: "In order to move to Birmingham we had to find a place where we could have a sense of community." Another resident says, "It was apparent right off the bat that this place had a strong sense of community, and most of the people that are here are community-oriented." The brochure that is included in the promotional packet with the DVD notes, "When you purchase a home in Mt. Laurel, you get more than just the house. You get a town—a community in every sense of the word."

The emphasis on community in this video is not the exception, but rather the rule in suburban promotions. In fact, the National Association of Realtors lists "community" as "one of the prime selling points on any property."[1] But the precise meaning of the term "community" is not entirely clear. The concept is more complicated than its use would suggest, and it conveys different things to different people. In the case of many suburban developments, community is presented as something that is hard to find in contemporary society. It is often invoked in a way that is very much in line with the nostalgic sensibilities examined in chapter 1. Potential buyers are asked to think fondly of the communities that they grew up in, remembering the good times but forgetting any negative aspects. For example, a nostalgic vision of community focuses on a sense of togetherness, happiness, and connection. But this vision conveniently overlooks the potentially negative consequences of community formation. Identifying a community usually involves identifying who will be included and who will be excluded. Those who are included are defined by their adherence to a set of norms, shared values, and similar identities. Those who fall outside these established norms are likely to find themselves excluded from the community.

The promotional materials demonstrate the significance of community in the construction of an ideal vision of suburbia. Recent fictional treatments of suburbia on both the large and small screens have picked up on this idea, often revealing the darker side of community by emphasizing the perils of conformity and exclusion. This chapter examines the suburban communities presented in the film *Far from Heaven* (2002) and the ABC television series *Desperate Housewives* (2004–2012), paying particular attention to the process of exclusion that is integral to the creation of such communities. In particular, I am concerned with two specific groups that have traditionally been excluded from the idealized vision of American suburbia: people of color and gays and lesbians.

Set in the 1950s in a suburb of Hartford, Connecticut, and employing the visual and performance styles of melodramas of that era, *Far from Heaven* tells the story of Cathy Whitaker (Julianne Moore), a housewife with a seemingly ideal life, including an elegant home with a large, well-landscaped yard, a handsome and upwardly mobile husband, and two well-behaved children. Her life falls apart when she learns that her husband Frank (Dennis Quaid) is gay, and she eventually finds herself developing a relationship with her black gardener, Raymond (Dennis Haysbert). The difficulties that these characters face as a result of homophobia and racism demonstrate how social exclusion can damage or even ruin the lives of those who do not fit in.

Desperate Housewives follows the lives of four women living on the same cul-de-sac, tracing the affairs, scandals, and mysteries that link the women, their families, and the surrounding neighborhood. Set in the present, but borrowing heavily from suburban iconography of the past, the series offers a more complicated picture of race, ethnicity, and sexuality than *Far from Heaven*, in part because of its much larger cast, and in part because of the complexity afforded by the ongoing, serial nature of the show. In addition to the white characters who make up the bulk of the cast, there is a Mexican American couple, Gabrielle and

Carlos Solis (Eva Longoria and Ricardo Antonio Chavira). The Solises employ two maids, both of whom are Chinese. Two African American women, Betty Applewhite (Alfre Woodard) and Renee Perry (Vanessa Williams), move into the neighborhood during the second and seventh seasons, respectively. And while the principal characters are straight, one of the housewives, Bree Van De Kamp (Marcia Cross), has a gay son named Andrew (Shawn Pyfrom). A gay couple, Lee and Bob (Kevin Rahm and Tuc Watkins), arrive in the neighborhood during the fourth season, and in the sixth season, seemingly straight Katherine Mayfair (Dana Delany) falls in love with another woman. The concerns about racial and sexual minorities are not always at the core of the narrative as they are in *Far from Heaven*, but the various minority characters on *Desperate Housewives* demonstrate the complicated nature of suburban conformity by showing that it is not always as simple as black and white, straight and gay.

Many suburban texts over the years have focused on distinctly white, heteronormative neighborhoods, helping to establish and maintain this image as a seemingly natural suburban norm. *Far from Heaven* and *Desperate Housewives* challenge the naturalized image of white heteronormativity by revealing the effort that goes into maintaining such norms, both in real suburbs and in fictional representations of suburbs. While the plots of both texts demonstrate the process of excluding individuals based on difference, the producers of the texts use stylistic devices such as lighting, color, music, and acting to convey subtle meanings that often subvert the messages conveyed at the level of plot. Though the plots establish and protect the heteronormativity of the suburbs, the exaggerated styles used in both *Far from Heaven* and *Desperate Housewives* reveal the artificiality and construction of any definition of "normal" and suggest that difference can never be eliminated. By highlighting the work that goes into preserving the illusion of homogeneity, *Far from Heaven* and *Desperate Housewives* reveal the damage that such efforts can cause to communities of all sizes.

Community and Citizenship

Community has been the focus of research by sociologists, anthropologists, geographers, urban planners, and political scientists, all of whom have demonstrated that despite its quotidian nature, community is far from being a simple concept. Sociologist Graham Day defines community as referring to "those things which people have in common, which bind them together, and give them a sense of belonging with one another."[2] Most thinking about the concept of community in the modern era—an era in which many people live more mobile lifestyles, often in large-scale urban settings—is based on Ferdinand Tönnies's distinction between community (Gemeinschaft) and society (Gesellschaft). As discussed in chapter 2, Gemeinschaft involves relationships based on coordinated efforts for a common good. Individuals know one another, care for one another, and share common ideals. Gesellschaft, on the other hand, involves individuals engaged in superficial, often short-lived relationships that are based on what they can get from one another. Many associate the impersonal, often temporary Gesellschaft with urban living, while Gemeinschaft is more closely connected to life in small towns and the suburbs that emulate them. Tönnies's ideas helped to popularize a notion of community as a natural outgrowth of close geographical and social relations, and also as a desirable phenomenon that is seemingly superior to the impersonal relationships often associated with modernity. The creators of *Desperate Housewives* and *Far from Heaven* make use of the tensions between suburb and city (Gemeinschaft and Gesellschaft) to define the spaces and residents of Wisteria Lane and suburban Hartford.

Community is a concept that is almost always used in a favorable way. Anthropologist Gerald Creed suggests that the positive values associated with community have led to its overuse, which has "turned the word into an empty, although inherently positive, signifier."[3] This is true of the promotions described at the beginning of the chapter, in which a vague concept of community is invoked but never defined, and yet is still presented as something to be desired.

The perception of community as inherently positive masks a variety of potentially harmful consequences. One such consequence is the exclusion that goes hand in hand with the creation of any community. In order to designate certain individuals or traits that are part of a given community, it is necessary to define those that are *not* part of it. Historian James Davis argues that attempts to create and maintain conformity necessarily lead to the identification of deviance, "for without deviance, there is no self-consciousness of conformity and *vice-versa*."[4] In other words, the difference between self and other must be constructed by a particular community in order to achieve cohesiveness. Anything that threatens group identity must be eliminated or at least neutralized.

The exclusion that is a part of community formation covers a wide range of situations. It may be small-scale, as in the case of an overweight child being ostracized in the lunchroom, or it may reach a much larger, national scale. Benedict Anderson draws a connection between small-scale communities and national identity in discussing his concept of the "imagined community." He argues that the development of a national identity is generally predicated upon the notion of community, but notes that a nation is necessarily composed of such large numbers of people that it would be impossible for everyone to know each other on a personal basis. Their sense of connection with one another is therefore imagined—they believe that they share commonalities that bind them together, and in living out this belief the bonds become a social reality.[5]

When Americans imagine themselves as a large, national community, the discussion of inclusion and exclusion inherent to community formation becomes a discussion of citizenship. As Linda Bosniak notes, "The idea of citizenship is commonly invoked to convey a state of democratic belonging or inclusion, yet this inclusion is usually premised on a conception of a community that is bounded and exclusive."[6] The communities in *Far from Heaven, Desperate Housewives*, and other suburban narratives therefore become spaces where broader questions and debates about citizenship can be worked through at a more personal level.

Contemporary social debates revolving around American citizenship are numerous. Immigration reform, for example, has become a talking point for many elected officials as well as those seeking office. The Secure Fence Act of 2006, created by Congress and signed into law by President George W. Bush, was partially intended to keep out illegal immigrants from Mexico, but opponents argued that taxpayer money should instead be put into reforming immigration policies to help people enter the country legally. The project was essentially halted a few years later by the Obama administration, but soon returned as a campaign promise of numerous GOP candidates during the 2012 presidential election cycle.

Unsatisfied with federal immigration policies, many states have recently enacted their own strict immigration laws. Some of these laws, including Arizona's (in 2010) and Alabama's (in 2011), were challenged by lawsuits from President Obama's Justice Department. In an attempt to provide a legal pathway to citizenship for the children of illegal immigrants, senators and representatives have introduced various versions of the DREAM Act (Development, Relief, and Education for Alien Minors), with opponents arguing that such a policy would only encourage illegal immigration. Citizenship concerns even reached the Oval Office when Donald Trump and other representatives of the so-called "Birther Movement" publicly questioned whether President Obama was a U.S. native and demanded that he produce a satisfactory birth certificate to prove his eligibility for office.

Questions of citizenship have also played a part in the debates about the rights of gays and lesbians. Many conservative groups have argued that allowing same-sex couples to wed will destroy the institution of marriage, and allowing gays and lesbians to serve openly in the armed forces will hurt the nation's military. Gay rights advocates have contended that bans on gay military service and same-sex marriage amount to treating gays and lesbians as second-class citizens rather than full participants in society.

Clearly, the concept of citizenship is complex and multifaceted, but at its core it signifies "belonging to and participation in a group or community—something that brings with it certain rights and obligations."[7] This chapter examines how *Far from Heaven* and *Desperate Housewives* work through notions of cultural citizenship—the right to full participation regardless of one's race, ethnicity, gender, religion, or other identity marker—by paying particular attention to the drawing of boundaries between inside and outside. This is only a small part of the larger conversation about citizenship, but the behavior of these fictional suburbanites gets to the heart of one of the most important questions about American citizenship—who is included and who is excluded?

Exclusion in Suburbia

Far from Heaven and *Desperate Housewives* dramatize the exclusion of racial, ethnic, and sexual minorities from suburban neighborhoods. While the stories themselves may be fictional, they are rooted in the long history of exclusion that has helped define American suburbia. As Robert Fishman points out, "From its origins, the suburban world of leisure, family life, and union with nature was based on the principle of exclusion."[8] People moved to the suburbs to get away from pollution, crime, overcrowding, and other negative aspects associated with city life. By excluding these attributes from the suburbs, residents hoped to create a better life for themselves and their children. The exclusion did not end with crime and pollution, but rather extended to individuals and groups of people whose race, ethnicity, or sexual orientation differed from the majority. Suburbia is often seen as a space populated by white, heterosexual couples and their families. This image did not come about accidentally—it is the result of many years of majority-enforced social norms and outright discrimination.

The most obvious exclusion has been of people of color. In many cases, these groups were excluded by actual laws and official government policies. For example, in the years leading up to World War I, racial zoning laws were not uncommon. In cities across the country, ordinances made it illegal for non-whites to move into certain neighborhoods that had an existing white majority. After the Supreme Court declared these zoning laws unconstitutional in 1917, real estate agents, developers, bankers, insurance companies, and homeowners began to find other ways of creating and maintaining segregated neighborhoods, particularly in the new suburban developments. They used both formal and informal methods, including ordinances, freeze-outs, buyouts, violence, threats, and intimidation to create and maintain all-white or nearly all-white communities.[9]

One formal way that people of color were excluded was through the use of restrictive covenants, "private agreements written into deed restrictions on the resale of property."[10] These covenants were usually drawn up by the developers of suburban spaces, and buyers would have to sign them before purchasing land, promising that even after they took ownership of their property (the house/land) they would agree to use that property only in specified ways. As Robert Fogelson's history of these covenants shows, the early versions were intended to protect property values by maintaining certain levels of aesthetic appeal, but by the early 1920s, covenants became a common tool for excluding racial minorities. Under a typical covenant, an owner was not only forbidden to sell to members of "undesirable" racial and ethnic groups (i.e., non-whites), but he was also forbidden to allow members of these groups (with the exception of gardeners and domestic servants) to occupy any part of the property.[11]

In the 1930s, the Roosevelt administration formed the Home Owners Loan Corporation (HOLC), primarily as a way of protecting homeownership in a time of economic turmoil. While the HOLC helped to protect homeowners by standardizing mortgage and appraisal practices, it also initiated the practice of redlining, which would have distinctly negative consequences for blacks and other minorities. Under this practice, neighborhoods were given a rating and an associated color designation to indicate the quality of the neighborhood. Neighborhoods with white residents, newer homes, and economic stability were ranked highly, and designated as green. Ranked at the lower end and designated as red were neighborhoods characterized by vandalism, run-down buildings, or populations composed largely of non-whites.

The rating practices of the HOLC had their biggest impact when they were adopted by financial institutions and even the U.S. government when making decisions about home loans and insurance. The Federal Housing Administration was a government body that insured long-term mortgage loans made by private lenders. With government backing, private lenders were more willing to offer loans to homeowners, because their own risk was lower. But because the FHA used the same practice as the HOLC, minority neighborhoods were at a disadvantage. Lenders were more likely to back the construction or purchase of homes in neighborhoods that were already white, because the FHA was more likely to insure them. As a result, white neighborhoods were able to build, buy, and improve homes, while non-whites saw their neighborhoods deteriorate.[12]

In 1948, the Supreme Court ruled in *Shelley v. Kraemer* that it was unconstitutional for state courts to enforce restrictive covenants that excluded individuals based on race and ethnicity. And the civil rights movement of the 1960s led to the 1968 Fair Housing Act, which sought to curtail the federal government's discriminatory housing practices. *Shelley v. Kraemer* and the Fair Housing Act provided some help, but they did not eliminate racial covenants (since it was only the state enforcement of such covenants that became illegal), nor did they put an end to other means of housing discrimination. As George Lipsitz notes, the practices of steering (real estate agents directing minority buyers only to homes in minority neighborhoods) and blockbusting (playing on white fears of racial change to promote panic sales at low prices and then selling those homes to minority residents at marked up prices) also continued long after the *Shelley* decision and the Fair Housing Act.[13] Although these practices have been all but eliminated today, their effects can still be felt, as generations worth of advantage and privilege take a long time to balance themselves out. Additionally, as Douglas Massey and Nancy Denton demonstrate, segregated housing "supports other racially discriminatory processes" in the realms of employment, social services, and education, the effects of which last for generations.[14]

Along with racial and ethnic minorities, the other social group that has traditionally been excluded from suburbia is gays and lesbians. Given the longstanding connection between the suburban home, the nuclear family, and clearly defined gender roles, suburbs have generally been seen as unfriendly spaces for gays and lesbians. The exclusion of non-heterosexuals has not generally come in the form of official laws or overt actions on the part of realtors and other homeowners—unless they are gays and lesbians who are also people of color, in which case they are doubly excluded. But for white gays and lesbians, the exclusion has been based more on social norms and mores that have made them feel distinctly unwelcome in suburban spaces.

The emphasis on family has its roots in the first wave of suburban growth in the United States, the late nineteenth century. During this time, advocates of suburban life repeatedly touted the benefits of raising a family in the suburbs. Catharine Beecher was one of the most outspoken of these writers, publishing numerous articles and books that sought to define appropriate roles for women, both in the home and in society at large. Much of her writing focused on the successful heterosexual coupling of a man who focused his life outside the home and a woman who turned her efforts to nurturing the family within the home, and she repeatedly suggested that the suburbs were the ideal space for this kind of lifestyle.

During the same era, and on through the suburban booms of the 1920s and 1940s, developers, promoters, and other commentators hailed suburbia as the ideal place to raise children. Home and garden magazines frequently ran articles about the subject, often drawing on doctors and scientists to give the ideology of suburbia the weight of scientific fact. An article published in *Suburban Life* featured a doctor commenting that if families with children were actually barred from the inner cities, "this might result in driving more families to the 'land of promise'—the suburban community—where they with their children rightly belong."[15]

Although research on early suburbs has found no evidence to suggest that developers explicitly tried to exclude homosexuals, the suburban focus on traditional nuclear families did not attract many singles or same-sex couples. Additionally, the lack of acceptance of homosexuality during the early years of suburbanization led most openly gay men and women to choose the relative anonymity of Gesellschaft-like city life over the Gemeinschaft-like life of suburbia. As gay populations in cities grew, gay bars, clubs, bookstores, and social networks developed in these areas. The suburbs' lack of such gay infrastructures further diminished their appeal to gay and lesbian residents. For those who did want to live in the suburbs, zoning laws often made it difficult for them to establish families. Although not aimed solely at gays and lesbians, the zoning restrictions of many communities prohibited homes from being occupied by more than two individuals who were not related by blood or marriage. While a gay couple could live together under such rules, adding children to the equation would put them in violation of the restriction, given the couple's inability to marry or adopt each other's children. The U.S. Supreme Court upheld such ordinances in *Village of Belle Terre v. Boraas* (1975), thus allowing individual communities to essentially exclude anyone who did not fit the traditional nuclear family model.[16] While some communities are eliminating such rules and others are simply not enforcing them, thousands of these ordinances are still on the books around the country.[17]

The image of the suburbs as a white, heteronormative space does indeed have a basis in reality. However, people of color and gays and lesbians have always been a part of American suburbia.[18] Their numbers have been relatively small, and they have often been segregated in their own separate suburbs or made to seem invisible or forced to live in the closet in mainstream suburbs, but they have nonetheless been present. And recent census data have shown increasing numbers of racial, ethnic, and sexual minorities in suburbs across the nation.[19] Despite the presence of minorities in real suburban spaces, media representations of suburbia over the years have constructed and reinforced the image of white heteronormativity by presenting little else. The bulk of television programs that accompanied the postwar suburban boom of the 1950s and 1960s, for example, revolved around white nuclear families. Programs like *The Adventures of Ozzie and Harriet* (1952–1966), *Leave It to Beaver* (1957–1963), and *Father Knows Best* (1954–1963) presented straight white families as the suburban norm. One notable exception from this era is *I Love Lucy* (1951–1961), which did eventually feature the Cuban-born Ricky Ricardo leaving New York for suburban Connecticut. However, this series differs from the others in that the Ricardos are clearly presented as urban transplants who are a bit out of place, whereas the all-white families in the other programs are presented as blending right in to their neighborhoods.

The trend continued into the 1970s and 1980s, during which time non-white television families generally lived in urban environments (*Good Times*, 1974–1979; *Sanford and Son*, 1972–1977; *The Jeffersons*, 1975–1985; *The Cosby Show*, 1984–1992) and whites lived in the suburbs (*Happy Days*, 1974–1984; *Family Ties*, 1982–1989; *Growing Pains*, 1985–1992). Films followed a similar path, with white families at the centers of films like *The Man in the Gray Flannel Suit* (1956), *No Down Payment* (1957), *The Graduate* (1967), *The Stepford Wives* (1975), *Back to the Future* (1985), and *The 'Burbs* (1989).

More recently, films and series have begun critiquing the processes of racial, ethnic, and sexual exclusion rather than simply perpetuating the segregation that results from such processes. Although *Pleasantville*

(1998) handles the issue metaphorically, the film features an unmistakable critique of the exclusion of people of color. *American Beauty* (1999) and *Big Love* (2006–2011) both feature characters that do not fit the traditional heteronormative nuclear family model. Additionally, series like *Weeds* (2005–2012) and *The Sopranos* (1999–2007), and films like *Happiness* (1998), *Little Children* (2006), *The Hours* (2002), *The Cookout* (2004), *Fun with Dick and Jane* (2005), and *Lakewood Terrace* (2008), all deal with the tensions created by racial, ethnic, or sexual differences in suburbia. *Far from Heaven* and *Desperate Housewives* serve as the focal points of this chapter because they both feature prominent characters of color and prominent gay characters, allowing them to explore multiple types of exclusion simultaneously. *Far from Heaven* highlights the social differences so often repressed in the 1950s melodramas that it references, making them the focus of the film's narrative. *Desperate Housewives*, with its eight seasons and large, ever-changing cast of characters, is able to depict a wide range of sexual, racial, and ethnic difference on its seemingly typical cul-de-sac. Both texts expose and critique the often invisible process of maintaining the suburban ideal of white heteronormativity that has dominated suburbia and its representation for decades.

Style as Façade

Before discussing any of the events that unfold in *Far from Heaven* or *Desperate Housewives*, it is important to consider the styles employed within these texts. As is the case with any film or series, the way in which the story is told is frequently as important as the story itself. Instead of using a naturalistic approach to subtly convey a sense of realism, the creators of *Far from Heaven* and *Desperate Housewives* use visual designs and storytelling devices that call attention to themselves as fabrications and thus help to create diegetic worlds that are well beyond the bounds of believability. The exaggerated styles used in these texts add significant layers of meaning that both enhance and complicate the meanings conveyed by the basic unfolding of events.

Both scholarly and popular responses to *Far from Heaven* have emphasized the visual style of the film, generally recognizing it as homage to the classic 1950s melodramas of Max Ophuls, Vincente Minelli, and especially Douglas Sirk. While director Todd Haynes adopts the style of these films, he reimagines them by openly addressing interracial desire and queerness, which were necessarily avoided or repressed in the earlier, Production Code–era films. *Far from Heaven* draws recognizable visual imagery and narrative developments from many films, including *Written on the Wind* (1956) and *Imitation of Life* (1959), but borrows most heavily from Sirk's 1955 film *All That Heaven Allows*, as well as from Rainer Werner Fassbinder's *Ali: Fear Eats the Soul* (1974), which was itself a remake of Sirk's film. Many critics have argued that Sirk's exaggerated style created an ironic sense of distance between the film and the audience, encouraging viewers to reconsider the ideologies seemingly conveyed by the plot.[20] Paul Willemen identifies Sirk's frequent use of mirrors in the mise-en-scène as an important element in this process, with the mirrors serving as a reminder of the fact that characters are always "putting on an act" in order to manage their social persona.[21] Other distancing techniques include the ironic use of camerawork and editing,[22] and an expressionistic use of color in costumes, set designs, and lighting.[23]

Far from Heaven draws on many of the techniques visible in Sirk's films. For example, characters are frequently framed by windows and doors, or reflected in mirrors. Cathy is standing in the doorway as she waves goodbye to her husband in the morning, and when she first sees Raymond, it is through the windows at the back of her house. When Cathy's daughter announces that she wants to be as pretty as her mother when she grows up, and when Cathy asks her husband about the progress of his psychiatric treatment, Cathy is shown as a mirror reflection, emphasizing the fragility of her image as a flawless wife and mother. Editing and camerawork are often used in an ironic way, as when the image of a happy family Christmas celebration is undermined by editing that "ensures that Cathy and Frank are never united in a single shot but are represented separately."[24] The use of color in the film is also similar to that of Sirk, as it helps to represent the desires of characters, to mark shifts in mood, and to associate particular spaces with acts of transgression and taboo. As Scott Higgins argues, "When Haynes uses his blue, yellow, red and green gels, he is consciously quoting and seeking to outdo Sirk, setting up the potential for ironic interference between events and our engagement with them."[25]

By drawing so heavily on the style of Sirk and other directors from the same era, Haynes significantly alters the setting of his film. Based on calendars and other references within the story, *Far from Heaven* takes place in the late 1950s. However, these characters and their lives are not placed within the 1950s as it actually existed, but within "the 1950s as mediated through an explicitly constructed fantasy."[26] Haynes's film is thus a reference to filmmaking of the 1950s as much as it is a reference to life in the 1950s, and it therefore comments not only on the state of race, gender, and sexuality during that era, but also on popular film's treatment or avoidance of those issues. By drawing so heavily on an obviously artificial construction, *Far from Heaven* encourages a reevaluation of our relationship to the Hollywood-influenced fantasies of the 1950s and suburbia.

Desperate Housewives is also highly stylized, though not in the exact same ways as *Far from Heaven.* The opening shot of the pilot provides a good example of the series' visual style. It is a crane shot of Wisteria Lane that begins high above the street and wide enough to see a handful of houses and the activities of people on the street. The houses are large and well kept, the lawns are neatly trimmed and meticulously landscaped, and the street on which they all sit is smooth and free of potholes. People walk, run, and drive along the street as the camera sweeps down for a closer shot of the narrator, Mary Alice Young (Brenda Strong). Unlike *Far from Heaven*, with its artificially gelled lights and extravagant costumes, the initial impression made by *Desperate Housewives* is somewhat closer to reality. However, the image is a little too flawless to be believed. Nothing is out of place. No utility lines or poles interrupt the view of the street. While the activity and presence of people on the street initially suggests a vibrant, friendly neighborhood, a closer inspection reveals how unlikely the scenario is. This is not a town square, after all, but a residential cul-de-sac, with ten to fifteen houses at the most. It is highly unlikely that a woman with a dog, a woman with a stroller, a jogger, two couples, a school bus, and a passing car would all converge in front of the narrator's house at the same moment—unless, of course, that moment was staged.[27] In this way, the opening shot is very reminiscent of the carefully constructed images of suburban streets that grace the pages of the promotional brochures described in chapter I. Thus the overall feel of Wisteria Lane (established by this shot, but developed throughout the series)[28] is almost plausible, but just a little too perfect to be taken at face value. Just as *Far from Heaven* presents an artificial version of the past, *Desperate Housewives* presents an artificial version of the present.

The manner in which the story is relayed to the viewer also helps to shape its interpretation. Full episodes and some individual segments are framed by comments from the narrator, Mary Alice, whose suicide sets the series in motion. Although she is not a part of the stories that develop, she has intimate knowledge of the families on the street and the overall way of life on Wisteria Lane. Her comments help the viewer to get to know the characters on a very personal level, but she is also able to point out the mistakes, secrets, and flaws of her friends. In this way, as Niall Richardson points out, "the beyond-the-grave narrator evokes a sense of critical distance, an ironic detachment commenting on the events unfolding."[29] Mary Alice's comments help create the sense that there is always more to the story than what the viewer sees on the screen.

Perhaps the most significant aspect of *Desperate Housewives'* style is the overall tone of the series, which is defined largely by its very camp sensibility. Although camp is a much-contested concept, most critics agree that it refers to both a mode of representation and a mode of interpretation that emphasize artifice and stylization.[30] Brett Farmer argues that camp is "a discourse of performativity par excellence, for it is first and foremost a discourse about performance and performative reiteration."[31] Because of its emphasis on artifice and performance, camp has the potential to highlight and comment on the performative nature of both gender and sexuality, and thus social identity as a whole, leading some to suggest that camp can be used politically in feminist and queer political movements.[32] The camp sensibility of *Desperate Housewives* is most obvious in the development of the primary housewives, who begin almost as stock female characters (the glamorous trophy wife, the harried stay-at-home mom, the cute and klutzy divorcee, and the accomplished Martha Stewart–esque homemaker), but take these roles

FIGURE 10. Pedestrians and vehicles converge in front of the narrator's house to create a charming but unrealistic moment on the small cul-de-sac of Wisteria Lane (*Desperate Housewives*). Frame enlargement.

to comically exaggerated extremes. Much like the too-perfect image of Wisteria Lane, these characters and their performances are too over the top to be taken at face value, and thus call attention to the performative nature of everyone and everything in the series.

The exaggerated styles of *Far from Heaven* and *Desperate Housewives* provide another take on the idea of the suburban façade. While some suburban narratives focus on characters putting up a front of normalcy to hide the truth about their lives (*American Beauty, Big Love*) and others feature a suburban world that is, at least to some characters, a recognizably fictional construction (*Pleasantville, The Truman Show*), these texts go in a different direction. They add another layer to the façade—one that is not apparent to the characters within the diegesis, but which is difficult for viewers to overlook. Rather than being just a portion of the story, this façade envelopes the entire story and all of its components, providing a constant source of tension that invites viewers to question the relationship between the fantasy and the reality of suburban American life and making it difficult, if not impossible, to take the stories' plot developments at face value.

Spaces of the Mainstream, Spaces of the "Other"

Both *Far from Heaven* and *Desperate Housewives* illustrate the process of exclusion, in part by highlighting distinctions between characters, behaviors, and spaces that fit in with the mainstream and are seen as normal, and those that do not and are thus labeled as deviant or "other." Within each text the definition of normal is established by those who are already a part of the community, and it rarely matches the lived experiences of most Americans. The stylistic choices made by the creators of these texts emphasize the constructed nature of normalcy in the fictional communities in which they are set, thereby calling attention to the construction of any notion of normal in American society.

One of the ways that both *Far from Heaven* and *Desperate Housewives* negotiate racial and sexual exclusion is through their use of space. *Far from Heaven* emphasizes the white, heteronormative nature of suburbia by depicting spaces that contrast with this image, appearing instead as black or queer spaces. The spaces depicted within the film illustrate what Michel Laguerre identifies as minoritized space. "Minority status is concomitant with minoritized space. It is the location where the identity of the minority person becomes spatialized."[33] Laguerre argues that minoritized space is socially constructed as inferior to majority space, and that spatially segregating people is crucial to the process of "othering" them in society. *Far from Heaven* emphasizes Frank's and Raymond's status as social "others," as well as their resulting exclusion from suburban life, in part by showing them in minoritized spaces that stand in contrast to the majority space of suburbia.

Frank occupies two significant spaces that can be identified as queer spaces: the gay bar and the movie theater. Although Frank's sexuality is hinted at earlier in the film (when he is arrested for "loitering"), his orientation is made more explicit when he is actually shown inhabiting these queer spaces. Given that "queer" has a variety of meanings—pejorative for some, radically activist for others—I should clarify my use of the word. In using "queer" throughout this discussion, I draw on the work of Alexander Doty, who suggests that queerness "is a quality related to any expression that can be marked as contra-, non-, or anti-straight."[34] The term "queer" is not limited to discussions of sexual activities, but can also describe spaces, attitudes, characters, styles, and behaviors that fall outside the norms defined by mainstream, straight society.

In his discussion of queer space, Aaron Betsky describes it as a "misuse or deformation of a place, an appropriation of the buildings and codes of the city for perverse purposes."[35] In other words, queer spaces are not generally built or designed with the intent of being queer spaces. They are instead pockets carved out of mainstream heteronormative space and put to use in the service of queer activities. Such activities range from illicit acts of public sex to the formation of an alternative queer community that is set apart from the majority culture.

Frank's first onscreen interaction with queer space is his visit to the downtown movie theater, which becomes a cruising space. As Frank stands alone in the dimly lit theater lobby, he watches two other men who also appear to be alone. One man stands at the base of the stairs, and the other stands near the concession stand. The men briefly make eye contact, and then disappear up to the balcony together. Although there is no explicit depiction of physical sexuality, both Frank and the audience understand that they have witnessed the opening moves of a sexual exchange, the details and conclusion of which are left unknown. As Betsky notes, the space of cruising is often difficult to see, especially for those who are not looking for it. "Its most fundamental characteristic is its ephemerality: it is a space that appears for a moment, then is gone, only to reappear when the circumstances are right."[36] This is the case with the theater, which is primarily a heteronormative space, attracting mainstream consumers who come to see the film that is being shown. But for a moment (and though we only see one such moment, the scene suggests that this is a semi-regular occurrence), the space is transformed into one that enables queer sexuality to appear, but only temporarily, and only for those who know what to look for. The queer space exists coterminously with straight space, yet manages to remain invisible to the heteronormative gaze.

At the conclusion of the screening, as Frank is walking out of the theater, he catches sight of the two men leaving together and walking down the street. He watches them turn a corner, and then he slowly follows them. When he rounds the corner, he finds himself in a dark alley. A small lamp and the glow of the moon provide just enough light to

FIGURE 11. The usually heteronormative space of the theater becomes queered by the clandestine acts of gay cruising that take place there (*Far from Heaven*). Frame enlargement.

make out the shapes of trash cans and the texture of the brick street. A door opens at the far end of the alley and a small patch of light spills out as the two men make their way inside. Frank continues to follow them, and after passing through the outer door and a dark hallway, he enters a dimly lit bar, populated entirely by men. Inside the bar Frank meets a man with whom he will soon have an affair.

Like so many gay bars, this one makes no attempt to announce itself to casual passersby. Nestled in a darkened alley, without even a light above its door, this is a space that basically hides in plain sight. It is a mere block away from the crowded movie theater, but it is so inconspicuous that it goes generally unnoticed. As Betsky notes, "The queer bar wears a mask that only fellow wearers can read."[37] Those who are in search of this bar can find it, but to anyone else it remains essentially invisible. This queer space differs from the movie theater in that it is more permanent. Although the activity within is likely to occur only during the nighttime hours, the bar never reverts to being a heteronormative space. Also, once inside the bar, patrons are shielded from the heteronormative gaze, creating a space of refuge. As Dereka Rushbrook points out, because gay bars generally remain "invisible from the population at large," they offer privacy and protection for their patrons, providing spaces for the exploration of identities and the formation of communities outside the mainstream.[38]

The theater and the bar provide Frank with the opportunity to explore and enact his homosexuality. These queer spaces are contrasted with the film's heteronormative spaces largely through editing. For example, the scene involving Frank's exploration of the theater and bar is juxtaposed with scenes of Cathy in the Whitakers' home. In the scene immediately preceding Frank's excursion, Cathy is chatting with the society reporter of the local paper, posing next to the family fireplace as a model of the ideal wife. The scene immediately following Frank's bar visit involves Cathy and three of her friends reading the article in the society page, which talks about Cathy's performance as a wife and mother. The women then move to a discussion of their husbands' love-making habits. Inserted in the middle of Frank's night out is a scene with Cathy, the firm but fair mother, putting her son to bed. All three of these scenes emphasize Cathy's heteronormative existence, and all three of them center that existence in the heteronormative space of the sub-urban home, highlighting the contrast between this space and the queer urban spaces that Frank inhabits.

The social privilege associated with Frank's status as a white, middle-class man allows him to inhabit almost any space he chooses, so long as he conceals his sexual identity in heteronormative spaces. Raymond faces a different challenge. Because his "otherness" is more clearly marked and visible, he is noticeably out of place in the spaces of white suburbia. Cathy even asks him what it's like "to be the only one in a room—colored, or whatever it was." Raymond replies, "There is a world, even here in Hartford, where everybody does indeed look like me. Trouble is, very few people ever leave that world." This comment positions the "black world" as somehow physically separate from the white world that Cathy inhabits. The difference between these two worlds is highlighted by a brief visit to a restaurant that Raymond describes as one of his "favorite spots." Eagan's Restaurant is situated next to a gas station and car wash (both of which appear to be staffed entirely by African Americans) in what seems to be a commercial strip along a well-traveled road. Aside from Cathy, the only white people visible in the scene are those who are waiting for their cars to be washed or refueled by the black attendants.

Cathy is once again used to help define this minoritized space. While images of her at home were previously juxtaposed with images of queer spaces, in this case her presence in the minoritized space helps to define it. As she enters the bar, the conversations in the room become quiet and everyone stares. Raymond tries to assure her that they are in a very welcoming place, but the curt responses from the waitress and a comment from another patron ("What do you think you're doing, boy?") clearly indicate that Cathy's presence is generating discomfort. Raymond is finally in a place where he could blend in, but because he is accompanied by a white woman blending becomes impossible.

Both the queer spaces and the black space in the film are marked by lighting and color. The theater and the bars are dimly lit, in contrast with the brightly lit spaces of the town square or the Whitakers' home or neighborhood. Additionally, all three spaces are dominated by very saturated red and green light and decor. As Sharon Willis notes, "This garish red-green combination of lighting and interior seems to mark disciplinary or *disciplined* spaces: the movie theater as protected space for furtive private acts, the gay bar and the black club as spaces closed off from the heterosexual and white worlds."[39] While all the spaces create a certain sanctuary for those excluded from the mainstream, their distinct segregation also functions to contain the inhabitants, helping to solidify their marginal status. By clearly defining limited spaces in which gays and blacks are welcome, *Far from Heaven* emphasizes the exclusion of both groups from the white heteronormative suburban community.

The spaces of *Desperate Housewives* are defined somewhat differently. Rather than depicting clearly bounded, segregated spaces to contain members of minority groups, the series draws a distinct line between the spaces of the city and the suburbs. The city is established as the more natural location of "otherness." Activities and behaviors that cause outrage on Wisteria Lane are presented as a regular part of life in the city, helping to draw the boundary between here and there, inside and outside, us and them. The vast majority of scenes in *Desperate Housewives* take place in the comfortable suburban cul-de-sac of Wisteria Lane and its surrounding neighborhood. The scarcity of urban images in the series makes them stand out that much more, allowing them to provide a distinct counterpoint to the veil of suburban serenity that dominates the series. One example of an activity that is naturalized in the city is crime. While there are plenty of crimes that happen right on Wisteria Lane (including arson, murder, drunk driving, statutory rape, and burglary), those crimes are played for their dramatic and comedic potential. In other words, they are made to seem shocking and out of place in this quiet neighborhood, and the juicy details of these activities form the roots of the scandals and secrets that drive the series' narrative.

The city, however, is presented as the more natural location for criminal activity. It is also presented as a space of poverty, in contrast to the affluence of Wisteria Lane. Both of these characteristics are displayed in the episode "Guilty," which features Bree and her husband Rex (Steven Culp) trying to get rid of a car that contains evidence of an accident involving their son. Bree decides that they should take the car to a "bad part of town" and leave the keys in the ignition, assuming that someone will steal it. When Rex questions the wisdom of their plan, Bree says, "This is the most impoverished neighborhood in the city. Trust me, somebody will steal the car." Within minutes someone hops in the car and drives off with it, upholding the expected connection between the city, poverty, and crime.

Similarly, in the episode "Come in Stranger," Susan (Teri Hatcher) is on a date with a police officer and rides along with him as he patrols an urban neighborhood, which Susan refers to as "Cracktown." After an argument, Susan storms away from the car and her date shouts, "Where are you going? It's not safe." She replies, "I'd rather take my chances on the street." The space of the city is again established as a place where crime and danger are to be expected, in contrast to the cozy Wisteria Lane.

These and other scenes in urban spaces establish the city as a space of otherness. It is a space where behaviors and activities that are shunned, frowned upon, and eliminated from the suburbs find their seemingly natural and acceptable place. This depiction in turn helps to define the suburbs as a more mainstream, "normal" space—a space from which otherness of all kinds must be excluded for the sake of preserving the established norm. I use the word "normal" in quotation marks to emphasize the fact that Wisteria Lane is only normal when seen through the eyes of the residents who are the central characters on the show. In other words, these women have constructed their own version of normalcy, and from their perspective (the perspective of the self-proclaimed mainstream) the distinction between "normal" and "other" is clear. However, when seen from the outside, Wisteria Lane is a parodic reimagining of previous representations of suburbia. Series creator Marc Cherry exaggerates the already unrealistic façade established by early suburban sitcoms, and then populates the hyper-real space with over-the-top characters in outrageous situations. This is not an attempt at mimetic realism, but an intentionally absurd exaggeration of the suburban ideal that has been circulated in media images for decades. So while the series' internal logic as realized by the housewives may present a version of what is or is not normal, the over-the-top, camp sensibility of the series reveals just how absurd this sense of normalcy is.

The boundaries between suburban Wisteria Lane and the city, inside and out, self and "other," may be vigorously policed, but they are certainly not impermeable, and though spaces may have a particular identity at a particular time, such an identity is not permanent. As an example, scholars of queer theory have argued that most of the world (particularly its public spaces) is blatantly heteronormative, but that there exists a potential for queering such spaces by disrupting the heterosexual hegemony that governs them.

Gill Valentine argues that the spatial heteronormativity defining most public spaces is never secure. She suggests that "the production of the heterosexual street is always under threat from sexual dissidents (re)negotiating the way everyday spaces are produced."[40] The cruising space of the theater in *Far from Heaven* hints at this potential for renegotiation, but because its queerness remains invisible to anyone who is not in the know, it does not fully disrupt the heteronormativity of the space. Lauren Berlant discusses the visible actions of the activist group Queer Nation, including the staging of miniature pride parades in suburban shopping malls as a way of inscribing alternative sexualities "in a safe space for suburban normative sexual repression."[41] Valentine, Berlant, and others suggest that one can queer a space by undermining or exposing the dominant norms that seek to maintain its heteronormativity.

On *Desperate Housewives* Bree's son Andrew provides an example of the potential imagined by these scholars and activists. One way that he does this is simply by being gay and out in his suburban neighborhood. Martin Dines argues that "by disrupting suburban-domestic [life] with the assertion of a homosexual presence, gay characters aim to undermine hegemonic heterosexism."[42] In the first season, Andrew makes out with another boy in his neighbor's backyard pool, surprising Susan, who is expecting to find her daughter making out with another boy. Against his mother's objections, Andrew continues to see his boyfriend, occasionally inviting him to spend the night. He even goes so far as to ensure that his mother will walk in on them in bed together, because he wants to get even with her for trying to control his life. By exploring his homosexuality under his mother's roof, and by making sure that she witnesses it, Andrew visibly injects queerness into the heteronormative space of the nuclear family home. This is especially significant in Bree's home, given how hard she works to present the image of a traditional home and family.

Andrew's efforts to destabilize familial order do not stop there. In the ongoing battle waged with his mother, he uses his youth and his sexuality as weapons. In the second season, when Bree does not want to allow him to become an emancipated minor, Andrew attempts to frame her for child abuse, knowing that a court would not force an abused child to live with his abuser. In this way he tries to break out of the confines of the heteronormative family. Later in the season, he seduces his mother's sex-addict boyfriend—in her bed.

Andrew's behavior seems to exhibit the potential for reshaping the suburban space of Wisteria Lane. By openly injecting queerness into the extremely heteronormative family home even as he tries to dismantle the bonds of his nuclear family, Andrew enacts much of what some theorists have suggested is necessary to queer heteronormative space. But the force of heteronormative hegemony is very powerful, and despite his aggressive attempts, Andrew's queering potential is hampered by his mother. Deciding that she can no longer deal with Andrew's behavior, Bree drives him away from Fairview, leaves him along the side of a road, and tells him that he is on his own. When he returns in season three (after spending some time on the streets of the city), his queerness has been muted (no boyfriend, no sexual exploits), and the space of Wisteria Lane seems to remain unchanged—at least for the time being.

Unlike a stand-alone feature film, which by necessity presents a relatively finite ending, the ongoing serial nature of *Desperate Housewives* provides an opportunity for further developments. Thus, while Andrew's queerness is temporarily silenced, it is not completely eliminated. By the fifth season, Bree has finally come to accept Andrew's sexuality, and even goes so far as to buy a house in the neighborhood for him and his partner. Another gay couple, Lee and Bob, also move into the neighborhood, and despite some initial squabbles with a few of the neighbors they eventually settle in as part of the community. Queer characters become a regular presence on Wisteria Lane, which at least partially queers the suburban neighborhood. This is not, however, the radical change that queer activists often call for. While gay men have become a part of the neighborhood, they have done so by mimicking the traditional pairings and family structures of the other residents on the street. These characters fit in because they essentially assimilate to the neighborhood rather than altering it in any substantial way. And despite the presence of these couples, heteronormativity is still a strong force in the neighborhood. When Katherine Mayfair begins her first relationship with a woman, she decides that she cannot bear the thought of all the neighbors staring at her and judging her. She is uncomfortable enough that she and her girlfriend decide to move away. The events of the series thus suggest that while individuals can partially disrupt the status quo, the heteronormative hegemony of suburbia is still very strong. Thus the project of queering the space of suburbia is not a one-time act, but an ongoing process.

Even when explicit expressions of sexual difference are expelled from the community, queerness is not eliminated from Wisteria Lane. The same argument can be made for the Hartford suburbs in *Far from Heaven*. Both *Desperate Housewives* and *Far from Heaven* feature plot lines that emphasize the removal/exclusion of queer characters, but the exaggerated style employed by the creators introduces queerness in other ways. The space of Wisteria Lane as created by Marc Cherry is an absurdly exaggerated version of the suburban ideal, while Todd Haynes's construction of suburban Hartford is a highly stylized homage to 1950s melodramas. The styles employed in both *Desperate Housewives* and *Far from Heaven* introduce a camp sensibility and a level of irony that make it difficult to take either story at face value. Even when characters who represent "otherness" (not only sexual, but also racial) are excluded from their respective communities, the "otherness" that exists at the level of style continues to pervade the texts, suggesting that no matter how hard a community tries to eliminate any traces of difference, it will always be present.

Invisible Minorities and the Protection of the Suburban Image

The concept of the flawless suburban community is certainly more of an ideal than a reality. Residents often work very hard to preserve the image of what Richard Sennett refers to as the "purified community."[43] This is essentially the belief that all members of a community are similar and share common ideals. People often choose to overlook the fact that this imagined sense of homogeneity obscures the discord and differences that actually define most communities. As cultural geographers James and Nancy Duncan note, most people are more interested in the image than the reality. "The sense of community that is longed for is more a symbol or aesthetic of community than the reality of close-knit social relations."[44] They also point out that "the presence of racially marked outsiders offends the aesthetic of homogeneity necessary to maintain the appearance of community."[45] The same can be said for homosexuals and ethnic minorities who present a visible difference (in terms of bodily appearance, dress, mannerisms, visible behavior, etc.). It is not always the presence of minority groups but their visibility that makes them offensive to the suburban community, because it is the visibility which threatens the suburban façade.

As both *Far from Heaven* and *Desperate Housewives* show, members of minority groups who are in some way able to make themselves less visible (or completely invisible) stand a better chance of avoiding being excluded from the community. However, these characters only become invisible to others within the diegesis. Because of the emphasis placed upon them, they become highly visible to the viewer, making them significant and powerful figures within their respective narratives.

One way that characters in *Far from Heaven* are able to make themselves invisible is by knowing and staying in "their place." By this I am specifically referring to the African Americans who work in and around the homes of the white suburbanites. Although the white families might be uncomfortable with black families living in the neighborhood as homeowners, they are happy to invite them in as laborers, since such a relationship reinforces existing racial hierarchies. In their study of Latino migrant workers in a New York suburb, Duncan and Duncan note that "their presence as servants . . . is naturalized as white privilege."[46] The same is true for the black characters in *Far from Heaven*. During a big party hosted at the Whitakers' home, some guests are discussing a political event of the period—the integration of schools in Little Rock, Arkansas. One of the guests says that something like that would not happen in Hartford, in part because "there are no negroes" in their area. This line is followed by an immediate cut to the reactions on the faces of three African Americans who are working as part of the catering staff. The man's comment suggests that as long as the black servants are upholding the privilege of the white residents and not causing any trouble, they basically disappear. But the visual emphasis on their hurt expressions reminds viewers that these people are indeed present and visible to those willing to acknowledge them.

The Whitakers' housekeeper, Sybil (Viola Davis), is another woman of color who does not cross the social boundaries set up for her, and therefore is able to remain essentially invisible. She works very hard for the Whitakers, helping to maintain the appearance of the home long after the family living in it has crumbled. While Cathy always treats Sybil with respect, one notable exchange between them reveals a level of ignorance on Cathy's part. When Sybil comments about the various church and charitable organizations that she is involved with, Cathy expresses surprise: "I think that's marvelous, Sybil, that you find the time, with all you do for us." Although her comment seems intended as a compliment, it also reflects Cathy's surprise in discovering that Sybil actually has a life beyond her role as the Whitakers' servant. For most of the white majority in this community, blacks are there to serve them and nothing more.

Raymond is an example of what happens to those who step outside their accepted role. In the early portions of the film, he goes about his duties as a gardener for the Whitakers and other families. He also runs a plant shop that sells the raw materials for the gardening work that he does. In both cases, he plays a crucial role in maintaining the suburban aesthetic that is so important to the local residents. As long as he continues in this role, he essentially blends into the landscape that he helps to create. When he moves beyond this role, however, he stirs up trouble. For example, Raymond attends the opening of an art show organized by one of Cathy's friends. He and Cathy discuss the appeal of modern art, and Raymond demonstrates an impressive knowledge of art from various eras as well as specific artists. As Cathy and Raymond chat, the other visitors to the exhibit openly stare and gossip. In part, they are shocked that Cathy and Raymond are on such "friendly terms," but Raymond's encroachment upon their territory obviously ruffles a few feathers as well.

Things become more serious after the local gossip spots Cathy and Raymond going into Eagan's Restaurant together. Word about their relationship spreads quickly, and before long both Cathy and Raymond feel the effects of their transgressions. But while Cathy becomes the subject of ongoing gossip, Raymond faces more serious consequences. His daughter is attacked by local bullies, people throw rocks through his window, and his business dries up as both blacks and whites abandon his shop and refuse to hire him as a gardener. While he was okay as long as he stayed "in his place," crossing societal boundaries made him too visible and thus a threat to the white hegemony of the community.

Another way that characters in these texts can make their difference invisible is to blend in or assimilate with the other members of the community. For Frank in *Far from Heaven* and Andrew in *Desperate Housewives*, staying in the closet is one way of blending in. Both characters conceal their sexual identity through careful management of their behavior, essentially performing heterosexuality as a way of making their difference invisible.

In the early part of *Far from Heaven*, before his secret is discovered by his wife, Frank makes use of the spatial boundaries in his life to essentially create two identities for himself. He follows a pattern that

FIGURE 12. Raymond (Dennis Haysbert) becomes more visible, and thus a problem, when he is seen chatting casually with Cathy (Julianne Moore) at an art show (*Far from Heaven*). Frame enlargement.

Wayne Brekhus identifies as common among gays living in suburbs where homosexuality is not welcomed or tolerated. Frank is what Brekhus refers to as an "identity commuter," meaning that he allows his gay identity to come out only in certain places, while playing up his heterosexual identity in the restrictive environment of his suburban home and community. Brekhus notes that identity commuters "use travel through space to mark off discrete chunks of their self."[47] Frank works very hard to keep his two identities spatially separated, which allows him to make his homosexuality essentially invisible within his regular suburban life. After Cathy catches him in the arms of another man and Frank promises to seek treatment for his "problem," Cathy helps to sustain the invisibility of his sexual identity by playing her part in the visible performance of heterosexual marriage. When Frank is no longer able to maintain the façade of the happy husband, he is unable to remain in the suburban community. He takes up residence in a small motel room with his lover while Cathy remains in the suburban home that they used to share.

During most of *Desperate Housewives*' first season, Andrew also remains in the closet, keeping his sexual identity hidden not only from friends and family, but from the audience. When he reveals his sexual orientation, Bree has a difficult time dealing with it, and she sends him away to a camp to try to "straighten him out." When the camp fails to change Andrew, and he throws that in Bree's face, she kicks him out of the family and physically removes him from the neighborhood. Although Bree blames Andrew's actions and not his sexuality, the end result is the expulsion of a queer character who refused to keep his sexuality in check. When Andrew apologizes and returns to Wisteria Lane in the third season, Bree accepts him back into her home. His acceptance notably coincides with the erasure of his sexuality, as he is no longer dating other men. While he is not completely closeted, he has made his queerness essentially invisible again, thus allowing him to remain a part of the community without disturbing its heteronormative façade.

When Andrew's sexuality visibly returns a few years later (after the five-year jump that occurs between the fourth and fifth seasons), it is in the context of a monogamous relationship with his eventual fiancé, Alex. Although he is out of the closet, his relationship status helps to make his minority status less visible in the community. Andrew and Alex, like Wisteria Lane's other gay couple, Bob and Lee, fit in the neighborhood in almost every way. They are white, affluent professionals who are monogamously coupled. Bob and Lee even have a showy outdoor wedding in the neighborhood and eventually adopt a daughter. Aside from their sexual behavior—which is one of the few activities that actually remains behind closed doors on *Desperate Housewives*—these couples are basically like any other family on the street. Their acceptance on Wisteria Lane mirrors the gradual acceptance of gays and lesbians in certain facets of American society. While some gay rights advocates have argued that acceptance based on "a politics of tolerance and assimilation"[48] amounts to little more than "partial citizenship,"[49] many gays and lesbians have used the argument that they are "just like everyone else" as a way to gain acceptance in suburban communities and many other contexts.[50]

In the case of racial and ethnic minorities, assimilation means becoming more like their white neighbors. For many ethnic groups in America's history, the act of buying a home and living in the predominantly white world of suburbia has been a significant step toward inclusion in the ever-shifting definition of whiteness. For example, Jeff

Crump notes that as Jews were "Americanized" by homeownership, "they achieved whiteness and were allowed to share in the benefits of suburban residence."[51] Similarly, Lipsitz notes that "the suburbs helped turn Euro-Americans into 'whites' who could live near each other and intermarry with relatively little difficulty."[52] If assimilating to the suburbs is an indication of the ability to assimilate into whiteness and American-ness, then the ability to blend in on Wisteria Lane would suggest broader implications for the Latino Solises and the African American Applewhites, who have very different experiences in the suburban community.

Gabrielle and Carlos Solis fit in very well on Wisteria Lane. As native-born Americans of Mexican ancestry, they do have a different ethnic identity from their neighbors, but they do not display the characteristics often attributed (via stereotypes) to other individuals of Mexican descent—specifically the recent immigrants (both legal and illegal) and migrant workers that whites often find threatening. These groups are stereotypically seen as poor or working class, and either unable to speak English at all or able to speak it only with a heavy accent. Gabrielle and Carlos are by far the wealthiest family on the block. Carlos is a high-powered businessman who likes to flaunt his wealth by purchasing expensive furniture, artwork, sports cars, and jewelry for his runway-model-turned-stay-at-home-housewife, Gabrielle. Their affluence and accent-free English distance them from direct association with the stereotypes often associated with Mexican immigrants and Mexican Americans, thus helping them gain access to the suburban mainstream. Their assimilation is so thorough that their daughter Juanita is shocked to learn that she is anything but white. In the sixth season's episode "You Gotta Get a Gimmick," Carlos and Gabrielle attempt to get their daughter into a private school. When the school administrator mentions that it has been a while since they last had a student of Mexican descent, Juanita looks startled and says, "I'm Mexican?! I thought we were American!" When her parents remind her that they are, indeed, American but that their ancestors came from Mexico, she says, "So we're like those people who sell oranges on the side of the road?" The family has become so immersed in white suburban culture that Juanita not only sees herself as part of the mainstream, but recognizes other Mexican immigrants as distinctly outside that mainstream.

The Solises' ability to blend is emphasized by their interactions with members of other social groups, and by way of contrast with Carlos's mother. They solidify their position in the community by treating members of other minority groups poorly. Lipsitz suggests that "one way of becoming an insider is by participating in the exclusion of other outsiders,"[53] and this is exactly what the Solises do, both intentionally and unintentionally. For example, they employ two Chinese maids, Yao Lin (Lucille Soong) and Xiao-Mei (Gwendoline Yeo), and they treat both of them terribly. Gabrielle makes it clear that cleaning the house is beneath her, but she has no trouble barking orders and criticism at the women who are hired to do it for her. And Carlos angers Yao Lin by ignorantly referring to her as Japanese. While these scenes are played for laughs, humorously inverting the usual stereotype of Hispanics as domestic workers, they also allow Carlos and Gabrielle to raise their own social status by putting another group below them.

In addition to mistreating the minority workers in his home, Carlos is also implicated in an illegal business arrangement that employs slave labor overseas. And completing the trend of mistreating other minority groups, Carlos is charged with assault and accused of committing a hate crime after he beats up two gay men. (He beats them up because he thinks they are sleeping with his wife, not because they are gay, but the end result is the same, as he contributes to the narrative punishment of non-normative individuals.) By blending in and often beating the white majority at their own games, as it were, Carlos and Gabrielle are able to make their potentially problematic ethnicity largely invisible and ultimately position themselves within the suburban mainstream.

As if to demonstrate that not all Latinos can blend in as well as Carlos and Gabrielle, Carlos's mother provides a stark contrast to the young couple. Mama Solis (Lupe Ontiveros) is more distinctly marked as an ethnic "other." She speaks with a Mexican accent and occasionally slips into Spanish during conversations with her son. She also watches Mexican telenovelas (which Gabrielle openly mocks), maintaining a connection to her ancestry through media consumption. In comparison to the neighbors on Wisteria Lane, Mama Solis sticks out like a sore thumb. Not surprisingly, she does not remain there for long—she is hit by a car and eventually dies in the hospital. Her otherness is eliminated from both the neighborhood and the narrative.

Mama Solis is not the only character who is unable to blend in. The Applewhites are also unsuccessful in any attempts at making their difference invisible. From her very first appearance on Wisteria Lane, Betty Applewhite is very visible. As a dark-skinned African American, her appearance is in sharp contrast to the lighter skin of her neighbors. But while her race may make her visibly different, this is not what prevents her from being welcomed into the neighborhood. Rather, it is her behavior. She moves into her new home in the middle of the night, which immediately starts the rumor mill and gets everyone wondering what secrets the woman must be hiding. Betty tries to go unnoticed by isolating herself, but this only draws more attention and prevents her from blending in.

Eventually, Betty's secret is uncovered. She believes that one of her sons killed a young woman, and in a misdirected attempt to protect him she decides to chain him up in the basement of her own home. She eventually learns that the true killer was her other son, who ends up being killed in a standoff with police, after which Betty moves away from Wisteria Lane.

The Applewhites' story is more complicated than simply being excluded because of racial difference, and their story differs from that of Raymond in *Far from Heaven*. Raymond is driven out of the community primarily because of racism and the fears that go along with it. In the eyes of the white suburbanites, Raymond embodies the dangerous black man who will bring crime and deviant behavior to the neighborhood and pose a sexual threat to helpless white women. Although Raymond does nothing wrong, the fear that he might is enough to make people exclude him—based solely on his race. The Applewhites, on the other hand, actually do bring trouble to the neighborhood. After all, Betty keeps one son locked in her basement while the other son (a murderer) holds Bree at gunpoint when she tries to stop him from running off with her daughter. The fears of white suburbanites are realized in a highly exaggerated fashion. In this way, the series draws on its over-the-top storytelling style to reveal just how absurd such fears are.

The Applewhites' story arc follows two familiar patterns with regards to African Americans in the suburbs. Viewed one way, theirs is the story of a black family who moves into a white suburban neighborhood, is unable to fit in, and eventually moves away. Viewed another way, it is a story of a black family who intrudes upon a white community, brings crime and violence with them, is eventually discovered and then run out of the neighborhood. The former repeats the true story of so many African American suburbanites, while the latter offers an absurd realization of racist fears and stereotypes about people of color and criminal behavior. Either way, the end result is the same. These African American residents are unable to make themselves invisible by assimilating into the neighborhood, and this eventually results in their exclusion from the community.

The question of visibility is very important in the context of minority status in these suburban narratives. In communities dominated by homogeneity in terms of race, class, and sexual orientation, individuals who fall into any minority category visibly disturb that homogeneity. Those who fit the majority ideal—white, middle class, heterosexual—are socially unmarked in these surroundings, and therefore become largely invisible. By this I mean to suggest that because they do not stand out as different, they blend in as part of the community. The characters in these texts who fail to achieve or maintain invisibility find themselves expelled from their suburban surroundings. The visible differences of Frank and Raymond in *Far from Heaven* and the Applewhites and Mama Solis in *Desperate Housewives* threaten the aesthetic of homogeneity. All of them end up either killed or driven out of the community—a reminder of the consequences faced by those who refuse or are unable to blend in. Individuals in certain socially marked categories can attempt to make themselves less visible by staying within the bounds of their socially determined roles, by assimilating to the behaviors and attitudes of the surrounding community or by hiding their difference behind the veil of the closet. Though these characters may become invisible to their neighbors, they remain quite visible to the viewer, serving as a reminder of the differences underlying the surface of any seemingly homogenous community.

From Community to Nation

The promotional brochure for Mount Laurel, Alabama, remarks, "A sense of community is more than living next to someone . . . it's deciding which fresh flowers to take to the neighbors for dinner Saturday night." The first half of this statement is certainly correct—community is much more than having neighbors. But the second half of the statement still does not provide a complete picture of the concept of community. As *Far from Heaven* and *Desperate Housewives* demonstrate, community is not always about liking your neighbors. The construction of a community involves a careful process of selecting the most desirable neighbors to ensure that you will in fact *want* to take them flowers and have dinner with them. Communities—suburban or otherwise—rely on the exclusion of undesirable outsiders as a way of creating a sense of internal unity.

The exclusion of a few individuals from a fictional suburb may at first seem to be a trivial concern, but *Far from Heaven* and *Desperate Housewives* reveal the workings of community creation at all levels. They offer a visible, concrete representation of a concept that often takes more abstract forms. Graham Day draws a connection between actual lived communities and imagined national communities: "In the imagination of their members, most communities operate in a similar way to nations, through the construction of close similarities and an underlying, seemingly essential, unity among those who 'belong,' and the exclusion of those who fail to meet these criteria."[54] The fictional residents of Wisteria Lane and suburban Hartford try to exclude those who disturb the façade of homogeneity, thereby constructing an imagined sense of unity among those who remain. This is essentially what happens at a national level as people work to define what constitutes citizenship in America.

Social debates about American citizenship are frequently led by those who are included as insiders. The outsiders are generally nameless, faceless others grouped together as "immigrants," "foreigners," or "illegal aliens," rather than being viewed as individuals, making it easier to draw lines between "us" and "them." *Far from Heaven* and

Desperate Housewives focus on identifiable individuals to depict acts of separation and exclusion at a more local, human level. The minority groups represented in *Far from Heaven* and *Desperate Housewives*, including gays and lesbians, African Americans, Latinos, and Asian immigrants, are among those engaged in ongoing struggles to achieve the rights and social acceptance that would allow them to enjoy full and equal citizen status in this country. *Far from Heaven* and *Desperate Housewives* give ample screen time to both insiders and outsiders in their respective suburbs, offering a complete picture of inclusion and exclusion in the formation and maintenance of a community. Drawing on the familiar nature of suburban life, these texts encourage viewers to consider their own role in small-scale social exclusion, and by extension the larger processes of citizenship.

Both texts use a variety of suburban and urban spaces as a way of setting the stage for acts of inclusion and exclusion. Spaces are distinctly marked and associated either with those who are accepted members of the given community or with those who are identified as outsiders. These distinctions help to establish a clear division between inside and outside and suggest that there are appropriate and inappropriate locations for difference, otherness, and challenges to the mainstream. While the spaces may mark separations, they do not eliminate difference but rather call attention to it. Even as characters within the narratives imagine a sense of unity, viewers are reminded that difference will always be present, even if it is temporarily moved around the corner. Characters within the narratives are also happy to tolerate differences that exist right under their noses, as long as those differences are made invisible through social customs and behavior. While assimilation, silent domestic service, or life in the closet may allow those who are different to blend in and thereby avoid disturbing a particular mainstream view of a community, both *Far from Heaven* and *Desperate Housewives* demonstrate the toll that this invisibility takes on those who are expected to disappear.

Forming a community, whether suburban, national, or otherwise, generally necessitates the creation of a false sense of unity and homogeneity. Norms do not simply exist—they are constructed over time and their maintenance requires a great deal of effort. Both *Far from Heaven* and *Desperate Housewives* make use of exaggerated visual and storytelling styles to present a version of normal that is anything but natural. They highlight the effort required to maintain social norms, thus questioning how anything can be seen as deviant when the supposed norm is so clearly an unnatural construction.

Far from Heaven and *Desperate Housewives* take important steps toward queering and diversifying the suburbs. Suburbia, after all, exists not only as a physical space but also as an idea embedded in the cultural imagination of the American people. The imagined version of suburbia is shaped in large part by the images of suburbs that circulate in popular media. While many suburban narratives reinforce the image of a white, heteronormative, middle-class space, *Far from Heaven* and *Desperate Housewives* help to alter the accepted image by emphasizing the heterogeneity of suburbia. By depicting difference as something that emerges from within, these texts serve as a reminder that gays and lesbians and people of color are not just now arriving in the suburbs—they have always been present. They have only been absent from the imagined suburban ideal, and it is this false image that these texts help to correct.

Many recent political debates have revolved around the dangers that certain "others" present to the unity of our nation, making exclusion a key concern in contemporary society. Politicians and pundits wage rhetorical battles over immigration, gay marriage, and homeland security, all of which focus on the threats posed by foreign workers, alternative sexualities, and potential terrorists. Excluding large groups of people, either by physically keeping them out of the country or by denying them full citizenship, is posed as the solution to these threats.

Images of suburban social exclusion may seem far removed from national debates about immigration and gay marriage, but as David Sibley points out, "Echoes of otherness travel backwards and forwards, reinforcing neighborhoods, providing electoral support for restrictive immigration practices, and legitimating foreign policy."[55] By depicting the process of exclusion that goes into the maintenance of a suburban community, *Far from Heaven* and *Desperate Housewives* rearticulate national attitudes and behaviors regarding the treatment of "others" in our culture. They serve as a reminder of the kinds of damages that are inflicted every day in the interest of preserving an illusion of national unity. But they also demonstrate that even if difference is not visible, it will always be present, and that the tensions created by the suppression of difference will always resurface. In this way, *Far from Heaven* and *Desperate Housewives* suggest that our desperate attempts to unify a nation of Americans may actually be doing more harm than good.

4

Desperate Husbands

The Crisis of Hegemonic Masculinity
in Post-9/11 Suburbia

In her book *Gendered Spaces*, Daphne Spain examines a variety of physical structures that range from domestic, professional, and educational to civic, commercial, and sacred. She argues that built environments in our society have historically segregated men from women, with some spaces being viewed as masculine and others as feminine.[1] Linda McDowell concurs, noting that the industrialization of Western societies in the 1800s led to a partial separation of home and work, helping to establish the ideology of separate spheres for men and women. Particularly for those in the middle class, "the home was constructed as the locus of love, emotion, and empathy, and the burdens of nurturing and caring for others were placed on the shoulders of women."[2] With the rise of residential suburbs in the twentieth century, the femininity associated with the home was broadened to incorporate suburban life in general. Suburbia came to be seen as a feminine sphere of consumption and reproduction, in contrast with the masculine public sphere of production.

Given the suburbs' associations with femininity, it is not surprising that many suburban narratives feature men whose masculinity seems threatened by suburban life. In older films like *The Man in the Gray Flannel Suit* (1956), *Mr. Blandings Builds His Dream House* (1948), and *No Down Payment* (1957), men find themselves struggling to manage the social, financial, and paternal expectations that are placed upon them as they make the transition from urban to suburban life. Masculinity

has continued to be a prominent theme in more recent suburban narratives, which often reflect the additional complications brought about
over the years by feminist, civil rights, and gay rights movements. Lester
in *American Beauty* (1999) tries to reclaim his youth and his masculinity by quitting his dull office job, standing up to his wife, buying a new
muscle car, smoking pot, working out regularly, and trying to seduce
a teenaged girl. In *The Ice Storm* (1997), Ben struggles to hold onto any
respect that he may have once had from his wife, his kids, his mistress,
and his neighbors, but he ends up breaking into sobs in the front seat
of the family car while his wife and kids look on in disbelief. In *Far from
Heaven* (2002), Frank tries mightily to fight off his attraction to other
men so that he can fulfill his expected role as father and husband,
while Raymond's ability to provide for his daughter is threatened by the
racism that surrounds him. *Revolutionary Road*'s (2008) Frank Wheeler
dreams of escaping the corporate grind for a more fulfilling life in Paris,
but he eventually succumbs to expectations of suburban marriage and
fatherhood. In *Big Love* (2006–2011), Bill struggles with the physical
and emotional demands of being a good husband to not one, but three
wives. In *Breaking Bad* (2008–2013), Walter resorts to extreme measures
in a desperate attempt to provide for his wife and children. All in all,
suburban narratives have repeatedly emphasized men whose domestic
surroundings are closing in on them, making it difficult for them to live
up to the expectations of masculinity placed on them by society.

Two notable films, *The Pacifier* and *Mr. & Mrs. Smith* (both 2005),
continue the trend of exploring suburban masculinity but depart significantly from most suburban narratives by drawing on a genre not
generally associated with suburbia—the action-adventure film. Similar
to suburban narratives, action-adventure films frequently take masculinity as a central narrative and thematic concern. However, in contrast
to the images of defeated suburban masculinity, action-adventure
films have generally focused on triumphant heroic masculinity, often
emphasizing violence as a means of proving dominance. This is not to
say that these films present masculinity as being without problems, but
they certainly emphasize the triumph over the turmoil. Recent popular films falling into this category have featured superheroes, pirates,
mythical warriors, government agents, and spies, and their stories tend

to play out in large cities or exotic locales far from the domestic tranquility of suburbia.³ *The Pacifier* and *Mr. & Mrs. Smith* move in a different direction, bringing the excitement of military heroics and undercover assassins to the seemingly mundane world of suburbia.

The Pacifier tells the story of Lt. Shane Wolfe (Vin Diesel), a Navy SEAL who is assigned to protect the family of a recently murdered Defense Department security expert. The government believes that the man was killed because of a nuclear defense program he was working on, and they are concerned that enemies may harm his family in an attempt to find out more information about the program. Shane is sent to the suburbs to live with the Plummer family, protect them from potential enemies, and search for any evidence of the missing defense program. Initially, Shane's version of masculinity seems out of place in the suburban domestic sphere, but by the film's conclusion, Shane emerges triumphant, saving not only the family and the defense program, but heroic masculinity as well.

Mr. & Mrs. Smith stars Brad Pitt and Angelina Jolie as John and Jane Smith, two professional assassins living cover lives as a typical suburban couple. At the beginning of the film, neither partner knows that the other is also an assassin, so they each work very hard to keep their secret identities hidden. When the two assassins are hired to kill each other, their secrets are revealed, and their relationship takes a series of surprising turns. In this case, the violent masculinity of John the assassin is not only in conflict with his domestic surroundings but is also threatened by the unexpected challenge presented by his equally dangerous wife.

By taking elements from the action genre, including particular versions of masculinity, and locating them in the domestic space of suburbia, *The Pacifier* and *Mr. & Mrs. Smith* raise important questions about the state of contemporary masculinity. While suburban narratives tend to depict the "everyman" as losing his grasp on masculinity, most action films reinforce the importance of maintaining the masculine traits of violence, aggression, and heroism. *The Pacifier* and *Mr. & Mrs. Smith* combine these two approaches in a way that draws attention to the uneasy fit between heroic masculinity and the domestic lives experienced by most American men. Although the conclusions of both films initially seem to reaffirm violent heroism as the epitome of masculinity in post-9/11 America, they actually do more to reveal the incompatibility of such masculinity within the domestic realms of American culture.

Masculinity—Always in Crisis?

Masculinity is a complicated concept that shifts and changes as you move from one culture to another or from one historical era to another. Even within a single time and place, the performance of masculinity can vary from one person to the next. As a result, any discussion of masculinity must actually be a discussion of masculinit*ies*. The films analyzed in this chapter, for example, feature men whose particular version of masculinity is defined in contrast to the masculinities of surrounding characters. R. W. Connell's influential discussion of plural masculinities provides a helpful framework for analyzing the characters in *The Pacifier* and *Mr. & Mrs. Smith*. Recognizing the range of masculinities present in our society, Connell argues that we must attend to the hierarchical nature of these masculinities, rather than assuming a more simplified power structure based on one form of masculinity which dominates femininity.

Connell identifies four basic categories of masculinity: hegemonic, complicit, subordinate, and marginalized. Hegemonic masculinity is defined as "the configuration of gender practice which embodies the currently accepted answer to the problem of the legitimacy of patriarchy, which guarantees (or is taken to guarantee) the dominant position of men and the subordination of women."[4] Hegemonic masculinity is historically contingent and thus varies in response to cultural shifts and societal changes. Because hegemonic masculinity is based on an idealized and exalted version of gender practice, often embodied by superheroes and other fictional characters, it is impossible for all (or even most) men to enact it fully. Complicit masculinity is the term that Connell uses to describe the large body of men who "have some connection with the hegemonic project but do not embody hegemonic masculinity."[5] These men may not achieve the ideal, but they support it and benefit from it by drawing on the power granted to them through patriarchy.

Hegemony suggests a form of cultural dominance and subordination, and in the case of masculinities Connell argues that it is homosexual masculinity that is subordinated to the hegemonic norm.[6] When gender practices intersect with other structures such as race and class, the hierarchy of masculinities becomes even more complicated. Hegemonic masculinity is constructed as both white and middle class, while masculinities falling outside that definition are considered marginalized.[7]

Various gender scholars have sought to revise Connell's framework, suggesting, among other things, that there should be more than just four categories, and that hegemonic masculinity might work in tandem with subordinate masculinities to reproduce patriarchy.[8] While the details of Connell's concept may still be up for debate, there are two components of his framework that are especially useful for this chapter's analysis: the recognition that masculinity cannot be reduced to a singular, monolithic form, and the attention to the hierarchies that define the range of masculinities. The tensions that exist between the different forms of masculinity and the struggle between groups to achieve and/or maintain dominance provides much of the comedic and dramatic conflict in the films that I examine in this chapter. In *The Pacifier*, Shane's masculinity is defined largely in contrast to the masculinity of other male characters, while in *Mr. & Mrs. Smith*, John's masculinity is defined in opposition to that of his suburban alter ego and to the gendered performance of his wife.

Because of its evolving nature, masculinity must be examined within specific cultural and historical contexts. Eras and events like industrialization, the Great Depression, World War II, and the feminist movement have all shaped understandings of American manhood and masculinity. Michael Kimmel has traced these shifts from the founding of the nation to the present day, and he argues, like Connell, that a history of manhood must "recount two histories: the history of the changing 'ideal' version of masculinity and the parallel and competing versions that coexist with it."[9]

Kimmel notes that at the turn of the nineteenth century, American manhood was rooted in landownership. After the industrial revolution, however, manhood came to be based on one's economic success in the marketplace. The potential for success was always balanced against the threat of failure, and though market performance has not always remained the primary marker of manhood, Kimmel argues that the tenuous nature of manhood has, indeed, remained. During different periods, manhood has been variously defined by military bravery, physical strength, athletic ability, and commitment to family, but in all cases, men have felt pressure to prove their manhood. It is this burden of proof that has defined much of what we consider manly behavior over the past two centuries.[10] The leading men in *The Pacifier* and *Mr. & Mrs. Smith* are characters who are driven by the need to prove their manhood within the seemingly feminine domestic sphere, often going to great lengths to do so.

As the work of Connell, Kimmel, and others demonstrates,[11] masculinity is a flexible concept that can adapt and evolve in response to changes in the culture of which it is a part. There is always another historical event or cultural shift that forces a reevaluation of masculinity and its position in our culture. The most recent threat to hegemonic masculinity has been largely economic. The recession that began in 2008, accompanied by high rates of unemployment, bankruptcies, and foreclosures, made it even more difficult for men to hold onto the masculine breadwinner role with which they have long been associated. But the economic crisis is just the latest in a long line of cultural changes and events that have threatened the dominance of hegemonic masculinity over the past few decades.

Many recent changes associated with masculinity have been in response to the 1970s feminist movement. Susan Faludi argues that some men have responded to feminism by fighting against what they see as an encroachment upon the privilege granted to them by the structures of patriarchy.[12] Kenneth MacKinnon notes that the main focus of the men's movement of the 1990s, with its self-help books and male-bonding retreats, "appears to be on the healing of wounds believed to have been inflicted on heterosexual men by gender relations."[13] Popular media responded to the apparent need to reassert manhood with magazines like *Maxim, Stuff*, and *FHM*, television programs like *The Man Show* (1999–2004), and even an entire television network (Spike TV), all of which reflected a shift toward consumption as a marker of masculinity.

For those men striving to align themselves with hegemonic masculinity, such media products provided a way of announcing such intentions. As if to prove that they had not gone "soft," millions of men began turning to pharmaceuticals like Viagra, Cialis, and Levitra to enhance their sexual performance. Although the drugs were intended to counteract a physiological dysfunction, the promotions and user responses often suggested that the drugs helped men recover their masculinity.[14]

As men desperately tried to prove their manhood with the help of men's retreats, conspicuous consumption, and pharmaceutical aids, the country was hit with an event that would impact all aspects of our culture, including our views of masculinity. When terrorists attacked the United States on September 11, 2001, the nation was left feeling shocked, wounded, and vulnerable. Although Americans had been hit by terrorists before, an attack of this magnitude was unprecedented, and it marked the beginning of the nation's "War on Terror." Within a year and a half, this war expanded to include not just those who had attacked on September 11, but also the regime of Iraqi dictator Saddam Hussein.

The initial images and news reports from the 9/11 attack emphasized a sense that the nation and its people had been violated. As Stacy Takacs notes, "Images of men, even soldiers at the Pentagon, screaming, running, and crying were particularly evocative of this sense of violation."[15] The nation's masculine façade had been damaged by the attack, but it wasn't long before images of reinvigorated masculinity began to replace those of the wounded victims. Amid the chaos, death, and debilitating destruction of the terrorist attacks, heroic firefighters and police officers valiantly went about the business of rescuing victims, often risking their own lives to do so. Stories about these rescuers dominated news coverage, and political leaders, including President Bush, repeatedly identified them as the heroes who would help heal the nation's wounds.[16]

When military campaigns got under way in Afghanistan and eventually in Iraq, images of heroic soldiers were added to those of the rescue workers as evidence of America's ability to fight back and repair itself. Although the wars faced resistance from a significant portion of the American population, they still produced a steady stream of images of military heroes. American masculinity needed to be made whole again, and the soldiers depicted in most of the images circulated during the war were "nothing if not competent, strong, and manly."[17] This was in stark contrast to the depiction of the dictatorial Iraqi regime and the terrorists, who were cast by political leaders and journalists as cowards, rapists, and barbarians who epitomized "the dark side" of manliness.[18]

While the masculinity of Americans was exalted and the masculinity of the terrorists was vilified in the popular press and political discourse, femininity was either completely absent or associated with victimhood. Middle Eastern women were depicted as oppressed and in need of liberation by American forces. And though many American women served their country in the armed forces, the one who received the most attention was Pfc. Jessica Lynch, who became famous when she had to be rescued from a hospital in Iraq. The endless recounting of Lynch's ordeal in news reports, documentaries, and dramatizations tended to highlight her "femininity, passivity, and vulnerability," which helped reinforce the perceived need for heroic masculinity during the conflict, and which also helped to justify the aggressive tactics that dominated U.S. foreign policy in the years following the 9/11 attacks.[19]

In general, public discourse immediately after 9/11 called for a remasculinization of the United States "in order to make us all less vulnerable."[20] Whether they were freeing people from rubble or liberating them from oppression and captivity, the rescuers and soldiers associated with the aftermath of 9/11 and the ensuing War on Terror provided a model for proving masculinity in a time when masculinity once again seemed to be in crisis.

Hollywood's Masculine Response

But how does the masculinity epitomized by the rescue workers of 9/11 or the soldiers fighting in the Middle East relate to images of masculinity in the entertainment industry? The work of film scholars Steven Cohan and Susan Jeffords is helpful here, as their investigations ask similar questions about masculinity at the end of World War II and the Cold War, respectively. Although the exact circumstances vary, there are some notable similarities in Hollywood's depictions of masculinity after World War II, the Cold War, and 9/11.

In a chapter from his book *Masked Men: Masculinity and the Movies in the Fifties*, Cohan investigates the redefinition of hegemonic masculinity following the return of soldiers from World War II. As he points out, "In the fifties, the domesticated breadwinner, commonly identified by the media as The Man in the Gray Flannel Suit, was responsible for legitimating the hegemony of the professional-managerial class."[21] He argues that films like *Pitfall* (1948), *The Seven Year Itch* (1955), and *The Man in the Gray Flannel Suit* (1956) depicted the need to eradicate the violence expressed by men in the war, replacing it with a more acceptable, domesticated masculinity. Common narratives of the time made home, not work or the battlefield or any other aspect of the public sphere, the place where masculinity was truly realized. This new ideal did not come without a price, however. Cohan points out that many of these films clearly depicted the heavy toll that living up to this domestic ideal took on men in the fifties.

Susan Jeffords looks to a different period with her book *Hard Bodies: Hollywood Masculinity in the Reagan Era*. Most of her discussion focuses on the militarized, excessive, muscular version of masculinity associated with 1980s action films, such as the *Rambo* series (1982, 1985, 1988), which she argues developed and projected an image of hard-bodied strength in the face of Cold War threats. She suggests, however, that this trend shifted in the early 1990s. With the Cold War finally over, the macho loner heroes of the previous decade were turning toward more domestic concerns, taking a particular interest in the family. Drawing on films such as *Kindergarten Cop* (1990), *Terminator 2: Judgment Day* (1991), and *Beauty and the Beast* (1991), Jeffords notes that "fathering became the vehicle for portraying masculine emotions, ethics, and commitments, and for redirecting masculine characterizations from spectacular achievement to domestic triumph."[22]

Both Cohan and Jeffords identify a shift from a violently heroic masculinity to a masculinity that revolves around home and family. Cohan focuses on World War II and the attempts that returning soldiers made to reintegrate themselves into society by way of the booming middle-class suburbs. Jeffords looks to the 1980s as a period of Vietnam recovery combined with Cold War anxieties, identifying a similar shift to more domestic masculinity following this era. Both scholars point to a tension between the heroic masculinity of war and the seemingly more complicated masculinity of home. Recent events have led to a similar tension.

The 9/11 attacks and the war in Iraq revealed an extraordinary degree of vulnerability, threatening the masculine ideal of self-defense and the nation's myth of invincibility. One cultural response to this threat was a resurgence of militarized, heroic masculinity. Firefighters, police officers, and soldiers were exalted as models of masculine behavior. Another response was an emphasis on domesticity, as Americans turned away from the traumas outside in order to focus on the family home, leading to what Faludi refers to as the "nesting nation."[23] While the eras described by Cohan and Jeffords emphasized a shift from military masculinity to domestic masculinity, the responses to 9/11 seemed to encourage both at the same time, which creates somewhat of a contradiction. After all, the majority of men in the United States were neither rescue workers nor soldiers, and far more men watched the war on the news than actually took any part in it. The patriotic masculinity exemplified by soldiers and rescuers was therefore not easily translated to the domestic lives of most men.

The post-9/11 era also differs from the periods discussed by Cohan and Jeffords in that while World War II and the Vietnam War were fought on foreign soil and focused national aggression on enemies halfway around the world, the War on Terror has repeatedly been portrayed as a war taking place in our own back yards. The outrage that followed 9/11 repeatedly focused on the fact that the attacks took place on American soil, and "homeland security" immediately turned into a national obsession. President Bush emphasized this in his speech on the fifth anniversary of the attacks when he said, "We face an enemy determined to bring death and suffering into our homes."[24] Protection of the nation became everyone's responsibility, not just that of the soldiers fighting overseas. This led to the awkward pairing of military machismo with domestic concerns, as the government suggested that the War on Terror would, in many ways, be fought at home.

Faludi points to a third post-9/11 response that differs from the eras following World War II or Vietnam—a backlash against weak men and strong women. She argues that the flip side of celebrating the return of heroic masculinity is laying blame for its disappearance in the first place. "The post-9/11 commentaries were riddled with apprehensions that America was lacking in masculine fortitude, that the masses of weak-chinned BlackBerry clutchers had left the nation open to attack and wouldn't have the cojones for the confrontations ahead." She notes that many pundits and columnists blamed feminists for this, claiming that "women's liberation had 'feminized' our men," leaving the nation weakened and vulnerable.[25]

The Pacifier and *Mr. & Mrs. Smith* articulate the contemporary anxieties about masculinity brought on (or at least amplified) by the 9/11 attacks and the War on Terror. Drawing on the traditional gender roles associated with the suburban home, they emphasize the interplay between the three responses to 9/11 that I have just identified: the celebration of heroic masculinity, the backlash against "weaker" versions of masculinity and strong women, and the renewed emphasis on domesticity. In different ways *The Pacifier* and *Mr. & Mrs. Smith* both make use of their suburban settings to work through these anxieties in an attempt to answer the same question—what should domestic masculinity look like in the post-9/11 era?

The Pacifier seems confident in its definition of desirable masculinity. It seemingly exalts militarized heroic masculinity, but the amount of effort required to do so reveals the tensions between this form of manliness and the domestic environment that it seeks to inhabit. *Mr. & Mrs. Smith* also presents a violent form of masculinity as heroic, but it complicates the situation even further by placing that masculinity in a position where it is threatened by the strength of an empowered female who performs many of the traits of heroic masculinity just as successfully as her male counterpart. Both films draw on the suburban intertext to establish expectations about appropriate masculinity, and then create humor based on the mismatch between these expectations and the actual behavior of the lead characters. One man is like a fish out of water while the other has to juggle the two halves of his double life, but both of them use the space of suburbia to explore the ongoing anxieties over how to prove domestic masculinity in the post-9/11 era.

Reaffirming Heroic Masculinity: *The Pacifier*

Of the two films examined in this chapter, *The Pacifier* works most literally to transform military masculinity into domestic masculinity. Unlike
the men in post–World War II films, Shane is not trying to adjust to suburban life after leaving the military. He is an active Navy SEAL sent to the
suburbs to carry out a mission. He therefore has no interest in shedding
his military mindset and instead treats the situation as he would any
other naval operation. Although this initially makes Shane seem out of
place, with the children taunting and disrespecting him, his heroically
masculine military expertise eventually allows him to save the day. *The
Pacifier* depicts hegemonic masculinity under siege and in crisis, but only
to allow it to transform and reestablish itself more firmly than before.

In many ways, *The Pacifier* borrows from previous films such as *Mr.
Mom* (1983), *Three Men and a Baby* (1987), and *Big Daddy* (1999), all of
which feature men who unexpectedly find themselves taking care of a
child or children. These films initially find humor in the reversal of traditional gender roles that results from men taking on the role of nurturer,
which our culture has constructed as the duty of women. By the end of
each film, however, the men adapt and learn to take care of the children, which not only sets up a happy and heartwarming ending but
also suggests that masculinity is able to expand to incorporate roles
traditionally associated with both men and women.

The Pacifier follows a similar trajectory but with some notable
alterations. While the earlier films feature men who are portrayed as
ordinary, or everymen, the protagonist of *The Pacifier* is a military hero
whose hyper-masculine persona is so exaggerated that he seems even
more out of place—not only in the role of nurturer, but in the domestic
sphere as a whole. Additionally, the film incorporates elements of the
action genre (to which Shane's masculine persona is better suited) by
placing the children in physical danger, thereby requiring Shane to
go beyond nurturing, employing violent heroics to protect the children. Like its predecessors, *The Pacifier* presents masculinity as flexible
enough to incorporate traditionally feminine traits, thereby doing the
work of both men and women. By exaggerating Shane's masculinity
to hyperbolic proportions, the film raises questions not only about

differences between genders, but also about differences between various forms of masculinity.

Shane's masculinity goes through four phases during the course of the film. First, Shane is established as a model of hegemonic masculinity. Second, his masculinity is questioned, ridiculed, and made to seem out of place. Third, Shane regroups and reestablishes his masculine control. Finally, Shane and his recovered masculinity save the day, restoring the domestic world to a state of stability. This evolution depicts a version of masculinity that faces threats and challenges but still manages to rebuild and maintain its dominant position.

Shane's masculinity is initially established through two primary means: the intertextual and extratextual star persona of Vin Diesel, and the performance of genre-coded heroic acts in the opening scene of the film. Before *The Pacifier*, Vin Diesel had starred in a series of action films including *Pitch Black* (2000), *The Fast and the Furious* (2001), *xXx* (2002), *A Man Apart* (2003), and *The Chronicles of Riddick* (2004). Through these films, Diesel had established himself as a hyper-masculine action star in the tradition of Sylvester Stallone and Arnold Schwarzenegger—a man who could rely on his size and strength to achieve and maintain a position of power.

The hyper-masculine image that Diesel brings to *The Pacifier* is reinforced by way of the film's opening sequence. In the first scene, Diesel's character, Shane, is organizing a group of Navy SEALs who are preparing for a rescue mission. Military-style snare drums fill the sound track as Shane barks orders to his fellow SEALs. His wetsuit is tight enough to reveal the muscular bulk of the body that it covers, and after Shane completes his speech, he finishes suiting up for the mission. Close-up shots show Shane affixing various weapons and devices to his wetsuit, including a knife, grenades, detonators, and an earpiece for communication. The weapons and gadgets serve to enhance the masculinity already presented by way of Shane's body. During the mission, Shane takes down a helicopter with an explosive device and outmaneuvers his enemies on a jet ski before finding and releasing the man he was sent to rescue.

The opening sequence not only depicts Shane's masculinity directly through his heroic actions, but it also situates him within the realm

FIGURE 13. The masculine identity of Shane (Vin Diesel) is initially established by way of his participation in a Navy SEALs rescue mission (*The Pacifier*). Frame enlargement.

of the military and within the action film genre, both of which have traditionally been dominated by men. Drawing on both traditions, the sequence positions Shane within a much larger system of dominant masculinity. His physical strength and aggressive demeanor allow him to tap into the power granted to him within the system of patriarchy. His status is threatened, however, at the end of the sequence, when he is shot by an unseen assailant, leading to his first-ever failed mission.

Although Shane recovers, the surprise attack has shown that he is not invincible. At the same time, his injury serves as a testament to his masculinity. He does not take on the role of a victim who has been defeated by his enemies, but instead returns to seek vengeance and finish the job he started. This further cements Shane's connection to the action genre, where the hero is frequently beaten, injured, and nearly broken, only to "emerge triumphant within the movie's narrative line."[26] By overcoming his injury and returning to his duties, Shane shows that his masculinity will not go down without a fight.

With a slight chink in his armor, Shane reluctantly agrees to the follow-up assignment that he is given: to protect the family of the man he failed to rescue. To make matters worse, this assignment places him far away from the heroic adventures associated with military service. He must carry out this mission in the domestic, feminized world of suburbia. Proving his masculinity in the world of Navy SEALs was easy for Shane, but proving it in the domestic sphere seems to be more difficult.

When he first enters this world, the masculinity that is a part of his persona quickly becomes a source of comedy, due to the fact that it is so excessive and out of place in its new surroundings.

The film draws many of its initial laughs from the well-worn idea that men just don't know how to take care of a house and kids. Following in the footsteps of the aforementioned *Mr. Mom, Three Men and a Baby, Big Daddy*, and others, *The Pacifier* includes comical images of Shane reacting in horror to the contents of the baby's diaper, dunking the baby in the toilet to clean it, and feeding the family food that is clearly not what their mother would normally give them. The film goes beyond the earlier films' suggestion that men are inherently unable to take care of kids. It suggests that Shane's particular brand of masculinity is incompatible with suburban domesticity.

For example, Shane attempts to bring his military tactics to the family home, barking out orders, giving the children code names, and basically running the family like a team of Navy SEALs. He announces that he has only one rule—everything must be done his way, and there is "no highway option." When Shane is unable to get the oldest son, Seth (Max Thieriot), to open his bedroom door, Shane kicks the door down. Walking out of the bathroom, Seth is appalled by Shane's actions: "Is this what you're trained to do? A 'shock and awe' on my door?" The clear reference to American military strikes and the inappropriateness of Shane's actions in this situation suggest that the military heroics associated with the War on Terror have no place in the domestic realm. Like the World War II veterans who had difficulty reintegrating into society after their tours of duty, Shane initially struggles to fit his military-trained masculinity in with the carefully constructed peaceful image of suburbia.

Shane's situation differs from the postwar men described by Cohan in one significant way. The men described by Cohan find their suburban lives to be a letdown after the excitement of the battlefield. Behaviors that were permitted during war were not permitted in suburbia, and these men had to repress their violent tendencies and take on the role of breadwinner and family provider. While Shane also finds his military style to be somewhat incompatible with suburban life, he finds suburban life to be anything but boring. Every moment is a new challenge, and rather than changing his behavior to fit his surroundings Shane incorporates elements of domestic life into his own behavior to show that his masculinity does, indeed, have a place in suburban life.

This becomes most apparent during a scene in which the family home comes under attack by masked assailants. Just after the oldest daughter, Zoe (Brittany Snow), tells Shane that the kids all hate him and that they do not need him around, two people crash through the window, wearing black from head to toe and performing martial arts moves. Shane initially fends them off with his bare hands, legs, and brute strength. Unlike the opening scene, this time Shane does not have his holster of weapons and gadgets to get him through the mission. Instead, he resorts to items associated with his new domestic role, fighting off his enemies with brooms, baby powder, hula hoops, and a stroller. Incorporating the trappings of domesticity into his display of masculine violence, Shane is able to protect the kids, earn their respect, and convince them that they do, in fact, need his assistance. Just moments before, Zoe had been chastising Shane for trying to replace their father, but as the kids huddle around him after the attack, Shane's new role within the family becomes clear. Following in the footsteps of earlier action films including the *Lethal Weapon* and *Terminator* series, "the white male protagonist is both a protector of domestic space and an iconoclastic loner, defending a family of which he has become a surrogate member."[27] He has successfully defended the family, but because the assailants escaped, there is still the threat of further attacks. The patriarchal protector is established as crucial to the family's survival.

Although the early scenes question the role of violent masculinity in suburban spaces, Shane is eventually able to prove that his tough-guy persona does, in fact, serve an important function—but only based on the internal logic of the film. After all, it takes a comically exaggerated threat—masked ninjas who crash into the house through a second-story window—to justify Shane's presence. The suspension of disbelief that makes the suburban ninjas seem plausible is also required to make Shane's violent masculinity seem appropriate. Situated within its post-9/11 context, the film offers a striking parallel to the Bush administration's policies of the same era. Critics of the War on Terror have argued that the Bush administration exaggerated the threat posed by Middle

Eastern terrorists in order to justify a violent response overseas and increased "security" (in the form of surveillance and suspicion of foreigners) at home. This military might, like Shane's hyper-masculinity, depends on an audience willing to believe in the threat as it is presented to them.

With Shane's heroic masculinity validated—at least within the logic of the film—the stage is set for him to save the day, the family, and even the nation. His primary task is to finish the job he started—protecting the family from harm while searching for the missing defense program. Not surprisingly, he is able to accomplish this task by using his military training, brute strength, and violence. But before the final showdown to resolve the crisis of the defense program, Shane (as the surrogate father figure) also manages to solve many of the other problems plaguing the family. Zoe has been unable to master the skills required to drive a car and is therefore unable to get her license. Lulu (Morgan York) and the other members of her Fireflies troupe are getting harassed by a group of boys who steal the cookies that they are trying to sell. Seth secretly wants to quit the wrestling team so that he can be in a production of *The Sound of Music.* Continuing the film's absurd logic, Shane manages to step in and solve all three kids' problems, applying his military training and mindset to each of their situations.

First, Shane teaches Zoe to drive—but not in the typical fashion. By the time he is done with her, she is able to maneuver the family minivan like a stunt driver, taking corners at high speeds and screeching (rather than gently coasting) to a stop as she finishes the obstacle course he creates for her. Shane trains Lulu and her friends in the martial arts so that they can defend themselves. And when the Fireflies are again harassed by a group of boys, they fight back, easily overwhelming their tormenters with high kicks and karate chops before tying them up with their own bandanas and forcing cookies into their mouths.

Shane teaches Seth to stand up for himself, rather than letting his peers and teachers bully him. First Shane sets an example by standing up to Duane Murney (Brad Garrett), Seth's vice principal and wrestling coach, who belittles Shane after learning that he is essentially working as a nanny. Realizing that Murney is nothing more than an insecure blowhard, Shane accepts his challenge to a wrestling match, ultimately pinning and humiliating Murney in front of a gym filled with cheering students, easily dominating the man who had dared to question Shane's masculinity. Not only does Shane show up the wrestling coach, but he also takes over the struggling production of *The Sound of Music*. The musical's director, with his lisp, tight clothing, and flamboyant mannerisms, is clearly coded as gay, and, after expressing his frustration with the poor quality of the performances, he quits his job and storms out dramatically. Shane witnesses this exit and volunteers to take over. When one of the actresses questions his qualifications, he launches into a confident speech. "I've directed rescue missions all around the world. . . . I've choreographed multi-pronged amphibious landings and stealth air attacks. Do you think I have the military proficiency to direct this production?" Seth and the other stunned performers overlook the absurdity of this logic and respond, "Yes, sir!"[28]

All these situations help to define and validate Shane's masculinity, in part by comparing him to other forms of masculinity that are shown to be "weaker" than his. Murney demonstrates a version of what Connell calls complicit masculinity. He believes in the ideal of hegemonic masculinity and strives to achieve it himself, but he is all talk, and Shane physically dominates him with very little effort. The drama director—coded as gay—enacts a subordinated form of masculinity. As Connell argues, "Gayness, in patriarchal ideology, is the repository of whatever is symbolically expelled from hegemonic masculinity," and it is often aligned with femininity.[29] As such, the director embodies everything that Shane is not. The ease with which Shane assumes the directorial duties (and, in fact, improves the production) suggests that the director's version of masculinity is not just different from Shane's, but inferior to it.

Shane can also be compared to the teenaged Seth, who is meek, insecure, and initially unable to stand up for himself. This is attributed to youth and inexperience, and Shane is happy to set him on the "right" path toward achieving the masculine ideal. In this way Shane is also shown to be superior to Seth's father, who apparently failed to teach Seth how to be a man. Within the logic of the film, this is hardly surprising, given that Seth's father was an intellectual who was captured and had to rely on Shane to rescue him. In a slight twist, Shane also teaches masculine skills to Lulu and her friends, allowing them to physically defeat the bullying boys who resemble a younger version of Murney—talking a big game, but unable to follow through when the girls fight back.

With their individual problems solved (through aggressive and often violent means), the kids are able to come together as a family, which becomes vital in the film's climax. Just when they think that everything is safe and back to normal, and just as Shane is set to open the vault containing the defense program, the enemy assailants return and are joined by Shane's boss, who is revealed as a traitor. Shane is knocked unconscious and the rest of the family is tied up and held hostage. Fortunately, thanks to Shane's training, the kids are able to escape by beating up their captor. While the kids go for help (with Zoe utilizing her aggressive driving skills to outrun an enemy pursuer, attract the police, and draw them back to the house), Shane regains consciousness and manages to fight off the enemies once and for all.

Shane's heroic masculinity, although beaten and questioned at the start of the film, fully recovers and emerges triumphant by the end of the narrative. His violent and heroic tactics—seen as necessary in war, but initially viewed as out of place in suburbia—prove to be well suited to domestic problems after all. This is not to say that Shane has not been changed by his domestic experience. After learning the steps to a children's dance that the toddler demands to see before going to sleep, Shane figures out that the dance contains instructions that will get him safely into the vault where the defense program is hidden. But once he gets to the program, he still has to resort to physical violence to keep it out of the enemy's hands. In the end, violence trumps sensitivity.

In this way, *The Pacifier* stands in contrast to many of the post–World War II suburban films. The soldiers returning from the war were generally expected to trade in their violent, wartime behaviors for the more peaceful pursuit of suburban family life. As Cohan describes, films of the era like *The Man in the Gray Flannel Suit* depicted this transition as difficult but necessary. Many men felt confined by their new roles as breadwinners and family men, but given the postwar "anxieties about the violence of returning veterans,"[30] those who did not conform to this image were often viewed as dangerous, leaving men little choice. Rather than exchanging his military aggression for domestic boredom, Shane merely transfers his brand of violent masculinity to the new setting. Again, this parallels the post-9/11 actions of the Bush administration, which not only stepped up military force to fight an official war overseas, but also bolstered a military presence and warlike atmosphere at home. The emphasis on homeland security was often justified by reminding people that terrorists could be living within our borders, potentially "in our back yard." While Shane's military masculinity initially seems inappropriate, the narrative shows that this is in fact the right choice, because it is the domestic front that comes under direct attack. Literalizing the possible threat of terrorists among us, the enemies threatening the Plummer family turn out to be their back yard neighbors. Without a ready domestic military presence, the film suggests, the family would have been vulnerable to an attack.

The threat in this film, however, does not end with the family. Shane's mission, after all, is not only to keep the family out of harm's way, but also to help find the missing defense program. These two tasks end up being merged into one, as the program turns out to be hidden in a vault beneath the family home. In this way, the film conflates protection of the family and its home with service to the nation. As discussed in chapter 2, the family has recently been the subject of intense debates, with some conservatives suggesting that "attacks" on the family (from liberal media producers, gay rights activists, etc.) are likely to lead to the collapse of the nation. This film celebrates violent, heroic masculinity as the best protection for both the family and the nation—but again, this is only plausible because of the outrageous scenario that the filmmakers have asked viewers to accept.

Additionally, the film conveniently resolves the contradiction between Shane's violent persona and his surroundings. After all, when Shane arrives, he is more than just out of place. He overreacts when he cannot find Seth (who is in the bathroom) and violently breaks down Seth's bedroom door. When he mistakes Zoe's boyfriend for an intruder, he physically assaults him. Shane's violent nature seems to be as much of a threat as anything else.[31] The film suppresses this by shifting the focus to an even bigger threat, which serves as justification for Shane's violent behavior.

During the process of revitalizing his masculinity and defeating the enemies, Shane does undergo something of a transformation. At first, he seems incapable of displaying any emotion or relating to people on a personal level. By the film's end, however, he has become a nurturing, caring father figure who protects the children out of love as much as out of duty. On the surface, it may seem that he has taken steps to move away from his position within hegemonic masculinity. But a closer look reveals that Shane has merely added this sensitivity to the characteristics he already possessed. He has not given up or shared any of the power or privilege afforded him by his hegemonic status. Instead, he demonstrates how hegemonic masculinity can expand and adjust in order to maintain its status. Shane enacts both masculine and feminine roles, thereby making the feminine seem almost unnecessary. Jeffords notes a similar trend in 1980s Vietnam War films and single-father sitcoms, pointing out that such narratives function not only by excluding women, but also by "effectively eliminating them altogether from considerations of value."[32]

This is emphasized by the absence of the mother, Julie Plummer (Faith Ford), throughout most of *The Pacifier*. Shane is initially asked to watch the kids while their mother goes to Switzerland to open a safe deposit box that is thought to have information regarding the secret defense program. In her absence, Shane becomes not only a surrogate father, but a surrogate mother as well. And as it turns out, he does a better job than she does. At the beginning of the film, the kids are misbehaving, skipping school, and causing trouble. Even with the help of a nanny, Mrs. Plummer is not able to keep the kids in line, or get them to school on time, or keep the house clean. Within a few days of his arrival (and with the loss of the nanny, who quits), Shane is able to master all these tasks and proves himself to be a better mother than Mrs. Plummer. The mother's absence has the effect of expanding masculinity's domain, giving Shane even more options than were already available within patriarchy.[33]

During the first part of its narrative, *The Pacifier* presents Shane as a model of hegemonic masculinity based on violence, aggression, and heroics, and then suggests that this kind of masculine performance has no place in the everyday world of most Americans. This tension cannot be completely resolved. To get around this, the film conveniently justifies Shane's behavior by shifting the focus to a constructed, external threat that makes Shane's heroic masculinity seem valid—especially when compared with the less successful versions of masculinity embodied by other characters in the film. By taking on the roles of both mother and father, Shane incorporates traditionally masculine and feminine characteristics to expand the bounds of hegemonic masculinity and save the day. Through its conflation of the family, the home, and the nation, *The Pacifier*—on its surface—suggests that although they may initially seem out of place, violence and aggression are crucial to the country's domestic safety and well-being. However, the effort required to suppress the tension between violent masculinity and domesticity and to justify the masculine response to a contrived, hyperbolic threat reveals the similar effort required to maintain the post-9/11 myth that has come to define the Bush era.

Gender, Genre, and Killers for Hire: *Mr. & Mrs. Smith*

Like *The Pacifier, Mr. & Mrs. Smith* features the unlikely coupling of an action-oriented narrative and a suburban setting. In this case, however, the protagonist is not faced with making a transition from a world where violent masculinity is rewarded to a world where it is questioned. Instead, John Smith attempts to live these lives simultaneously by carefully separating his work (which requires violence and aggression) from his suburban home life (which necessitates a much more restrained version of masculinity). This balance seems to come easily for John until his two worlds collide, and he is forced to enact one version of masculinity in the surroundings usually reserved for the other. This clash of masculinities, coupled with a threat from an empowered woman, demonstrates the constant struggle to define appropriate gender performances in particular spaces and periods.

Mr. & Mrs. Smith borrows heavily from the 1994 film *True Lies*, but it raises the stakes in important ways. The earlier film features Arnold Schwarzenegger as Harry Tasker, a government agent whose cover involves living a seemingly typical suburban life with a wife and daughter who know nothing of his secret career. Like John Smith, Harry works very hard to keep the two halves of his life separate. But when his wife, Helen (Jamie Lee Curtis), and daughter, Dana (Eliza Dushku), are unexpectedly drawn into the world of espionage, Harry must reveal his secret identity in order to protect his family.

Mr. & Mrs. Smith also features a man with a secret identity (in this case, as an assassin) whose cover involves living the life of a typical suburbanite. The film departs significantly from *True Lies* in that John's wife, Jane, is not a bored housewife, but a rival assassin. Both films ultimately focus on repairing broken relationships. As Peter Krämer points out in his discussion of family action films, the spectacular events of *True Lies* act like a family therapy session, working to reunite father, mother, and daughter as a happy family.[34] Similarly, the battle between John and Jane Smith does not destroy their marriage but instead revives it. When John and Jane are hired to kill one another, they engage in a battle that initially looks as though it will destroy their marriage, but it eventually brings them together as they unite to fight their common enemies.

True Lies and *Mr. & Mrs. Smith* are similar in that both Harry and John lead professional lives that constantly place them in danger. Exaggerating the traditional separation of spheres, they also work very hard to keep their professional lives separate from their home lives, but they eventually find it impossible to keep the two worlds from colliding. For Harry, the collision of his professional and domestic lives gives him the opportunity to reaffirm his masculinity by coming to the rescue of his wife and daughter. John Smith finds himself in a more complicated position, because the biggest threat to both his life and his masculinity comes from his wife, thus making it harder for him to prove his masculinity.

The narrative of *Mr. & Mrs. Smith* combines elements of two primary genres—action-adventure and domestic melodrama. On one hand, this is the story of two lethal assassins carrying out a series of missions. Initially, they carry out their jobs by killing the targets they have been assigned to eliminate, but eventually they are forced to defend their lives when they themselves become the targets. This part of the story has all the trappings of an action film, including gunplay, explosions, fights, and chases, all of which are highlighted in the film's trailers and other promotional materials.

On the other hand, this is also the story of a husband and wife who have reached a difficult point in their relationship. They must face and work through their personal conflicts if they want to be able to salvage their marriage. This part of the story fits well within the category of domestic melodrama. As various media and literary scholars including Peter Brooks and Thomas Elsaesser have argued, melodrama is defined in part by stories that appeal to audiences' emotions by focusing on the interpersonal relationships of a small number of characters. The characters' heightened emotional responses to events tend to be marked by a pattern of rising and falling that extends seemingly mundane situations to exaggerated proportions. Larger social and ideological issues are reconfigured as interpersonal conflicts and worked through on an intimate scale. Stylistically, melodrama frequently relies on metaphor, gesture, and mise-en-scène even more than dialogue to convey the heightened emotions and inner states of its characters.[35]

Within the broader category of melodrama, the domestic or family melodrama focuses on familial conflict and its resolution, frequently calling the institution of family into question even while offering the family as a solution to social problems.[36] Domestic melodramas tend to stay within a contained setting, either in a middle-class home or small community, with this setting often becoming oppressive to main characters.[37] Family melodramas reached the height of their popularity in American cinema during the 1950s, epitomized by films such as *Rebel without a Cause* (1955), *Written on the Wind* (1956), *Cat on a Hot Tin Roof* (1958), *A Summer Place* (1959), and *Splendor in the Grass* (1961), but the tradition lives on in more recent films like *The Ice Storm* (1997), *American Beauty* (1999), and *Little Children* (2006).

While some scholars have placed melodrama and action in opposition to each other,[38] others have argued that melodrama (as a mode, and not a distinct genre) is actually a crucial component of any action film.[39] Either way, action and domestic melodrama stand as recognizable categories that carry with them certain conventions and expectations. Along with standard plot structures, there are settings, character types, visual and musical styles, and other narrative elements associated with each genre. The performance of gender is one such element. The conventions of action films and melodramas dictate that men and women will behave in particular ways, and while action films have typically been aimed at men, melodramas have historically targeted women. By bringing the two genres and their respective gender expectations together in the same film, *Mr. & Mrs. Smith* highlights the performativity of gender as it relates to the situations and settings of both genres.

The action genre has, by and large, been dominated by men. Over the years, the genre has produced such stars as Sean Connery, Clint Eastwood, Arnold Schwarzenegger, Mel Gibson, Bruce Willis, Jackie Chan, and Vin Diesel. Leading men in action films have typically been mature, heterosexual, independent men. They may develop a love interest during the film, but rarely do they have family commitments to tie them down. The 1980s saw a tendency toward especially muscular action heroes who often demonstrated their masculine prowess through the spectacle of their pumped-up bodies.[40] In the 1990s, action heroes began to shift their focus and motivation toward family concerns, but for the most part they maintained their hypermasculine personas.[41]

Women have certainly not been absent from the action genre, but they have had an even more complicated history in it than men. For instance, many serials of the early twentieth century—most famously *The Perils of Pauline* (1914)—placed women in heroic roles at the center of action-adventure narratives. However, as Ben Singer points out, "The genre is paradoxical in that its portrayal of female power is often accompanied by the sadistic spectacle of the woman's victimization."[42] As the action genre evolved during the latter half of the twentieth century, women's victimization became a more common element than women's empowerment.

Over the years women have frequently been relegated to the sidelines of action films, serving as either love interests, sidekicks, or damsels in distress. Along with the continuation of these trends, the 1980s and 1990s saw the rise of strong heroines who took center stage in their own action narratives. Citing *Aliens* (1986) and *Terminator 2: Judgment Day* (1991) as prime examples, Yvonne Tasker argues that the first of these women reinforced their masculine position in the narrative by demonstrating traditionally masculine physical traits, such as large muscles and brute strength.[43] More recent texts have emphasized heroines who not only perform the same violent stunts and daring feats as male action stars, but who also emphasize their femininity through appearance and behavior. They are all conventionally beautiful; they often wear clothing that accentuates their figure; and, when necessary, they can use sexual allure as a weapon in their missions. Examples of this trend include *Xena: Warrior Princess* (1995–2001), *Buffy the Vampire Slayer* (1997–2003), *Lara Croft: Tomb Raider* (2001) and its sequel *Lara Croft Tomb Raider: The Cradle of Life* (2003), *Charlie's Angels* (2000) and *Charlie's Angels: Full Throttle* (2003), *Alias* (2001–2006), *Wanted* (2008), and *Salt* (2010). These women have moved into roles and taken on characteristics usually associated with men, but they retain many of the markers of traditional femininity. They provide a counterpoint to characters like *The Pacifier*'s Shane, whose hegemonic masculinity expands to absorb markers of femininity. This push in the other direction may not put the women on equal footing with their male counterparts, but it does suggest that the ongoing expansion of masculinity will not go unchallenged.

During the action sequences of *Mr. & Mrs. Smith*, both John and Jane live up to the expectations established for their gender by previous action films. John is strong, cocky, quick with his gun and any other weapon, and can knock a man unconscious with his bare hands when necessary. Jane, too, is a skilled fighter, a weapons expert, and confident in her abilities, but she also has a great deal of feminine sex appeal, which is regularly emphasized. Angelina Jolie's presence in the role builds on her earlier performances as Lara Croft, a character who also blended violence and hyper-feminine sexuality. The action personas of the two characters are captured on the film's promotional poster and DVD cover. The title of the film is in the middle over a white background, with the film's stars on either side, both leaning their backs against the edge of the frame and looking confidently at the camera. Both are dressed in black, and each is carrying a gun. But while Pitt's outfit is a black suit, Jolie is dressed in an evening gown that hugs her curves and is slit up the thigh. The positioning of her body (one leg is raised, with the heel resting on the wall behind her) exposes the majority of both of her long legs. While Pitt holds his gun in his hand, Jolie's

FIGURE 14. The image on the cover of the *Mr. & Mrs. Smith* DVD establishes both characters as dangerous while also emphasizing the sexual allure of Jane Smith (Angelina Jolie). Author's personal collection.

gun is tucked into a garter around her thigh. Both actors/characters are presented as dangerous and potentially violent, with Jolie being hyper-sexualized in addition.

This promotional image is very much in line with the characters as they play out in the action portion of the narrative. However, as previously mentioned, the film also tells a familiar story of a marriage in trouble, a staple of the domestic melodrama. The first and last scenes of the film feature John and Jane sitting side by side in separate chairs, looking at and talking to an unseen therapist. They discuss the fact that their marriage (five or six years—they can't agree on how long it has been) has hit a rough patch. While they used to find each other exciting, they now feel trapped in a boring, domestic rut. They talk *at* each other but not *to* each other as they stand at their separate sinks in the morning, brushing their teeth.

The failing marriage storyline, highlighted and bookended by the therapy scenes at the beginning and end of the film, draws on the tradition of domestic melodrama, and the characters' gendered performances reflect this. The characters' identities are defined largely by way of their adherence to expected domestic roles, which differ greatly from the expectations of action heroes and heroines. Films like *All That Heaven Allows* (1955), *East of Eden* (1955), *No Down Payment* (1957), and *Home From the Hill* (1960) helped to establish gender roles as a central occupation of domestic melodramas. Liebman argues that these and other films (as well as television series like *The Adventures of Ozzie and Harriet*, 1952–1966; *The Donna Reed Show*, 1958–1966; and *Father Knows Best*, 1954–1963) established and reinforced particular gender roles in both adults and children. Men were the heads of the households, while women kept those households running smoothly by supporting the men and taking care of the children. Men proved their masculinity not through violence or physical strength, but through their ability to enact the role of breadwinner and provider. Women, though not unattractive, were generally not overly glamorous or hypersexualized, but demonstrated their femininity through domestic tasks such as cooking, cleaning, and attending to the family's needs. Liebman argues that 1950s melodramas repeated these images again and again, "continually reminding the viewer that the key to secure family life lay in a strict adherence to social-sexual codes and dictates."[44] The pressures to live up to these gendered ideals often created the conflicts driving the melodramatic narratives. This difficulty in fulfilling the gendered expectations of domestic life has continued to play an important role in contemporary melodramas, as evidenced by such recent films as *Happiness* (1998), *Far from Heaven* (2002), and *Revolutionary Road* (2008).

Mr. & Mrs. Smith is quickly connected to these recent domestic melodramas by way of its suburban setting, a family-centric space that helps to set the stage for the familial conflict about to unfold. After the opening therapy scene and a series of flashbacks to the early stages of John and Jane's relationship, the narrative returns to the present. The establishing shot for this segment is a long shot of John and Jane's street. It is lined with spacious homes, mature trees, and SUVs along the curb. A woman walks her dog, a man rakes his leaves, and another man jogs down the sidewalk. A school bus drives away as the paperboy rides his bike past John, throwing the morning paper at his feet as he passes. This peaceful, safe, family-oriented (and some would argue boring) space is clearly established as suburban—the ideal setting for a domestic melodrama.

Much of the conflict and comedy of the film comes from the clash of codes brought on by the blending of action and melodrama. In one early sequence, John and Jane each leave the house to secretly carry out an assassination. John shoots four men in the back room of a bar, and Jane breaks a man's neck with her bare hands before rapelling off a hotel balcony. They both then return home, freshen up, and turn around to go to a neighborhood party. At the party, Jane mingles with the other suburban women, making small talk about babies and kitchens and husbands' promotions, while John talks to his neighbors about stocks and cigars. They perform the roles of suburban husband and wife, which seem all the more mundane and absurd when juxtaposed against the action sequences that immediately precede the party scene.

Essentially, the film is an example of genre hybridity, or what Christine Gledhill refers to as "boundary encounters and category mixing."[45] The juxtaposing of different genres highlights the different codes that make up those genres, including particular gender expectations. This is particularly true in the case of *Mr. & Mrs. Smith*, since it blends two genres that have traditionally been associated with and even addressed to masculine (action) and feminine (melodrama) audiences. With both characters shifting back and forth between the masculine, public world of the action genre and the feminine, domestic world of the melodrama, the film calls attention to the different ways that gender is performed in each genre. Like many other men in suburban melodramas (including *American Beauty*'s Lester Burnham, *The Ice Storm*'s Ben Hood, and *Far from Heaven*'s Frank Whitaker), John is somewhat confined by his domestic surroundings and has a hard time proving his manhood through any means other than earning power. Unlike most of those men, however, John has the opportunity to prove his manhood through the violence and aggression that define his secret life as an assassin. In this way, John is able to shift back and forth between hegemonic masculinity and complicit masculinity. The fact that his cover identity, the one that is created specifically to be as normal as possible, is in line with complicit masculinity, while his secret identity demonstrates hegemonic masculinity, serves as a reminder of how few men actually embody hegemonic masculinity. It is for most men merely a fantasy, but keeping that fantasy alive as an ideal is what allows so many men to draw on its patriarchal power.[46] John Smith makes this fantasy a reality each time he abandons the norms of suburban domesticity to slip into his secret life.

Placing John and Jane's cover identities in the seemingly mundane world of suburbia situates the story as part of a larger trend in suburban narratives. The previously mentioned *True Lies* offers a similar setup, placing a secret agent undercover in the suburbs because the extreme ordinariness of suburban life helps to make his true identity almost unthinkable. Similarly, *The Incredibles* (2004) features a family of superheroes forced to abandon their powers and live anonymously in the suburbs as part of the "superhero relocation program" after the government decides that superheroes are a menace to society. Action superstar Jackie Chan stars as a Chinese spy working for the U.S. government and living an undercover life as a suburban pen salesman in *The Spy Next Door* (2010). Individual episodes of various spy and detective series, including *Mission: Impossible* (1966–1973), *The Man from U.N.C.L.E.* (1964–1968), *The X-Files* (1993–2002), and *Alias* (2001–2006) have featured their agents going undercover as suburban residents in order to carry out their missions or search for clues without being noticed.[47] Using the suburban camouflage for slightly different purposes, the fourth season of the Showtime series *Dexter* (2006–2013) features the titular character adopting the role of suburban husband and father as a way of concealing his secret life as a serial killer, even as he hunts another serial killer who is also masquerading as a suburban family man. In all cases, the suburban environment is seen as the perfect hiding place because of its status as unremarkable and ordinary.[48] All the characters leading a secret life, including John and Jane Smith, seem to follow the advice that Mrs. Incredible (voiced by Holly Hunter) gives her frustrated young son when she tells him, "Right now, honey, the world just wants us to fit in, and to fit in, we've just gotta be like everyone else."

The covers adopted by John and Jane are themselves quite gendered. As previously mentioned, when they are in their neighborhood, John and Jane play the role of the traditional suburban couple. While Jane does have a full-time job, she still manages to take responsibility for putting dinner on the table every night and is clearly concerned with the appearance of the house, fussing over drapes, upholstery, and carpets. John, on the other hand, merely eats the meals that Jane puts in front of him before retiring to his room to watch televised sports. Even their weapons are hidden in gendered spaces: John's guns, knives, and stash of money are hidden in the back yard beneath the tool shed, while Jane conceals her trove of weapons in a secret compartment inside the oven. In this way, the gendered spaces of the suburban house emphasize the gendered performances of the lead characters.

It would be incorrect, however, to suggest that the suburban cover story is the only masquerade, and that it hides the "true" identities of the Smiths. Even when they are working, their jobs often require them to assume alternative identities as a way of getting close to their targets, and these performances also tend to be gender-coded. For example, when they sneak out of the house to pull off jobs before the neighborhood party, John assumes the role of a stumbling drunk who weasels his way into an all-male back room poker game, while Jane goes undercover as a dominatrix call girl, complete with leather bustier and fishnet stockings. When the time is right, they each change their personas immediately to become ruthless assassins, before changing again to return to their suburban personas.

The ease with which both John and Jane slide in and out of their roles (and the gendered attributes that accompany them) highlights the fluidity of gender performance in general. In doing this, the film suggests that there is no true self (gendered or otherwise) and that any identity is merely a performance. John and Jane wear the masks of hyper-masculinity and hyper-femininity when it suits their needs, but these identities prove to be unstable in the long run. As Chris Holmlund suggests, the ramifications of gender masquerade differ for men and women, based on differences in power.[49] Men, after all, have more to lose if their masculinity is shown to be nothing but a façade, and therefore the exaggerated performance of hyper-masculinity often reveals anxieties about the precariousness of masculine power. This is emphasized in *Mr. & Mrs. Smith* due to the fact that Jane (in her role as assassin) enacts many characteristics of masculinity just as well as her husband—if not better. Although our society commonly equates masculinity with maleness, Judith Halberstam reminds us that "what we understand as heroic masculinity has been produced by and across both male and female bodies."[50] John is in danger of being defeated by what Halberstam refers to as "female masculinity." While many action heroes feel the need to prove their masculinity, rarely do they do so in competition with a woman who is also enacting masculinity.

The competition between John and Jane may initially push them apart, but it is also what eventually brings them back together. The showdown in their home, although violent and aggressive, is also highly erotic, and instead of ending in the death of either character, the fight morphs into a heated session of rough sex. The scene offers an exaggerated version of any couple whose chemistry is recharged by a particularly passionate fight. It also calls to mind the underlying homoerotic desire that is sublimated in traditional action-adventure films. The bulk of action films over the years have featured men as both heroes and villains, and they frequently develop rather obsessive relationships with one another. The banter, physical contact, and passionate emotions that connect these heroes and villains raise the specter of homoerotic desire, which is then typically displaced onto the body of a woman over whom the two men are fighting. In this film, the desire that exists between the two combatants does not need to be displaced or suppressed, instead spilling over into passionate lovemaking. This is made possible in part by the persona that Angelina Jolie brings to the film. Established as a woman whose hyper-feminine appearance gives way to hyper-masculine physicality, she is able to fill the roles of both nemesis and love interest. In this way, the film subtly reveals the effort that most action films undertake in order to displace the threat of homoerotic desire, as required by the codes of the genre.

The competitive nature of John and Jane's relationship is also central to the messages embedded within the film. John is forced to prove his masculinity in the face of a direct threat from a strong, empowered woman. In this way, the film draws on the melodramatic mode of recasting broad social issues through individual characters. As Thomas Elsaesser points out, a significant characteristic of melodrama is that it "can successfully shift explicitly political themes onto a personalized plane."[51] John represents the millions of men who feel threatened by feminism and the empowerment of women. But unlike *American Beauty*, for example, where the empowered woman is portrayed as castrating and domineering (dangerous on an emotional or psychological level), this film extends the threat so that John's life is actually in danger. The threat to masculinity is made visible in the body of Jane, the woman who seeks to usurp the masculine power that John possesses. In this way, the film carries a slightly misogynistic tone. Although John and Jane have the exact same assignment (to kill each other), are generally presented as sympathetic characters, and eventually end up working as a team, the film favors John slightly, partially casting Jane as the villain.

Jane's negative portrayal is carried out in two specific ways—through discussions that John has with his friend and co-worker Eddie (Vince Vaughn), and through interactions between John and Jane. Eddie is very clearly anti-women. Although he lives with his mother (whom he defends as a "first-class lady . . . she cooks, she cleans, she makes [him] snacks"), he clearly has negative feelings about Jane and other women. When he invites John to a "dudes only" barbecue, and John says that he'll check with his wife, Eddie harasses John about even considering his wife's input. After John discovers that his wife is trying to kill him, he goes to Eddie's place to crash for the night. When he tells Eddie what happened, Eddie says, "At least Jane was a man about it. At least she was up front about it—but they all try to kill you. Slowly, painfully, cripplingly, and then wham—they hurt you." Later, Eddie says, "You gotta take this bitch out head on . . . this broad is not your wife, she's the enemy." Eddie is clearly a source of comic relief in the film, with Vaughn drawing on the overgrown-yet-immature frat boy persona that he has developed in films like *Old School* (2003), *Dodgeball* (2004), and *Wedding Crashers* (2005). This persona (a noticeably flawed version of complicit masculinity) also helps to establish John's performance of masculinity as being closer to the hegemonic ideal. Despite Eddie's comic delivery and childish behavior, he gives voice to the anxiety and resentment that John may feel but cannot express without compromising his own heroic persona.

Jane gets a very different response when she tells her associates that her husband has targeted her. They express surprise and sympathy, but they say nothing bad about John—only that she has to kill him, and that nobody is better at that than she is. While Eddie presents John as the victim and Jane as the enemy, Jane's associates treat John as just another target, and Jane as a ruthless killer who can easily knock off her own husband.

Interactions between the two also tend to favor John. After discovering each other's true identities, Jane drives away from the house, and John chases her through the neighborhood on foot. At one point he trips and accidentally fires his gun at Jane's car. In response, she very intentionally tries to run him over. Later, when she thinks she has John trapped in an elevator loaded with explosives, Jane tells John that he must either promise to leave town or she will kill him. He refuses and basically challenges her to kill him—which she attempts to do. As it turns out, John had rewired some cameras to create the illusion of actually being in the elevator, and therefore he is unharmed by Jane's actions. Jane does express a hint of regret, but the fact of the matter is that she actually took the final step in an attempt to end his life. And when the two have a showdown in their suburban home, both of them attempt to kill each other in a variety of ways. But at the end of the fight, they end up standing eye to eye, each one pointing a gun at the other. After thinking for a second, John decides that even though she is the enemy, he cannot kill his wife, and he lowers his gun. Although Jane eventually gives in as well, she holds out longer, maintaining her aggressive stance long after John has given in to love and compassion.

While it is true that John and Jane eventually make up and join forces to fight off their mutual enemies, it is hard to erase the misogynistic treatment that Jane receives in the early part of the film. This is yet another way in which *Mr. & Mrs. Smith* draws on the melodramatic mode. As Laura Mulvey notes, "The strength of the melodramatic form lies in the amount of dust the story raises along the road, a cloud of overdetermined irreconcilables which put up a resistance to being neatly settled in the last five minutes."[52] In other words, although melodramas may provide a sense of closure, they have opened up too many ideological struggles to be able to contain everything with a happy ending.

In the end both characters are identified with particular gender norms based on the two genres present in the film. The clashing of these two genres leads to a constant shifting of gendered performances by both John and Jane, and this gender fluidity and masquerade points to the anxieties about gender that currently exist in our society. But while both characters are paid killers and suburbanites, and should probably merit equal amounts of sympathy, Jane is clearly portrayed as presenting the bigger threat with her gender transgressions, once again highlighting cultural anxieties about the place of manhood and masculinity.

Absurd Domestic Masculinities

Masculinity is never easy to define, and there will always be multiple versions of masculinity present in any given time and place. The United States in the post-9/11 era is no exception. Onscreen constructions of masculinity during this period include a wide range of possibilities. Action-adventure films offer a fairly straightforward and unabashedly heroic masculinity. Domestic melodramas offer men whose tenuous grasp on masculinity relies on their ability to provide for their family. Some narratives present men who are damaged or broken by the events of 9/II or some other traumatic situation. The series *Rescue Me* (2004–2011), for example, provides a contrast to the celebration of invincible 9/II heroes by telling the stories of New York firefighters who have trouble dealing with the emotional aftermath of the terrorist attacks. The film *Reign over Me* (2007) focuses on a man who is trying to rebuild his life after losing his family on 9/II. In *24* (2001–2010), Agent Jack Bauer (Kiefer Sutherland) tries to deal with the traumas of lost friends and loved ones while fighting against terrorists and government corruption in a seemingly never-ending quest for justice. And Jack Shepherd (Matthew Fox) of *Lost* (2004–2010) faces personal demons while trying to provide strength and leadership for a group of fellow plane crash survivors on a remote island. Meanwhile, in sitcoms and romantic comedies of the era, men face the same amusing obstacles that men in these genres have always faced: misunderstandings, love triangles, misbehaving children, and so forth. I am not arguing that the films examined in this chapter represent the definitive version of post-9/II masculinity, as it is clear that no such thing exists. The films do, however, bring together competing narrative trends in a way that highlights the difficulty and even the absurdity of embodying all the components of the masculine ideal that is celebrated in American society.

The Pacifier and *Mr. & Mrs. Smith* depict men who epitomize the tough, aggressive, heroic masculinity modeled by soldiers and other 9/II heroes, but both characters face challenges that threaten their dominance. Shane's masculinity is threatened primarily by the fact that he must take on traditionally feminine roles and perform them in a feminized space. John's masculinity is threatened by the fact that his wife has taken on her own masculine traits, and she is able to prove that she handles them just as well as he does. While Shane is in danger of having his masculinity diluted by femininity, John is challenged by his wife's embodiment of female masculinity.

Each of these films defines the hegemonic masculinity of its main character by way of contrast. In *The Pacifier*, Shane's masculinity is made to seem more impressive when he is compared to Murney, Seth, Mr. Plummer, and the drama director. John Smith is defined in contrast with Eddie, Jane, and the Smiths' bland suburban neighbors. By providing a range of unacceptable/illegitimate masculinities, these films help to valorize the hegemonic status of heroic, violent masculinity as enacted by men, while simultaneously demonstrating the anxieties provoked by these alternative versions of masculinity.

Both films draw on their suburban settings and a combination of genres as a way of highlighting the anxiety about masculinity and mining it for laughs. While suburban spaces have often been the setting for family comedies and melodramas, the action genre has tended to focus on more public, open spaces. In the late 1980s and 1990s, some action films such as the *Lethal Weapon* series (1987, 1989, 1992, 1998) began to feature their heroes being attacked in their own homes and then needing to defend those homes.[53] However, these were generally isolated scenes, and the majority of the films still played out in non-domestic spaces. Mark Gallagher notes that "most action films negotiate domestic and family concerns by mapping these issues cursorily onto the active, public, male sphere."[54] *The Pacifier* and *Mr. & Mrs. Smith* move in the opposite direction, bringing the masculine action genre home to the suburbs. This unexpected combination is a significant source of humor in both films, particularly when it involves the attempted containment of heroic masculinity within the bounds of suburban life.

Placing these films in their post-9/11 context, the suburban home can be read as a metaphor for the nation. In both films, the suburban space comes under attack from enemies within, necessitating enhanced security measures to prevent further damage. This parallels the national post-9/11 anxieties about terrorists living within our country, ready to strike at any moment, and the resulting need to take preventive measures. In this context, the heroic masculine behavior that Shane and John display in the domestic world of suburbia echoes much of the nation's aggressive foreign and domestic policy. Just as the Bush administration turned some of its military might to focus on domestic concerns (homeland security), these films suggest that violent, aggressive, heroic forms of masculinity—once reserved for the open, public sphere—must now be used to protect the domestic sphere as well.

It would be incorrect to suggest that these films merely reinforce the ideologies embedded in the Bush administration's domestic policies. As Robert Ray suggests, Hollywood movies often contain competing messages, allowing audiences to "have things both ways."[55]

Ideologies can be criticized and celebrated in the same narrative, thus creating a sense of ambiguity. These films are no exception. While both films do feature hyper-masculine men who solve their suburban domestic problems with violence, force, and aggression, the films also find a great deal of humor in the fact that this form of masculinity is so out of place in the domestic realm. Despite their tidiness, the films' conclusions cannot completely negate what has come before them. As Ray suggests, audiences use movies to confirm their own predispositions, and these films allow audiences to either mock or celebrate excessive masculinity.[56]

By simultaneously exalting and ridiculing heroic masculinity, *The Pacifier* and *Mr. & Mrs. Smith* reveal the anxieties surrounding masculinity during the post-9/11 era. Media images of the 9/11 rescue workers and the soldiers fighting in Iraq and elsewhere reestablished the value of a militarized, heroic masculinity, but they raised questions about how men who were not soldiers, police officers, or firefighters could prove their masculinity. On their surfaces, *The Pacifier* and *Mr. & Mrs. Smith* suggest that heroic masculinity can be transferred to domestic concerns with desirable results. However, in order for these films to reach this conclusion and provide the tidy closure and happy endings expected of action films and family comedies, they must suppress the absurdity of hyper-masculinity in the domestic realm. They do this by constructing threats to the home that are even more absurd (ninja neighbors or a killer-for-hire wife) to make the violent, masculine response seem justified. In this way the films reveal the effort required to justify many of the domestic policies of the post-9/11 Bush administration, as well as the ongoing effort required to maintain the dominance of hegemonic masculinity.

5

Protecting the Suburban Lifestyle

Consumption, Crime, and the American Dream

In an episode of the legal drama *Close to Home* (CBS, 2005–2007) entitled "Land of Opportunity," a real estate mogul is being interrogated
by a district attorney regarding some questionable business practices
that allegedly caused home buyers to default on their loans and lose
their houses. Proclaiming his innocence, the man says, "I'm in the business of putting hardworking people in their dream homes." He goes
on to say, "You can't criminalize business in the land of opportunity."
Moments later, one of his associates, also being questioned, says, "We
got into this because it made us feel good. Not the money—putting
people into houses, I mean. The American Dream." Meanwhile, people
who purchased houses from these men are losing their homes to foreclosure and facing complete financial ruin, leading one man to crash
his car into the front window of an appraiser's office to show his anger.
These and other scenes in the episode capture something that is often
overlooked in suburban television narratives—the fact that getting and
keeping a home in the suburbs is far from easy.

While early suburban films including *Mr. Blandings Builds His
Dream House* (1948), *The Man in the Gray Flannel Suit* (1956), and *No
Down Payment* (1957) offer dramatic depictions of suburbanites' financial struggles, television programs from the same era generally avoid
such concerns. Light-hearted domestic comedies like *Father Knows Best*
(1954–1963), *Leave It to Beaver* (1957–1963), and *The Donna Reed Show*
(1958–1966) feature families living comfortably in the suburbs. Their

middle-class status is taken as a given, is rarely contrasted with different socioeconomic situations, and is never threatened. As Mary Beth Haralovich notes, these shows "rarely make direct reference to the social and economic means by which the families attained and maintain their middle-class status." She argues that by effacing the social differences that produced suburban neighborhoods, these programs "naturalize the privilege of the middle class."[1] The hard work that is involved in maintaining the middle-class suburban lifestyle is obscured or made invisible in these programs. Over the years, narratives dealing with socioeconomic status have generally been reserved for working-class television families, like the Evans family of *Good Times* (1974–1979) or the Conner family of *Roseanne* (1988–1997). Meanwhile, the assumption of easy middle-class stability continued to be the norm for suburban families on programs like *The Brady Bunch* (1969–1974), *Happy Days* (1974–1984), *Growing Pains* (1985–1992), and *Home Improvement* (1991–1999).

More recently, television programs both comedic and dramatic have taken a different approach by revealing and emphasizing the work involved in maintaining the suburban middle class lifestyle. In various ways, shows like *The Sopranos* (1999–2007), *Arrested Development* (2003–2006), *The Riches* (2007–2008), *Breaking Bad* (2008–2013), and even *The Real Housewives of Orange County* (2006–) demonstrate the challenges of maintaining a middle-class lifestyle and the lengths to which some people will go in order to achieve and protect that status. For two series in particular—*Weeds* (2005–2012) and the aforementioned *Close to Home*—the preservation of a suburban middle-class way of life is the driving force behind the actions of the protagonists and the development of their respective narratives. In *Weeds*, a single mother turns to dealing marijuana in order to maintain a privileged lifestyle for her family. In *Close to Home*, a young attorney prosecutes criminals who threaten the very lifestyle that so many suburbanites have come to take for granted. Examining these two series together is helpful because they are essentially two sides of the same coin. *Weeds* focuses on characters who are trying to maintain class status through consumption, and it reveals how class-based anxieties and the desire to consume can lead to crime. *Close to Home* functions as a response to this, showing how crime can destroy the middle-class suburban lifestyle that people are so desperate to achieve and maintain.

The basic concepts of both *Weeds* and *Close to Home* encourage an intertextual engagement with the suburban narratives that came before them. These two programs provide a counterpoint to the many texts that present suburbia as a space where middle-class status is a given, and thus does not require any drastic measures to maintain it; where consumption is a part of life to be celebrated, not questioned; and where criminal behavior is essentially nonexistent. The comedic and dramatic impact of these recent programs relies on the recognition of their contrast with earlier suburban narratives. All the texts examined so far in this book feature characters who are engaged in some kind of social or emotional work to preserve the façade of suburban perfection. *Weeds* and *Close to Home* emphasize that work by taking a more literal approach, revealing the paid and unpaid labor required to maintain the façade, as well as some of the illicit activities that threaten to destroy it.

This chapter examines the complex relationships between work, crime, and the suburban American Dream as they play out in *Weeds* and *Close to Home*. While *Weeds* emphasizes the maintenance of economic status, and *Close to Home* focuses on upholding moral values and preserving suburban safety, they both feature women working as hard as they can to protect their own version of the American Dream. Although these programs deal with similar themes in similar settings, they represent very different genres and narrative tones, thus helping to highlight some of the conflicts that are inherent to the ideology of the American Dream. By revealing the work that goes into protecting suburban middle-class privilege, these series show how precarious that privilege is, and how easily it can be taken away.

Consumption, Class, and Suburbia

The Showtime comedy series *Weeds* focuses on Nancy Botwin (Mary-Louise Parker), a recently widowed housewife living in the suburban Southern California community of Agrestic. After the loss of her husband, she is faced with the challenge of continuing to provide her two teenage sons with the lifestyle they have always known. They live in an enormous, well-furnished home in an affluent community, and they have always been able to afford anything they desire. Faced with mounting bills and increasing debt, yet determined to ensure stability for her sons, Nancy begins selling marijuana to other residents of her posh neighborhood. As business takes off, she faces new challenges, including spats with her suppliers, troubles with her cover business, and run-ins with the law, always trying to keep her head above water. During its first three seasons (before Nancy pulls her family out of Agrestic to start a new life), the series offers a satirical look at American life as epitomized by the suburban American Dream, raising many questions about the interconnections between legitimate work and criminal behavior in a consumer-oriented society.[2] *Weeds* taps into a longstanding connection between suburbia and the consumer-oriented, middle-class lifestyle, and it is worth discussing this connection before examining how *Weeds* engages with it.

Scholars and cultural critics have identified the American suburb as an ideal space for consumption, noting that the purchase of the single-family detached house is only the first in a series of consumptive acts that define what it means to be a suburbanite in this country. During the first American suburban boom in the 1920s, advertisers began to go after the suburban market, specifically promoting "the private suburban dwelling as a setting for other purchases,"[3] like appliances, furniture, and automobiles.

In the years following World War II, as returning soldiers and their families drove massive postwar suburban development, advertisers and manufacturers specifically targeted these new suburbanites, encouraging them to buy more and more goods to fill up their new dream homes. In 1957 the publishers of *Redbook* produced a short film entitled "In the Suburbs," which sought to convince potential advertisers that the readers of *Redbook* were heavy consumers, and thus desirable advertising targets. The film describes *Redbook*'s audience, primarily young suburbanites, as "an energetic lot . . . a carefree lot" who have "come into their purchasing stage." Their suburban life is described as a "happy-go-spending world, reflected in the windows of the suburban shopping centers where they go to buy." In her historical account of postwar consumer culture, Lizabeth Cohen points out that the suburban home itself became "the quintessential mass consumer commodity, capable of fueling the fires of the postwar economy while also improving the standard of living of the mass of Americans."[4]

Although all suburban residents were invited into the consumer-oriented lifestyle, women were especially targeted. Dolores Hayden suggests that "the private suburban house was a stage set for the effective gender division of labor," with men acting as homeowners and women serving as "home managers." Part of the housewife's duty was to purchase the necessary appliances and consumer goods to create a comfortable domestic retreat for her husband, making "consumption seem to be as crucial as production"[5] in the balance of family economics. Betty Friedan, in her classic wake-up call to suburban women, *The Feminine Mystique*, laments the fact that housewives have been seen first and foremost as consumers, noting that "the really important role that women serve as housewives is *to buy more things for the house.*"[6] Friedan also discusses the fact that researchers for a leading women's magazine divided housewives into categories ("true housewives," "balanced homemakers," and "career women") to help identify those most likely to consume in large quantities.[7]

As advertisers and manufacturers tried to motivate suburbanites to consume, early television representations of suburbia reinforced the consumer ideal with its endless depictions of suburban comfort and happiness through consumption. The lives of the early suburban television families like the Andersons (*Father Knows Best*), the Stones (*The Donna Reed Show*), and the Cleavers (*Leave It to Beaver*) often revolved around the acquisition of consumer goods, and the happiness that came with them. As Nina Leibman points out, "The matter-of-fact use and accumulation of consumer items in conjunction with the implication that such luxuries are not extravagant but the norm served as a reiteration of the purchasing practices necessary to ensure understated comfort."[8] Her study of the most popular suburban sitcoms of the 1950s reveals that one in eight episodes revolved around the purchase and/or use of consumer items.[9]

In his historical account of television sitcoms, Gerard Jones attributes much of this consumer activity to the relationship that early television had with sponsors. As an example, he points to the early seasons of *The Adventures of Ozzie and Harriet* (1952–1966), which were sponsored by Hotpoint and which featured a disproportionate number of scenes in the kitchen, "to better show off the snazzy appliances."[10] George Lipsitz develops the link between suburbia and consumption in his discussion of *The Goldbergs* (1949–1956) when he notes that after the title family moved from the city to the suburbs, "consumer purchases and fears of installment credit took center stage."[11] In all these series, families' lives were made easier by their newly purchased appliances, and children learned lessons about saving money to buy consumer goods, creating the image of a space where people were defined by their consumption habits.

Acts of consumption are frequently viewed as markers of a particular class status, and because of the consumption habits associated with suburban life, suburbia has come to be seen by many as the space of the middle class. Both suburban life and middle-class status have been normalized in America, even though there are large segments of the population falling outside these boundaries. Barbara Ehrenreich argues that "in our culture, the professional, and largely white, middle class is taken as a social norm—a bland and neutral mainstream—from which every other group or class is ultimately a kind of deviation."[12] Whether or not they know how to define middle class, the bulk of Americans see themselves as fitting into such a category.

In his historical account of the connections between the real estate profession and the creation of a middle-class identity, Jeffrey Hornstein demonstrates the importance of homeownership in creating that identity. He notes that professional real estate organizations in the first half of the twentieth century saw it as their duty to make homeownership available to more people, seeing it as the "special moral burden of their occupation."[13] As more and more individuals purchased single-family houses, homeownership became a prerequisite for middle-class status. Hornstein says that by the start of the 1950s, "to be middle class meant, at least, to own—or to aspire to own—a home of one's own."[14] The bulk of new home development from the postwar era to the present has been in suburban spaces, forever intertwining middle-class status, homeownership, and suburban life.

In recent years, however, fears of a shrinking middle class have had a significant impact on the national psyche. While everyone seems to want to believe that they are middle class, recent societal shifts and redistributions of wealth have made it more difficult for families and individuals to maintain their socioeconomic status. Census reports reveal that in the past twenty years, those Americans who are economically in the top 5 percent have experienced income increases at rates far higher than anyone else.[15] Robert Frank argues that because Americans take spending cues from those above them on the economic scale, increased consumption by wealthy individuals leads others to believe that they must also consume more. He notes that "increased spending at the top of the income distribution has imposed not only psychological costs on families in the middle, but also more tangible ones. In particular, it has raised the cost of achieving goals that most middle-class families regard as basic."[16]

To help fund their increasing consumption, many are depending more heavily on credit providers. Alladi Venkatesh argues that an "elaborate credit system" is necessary to sustain the "advanced state of consumer culture" that currently defines suburban America.[17] As people sink further into debt (in the form of mortgages, car loans, credit cards, etc.) they become more concerned about their ability to keep up. As Ehrenreich notes, "Whether the middle class looks down toward the realm of less, or up toward the realm of more, there is the fear, always, of falling."[18]

Fanning the flames of middle-class anxiety are the repeated warnings coming from the news media and popular press. Diana Kendall suggests that "the idea that the middle class is in peril is a key framing device for news stories about politics and the economy."[19] Whether it is because the wealthy are cutting into middle-class incomes (by outsourcing jobs and downsizing American companies) or because the poor are getting unfair assistance (receiving financial support not available to the middle class), these reports make it seem that the middle class is under constant attack. During the long run of his nightly program on CNN, host Lou Dobbs repeatedly warned viewers about the ways that big business and the government are harming the middle class. His 2006 book, *War on the Middle Class*, makes a similar case for the bleak future of middle-income families. *The Two Income Trap: Why Middle Class Mothers and Fathers Are Going Broke* (2003), by Elizabeth Warren and Amelia Warren Tyagi, and *Screwed: The Undeclared War against the Middle Class* (2006), by Thom Hartman, are just two more examples of recent mass-market books that have fueled fears about a collapsing middle class.

Those fears became a reality for many Americans with the mortgage crisis of 2008 and the recession that followed. During the period from 2006 to 2009, the mortgage delinquency rate and the foreclosure rate in the United States both doubled.[20] Home values plunged while unemployment rates rose. From 2008 to 2010, the number of personal bankruptcies filed in U.S. courts jumped by nearly 39 percent.[21] As total student loan debt climbed to over one trillion dollars,[22] student loan default rates also rose, with the Department of Education reporting that of the 3.6 million Americans who began paying back students loans in fiscal year 2009, 8.8 percent defaulted within two years, up from 7 percent the previous year.[23] According to U.S. census data, the median household income dropped 6.4 percent between 2007 and 2010. In 2010 the family poverty rate was 11.7 percent, and 16.3 percent of Americans were without health insurance.[24]

In response to these and other growing economic crises, President Obama offered a number of proposed solutions, including a plan for universal healthcare and an attempt to stabilize the national economy by eliminating certain tax breaks that benefit the country's ultra-wealthy. Many conservative politicians responded to Obama's proposals by attempting to label him as a socialist who engaged in class warfare, and thus a threat to free market capitalism and the American Dream itself.[25] Identifying the ultra-wealthy as "job creators" and "business leaders," they argued that raising taxes on the wealthy discourages entrepreneurial spirit.

While not officially organized as part of the Republican Party, the Tea Party movement emerged as a powerful force during the 2010 election cycle, in part by challenging the economic policies of President Obama and congressional Democrats. Citing "Free Markets" as a core value of their cause, the Tea Party Patriots (one of many voices in the rather diffuse movement) argued that the existing structure of government inhibited "the pursuit of individual and economic liberty."[26] While Tea Party candidates suggested that scaling back government involvement in the economy would allow a return to prosperity, opponents argued that it was an overly free and unregulated market that caused the problems in the first place.

With politicians and pundits arguing over the best path to recovery, individuals and families faced the realities of declining socioeconomic status—and the suburbs have not been immune. Although suburbia has long been viewed as the ideal space to demonstrate economic success and growth, the recent economic troubles have emphasized the vulnerability of this way of life. According to a 2010 report from the Brookings Institution, between 2000 and 2008 suburban poverty increased five times faster than urban poverty, and by 2008 almost one-third of the nation's poor was living in suburban communities.[27] Even for those able to hold onto their middle-class status, the threat of losing that status has become increasingly real.

The fears and anxieties associated with maintaining a consumption-driven, middle-class suburban lifestyle are a recurring theme of *Weeds*, which debuted at the height of the housing bubble, when signs of the coming collapse were beginning to appear. By way of its heroine, Nancy Botwin, the series explores various aspects of the complex situation facing many Americans, suggesting that while a free market and entrepreneurial spirit may lead to success for some people, that success often comes with unexpected costs for society. My analysis focuses on three elements of *Weeds*' narrative: its depiction and critique of consumer culture, the relationship between crime and the American Dream, and the blurring of moral boundaries.

Weeds presents a rather complicated view of the excessive consumption that has come to define American life, seemingly critiquing such consumption but ultimately reinforcing it. One example of the critique of consumption comes in the opening credit sequence. The very first image in the sequence is a collage of smaller images that look as though they were taken from a promotional brochure. The phrase "Agrestic Luxury Homes" appears on the left side of the screen, surrounded by sketches of houses and diagrams of floor plans—the kinds of images that real estate agents use to sell a community that has not yet been built. More than anything, they are used to sell a way of life. Thus, the opening image establishes the ideas of buying, selling, and consuming in a suburban community. The word "luxury" establishes the level of consumption that one can expect in this community.

The title sequence is set to the Malvina Reynolds folk song "Little Boxes," which was written in the early 1960s as a critique of suburban conformity. As the lyrics lament the fact that the houses and people who inhabit them "all look just the same," the sequence offers images of gas-guzzling SUVs driving the neighborhood streets and businessmen guzzling coffee as they exit a chain coffee shop. Taken together, these words and images present a picture of a space built around consumption. This is not a story of one person or one family and their consumer goods. Consumption is the rule for everyone in the community, and keeping up with the neighbors is seemingly defined by one's rate of consumption. By incorporating Reynolds's lyrics, the opening sequence revives the concerns of postwar critics who felt that consumer culture and mass suburbanization would turn everyone into conformist clones.

The opening scene of the pilot episode continues the theme started in the credit sequence, offering numerous references to the consumption-oriented life in Agrestic. The scene takes place at an elementary school PTA meeting, where Nancy is presenting her recommendation that canned sodas be removed from the school's vending machines and replaced with water and fruit juices. She argues that the children "shouldn't be guzzling sugar and chemicals," but clearly has no problem with the basic idea of vending machines in an elementary school. As the debate over convenience beverages continues, some of the women at the meeting gossip quietly about how Nancy is handling the loss of her husband. One woman says, "I think she got a little Boty between the eyes." In response, another woman says, "She probably treated herself, poor thing." This reference to a non-essential cosmetic procedure—a form of medicine as consumer good—reveals its status as both desirable and expensive. Getting Botox is seen as a way of "treating" oneself in a time of distress. The double meaning of the word "treated" conflates the medicinal nature of Botox with its status as a self-indulgence available only to those with plenty of disposable income. Moments later, one of the women admires Nancy's designer purse (which Nancy

FIGURE 15. Nancy (Mary-Louise Parker) and Celia (Elizabeth Perkins) argue about appropriate vending machine contents while other women at the PTA meeting gossip about Nancy's purse, kitchen, and possible cosmetic surgery (*Weeds*). Frame enlargement.

later reveals is a knockoff, used to perpetuate the image of being able to consume at will), while another comments on the money Nancy and her late husband spent on their new kitchen, which she says "turned out gorgeous."

On one hand, this scene presents a group of catty women whose gossip revolves around Nancy's consumption habits, suggesting that consumer culture is trivial and superficial. At the same time, the backdrop for this gossip session is a seemingly serious discussion not of whether children should be purchasing items from a vending machine in the school, but about what kinds of products should be available for them to purchase. Consuming is clearly a defining behavior for all the residents of Agrestic. This opening scene is representative of the entire series, which is filled with images of conspicuous and excessive consumption. From the SUVs and sports cars driven by local residents, to Nancy's constant consumption of iced coffee and canned cola, to the faith healer given to one of Nancy's friends as a get-well "gift," to the recreational use of marijuana, *Weeds* presents a suburban lifestyle that is saturated with consumption.

The series' primary critique of excessive middle-class consumption emerges in the juxtaposition of Nancy's life in Agrestic with the life of her supplier, Heylia (Tonye Patano), and Heylia's nephew Conrad (Romany Malco). Nancy often stops by Heylia's house to pick up her supply of pot, and both the neighborhood and the individual house are a far cry from what exists in Agrestic. Heylia's house is a working-class house. While Nancy's kitchen is spacious and elegant, Heylia's kitchen (a space of business and socializing) is small, crowded, and primarily functional. She and Conrad measure ounces of weed on the kitchen table, and Heylia always has something cooking on the stove. The family is not poverty-stricken, but they also do not have a great room with a skylight, a back yard pool, or an atrium in their home, as the residents of Agrestic do. Heylia's house sits on a trash-laden street and is protected by a tall chain-link fence.

Many scenes cut directly from Nancy's home and neighborhood to Heylia's home and neighborhood to highlight the differences between them. Heylia may not be surrounded by extravagant consumer goods, but she and her family seem to get along just fine. Juxtaposing her lifestyle with Nancy's highlights the fact that many of the items and services Nancy believes she needs are nothing more than desires and expectations based on the life to which she has grown accustomed.

The contrast between Nancy and Heylia also draws attention to the parallels that exist within *Weeds* between distinctions based on class and distinctions based on race and ethnicity. Unlike *Far from Heaven* and *Desperate Housewives*, *Weeds* does not emphasize the process of excluding people of color from the community, but rather takes that exclusion as a given. Although the community of Agrestic does seem to have a few Asian American residents, black characters like Heylia and Conrad live in neighborhoods outside Agrestic, while Hispanic characters provide domestic service. At one point, Nancy's friend Celia (Elizabeth Perkins) even says quite plainly, "In Agrestic, the people are white, and the help is brown, not black." As part of its commentary on suburbia, *Weeds* not only assumes the exclusion and subordination of most people of color, but also uses that separation as a way of making class differences even more obvious. Although Nancy struggles to maintain her privileged, suburban lifestyle, the series argues that there are many people who never even have the opportunity to live the life that she is afraid of losing. *Weeds* clearly depicts race and class as intertwined, but for the purpose of this chapter, I focus my comments on the economic issues that are brought to the surface, working from the assumption that, in *Weeds'* suburban diegesis, people of color are also poor or working class.

On the surface, *Weeds* seems to be criticizing the consumer culture and class stratification that have become associated with American suburban life. To a certain extent, this is true. Many scenes do depict conspicuous and excessive consumption as something to be ridiculed— something that unfairly divides society into the "haves" and the "have-nots." But at the same time, the audience is being asked to sympathize with a woman whose central concern is maintaining a lifestyle defined by the very consumption that is supposedly being ridiculed. Nancy is, after all, the series' central protagonist, and while she may have some annoying quirks, she is generally presented as a likeable woman that viewers should root for. By comparing Nancy's life with Heylia's, the series encourages viewers to ask why Nancy is any more deserving of the good life than Heylia. But in the long run, it is Nancy who is presented as being "just like us," and while the audience may be asked to reflect on their consumption-oriented lifestyle, they are also encouraged to fight to protect it, just as Nancy does. Nancy's behavior reflects a belief that Keith Hayward suggests pervades contemporary society— the belief that we have "an implicit *right to consume*."[28] So while *Weeds* initially seems to critique middle-class consumption, it eventually reinforces consumer culture as something worth protecting at all costs.

Crime and the American Dream

Nancy starts out as a small-time dealer, but she eventually develops her business to the point where she has a group of people working beneath her, helping to create, grow, and sell new strains of marijuana to an increasingly large client base. The bigger her business gets, the more trouble comes her way. The criminal activities with which she is involved escalate rapidly from misdemeanors to felonies, as murder and other violent crimes become part of her small-business world. All this happens because of her desire—one that most of the audience likely shares—to live the American Dream.

Weeds emphasizes desires and fears that are also raised by many other contemporary suburban narratives. HBO's hit series The Sopranos, for example, features a mob boss whose criminal dealings afford him and his family an enormous house in a posh New Jersey suburb. The FX series The Riches, which used promotional taglines like "It's a Wonderful Lie" and "They're stealing the American Dream," features a family of con artists who assume the identity of a recently deceased couple and move into their new suburban home, maintaining the lifestyle through a series of increasingly elaborate cons. In Fox's Arrested Development, a dysfunctional family is forced to live in the model home of a barren, unfinished suburban development after the family's patriarch, a housing developer, is accused of pocketing millions by defrauding his company's investors and building tract houses for the Iraqi government. AMC's Breaking Bad features a terminally ill high school chemistry teacher who begins producing methamphetamine so that he can set aside money to provide for his family after his death. In the 2000 film Traffic, a suburban housewife protects her home and family by diving into the drug trade after her husband is taken to jail. And the 2005 film Fun with Dick and Jane features a suburban couple who lose their jobs and then turn to armed robbery in order to keep up the payments on their home and lifestyle. All these examples feature middle-class individuals whose share of the American Dream is dependent on their success in criminal activities.

The term "American Dream" has slightly different meanings for different people, thus making it difficult to pin down a precise definition. As John Archer points out, despite the common use of the phrase in media, marketing, and political campaigns, "it is seldom defined," yet "widely understood."[29] Perhaps the vagueness of the concept is what gives it such power, since it allows individuals to focus on their own aspirations, while allowing marketers and storytellers to invoke those individualized aspirations simply by using the term. Messner and

Rosenfeld sum up the concept well by saying that the American Dream "refers to a cultural commitment to the goal of economic success, to be pursued by everyone under conditions of open, individual competition."[30] While Messner and Rosenfeld are rather vague about what constitutes "economic success," Hornstein offers more precision: "Thanks in large measure to organized real estate brokers' cultural and political work, the single-family home on a quarter-acre lot in a low-density suburban development became the 'American Dream,' and the vast majority of Americans bought into it."[31] Based on either the broad idea of economic success, or the specific image of suburban bliss, Nancy and her husband had achieved the American Dream. When that dream is threatened, Nancy does what she can to protect it.

Cast in the most positive light, the American Dream encourages people to work hard, because hard work is said to bring financial success. However, it can also lead some to turn to crime, as criminal behavior is often seen as the quickest or easiest way to achieve the goals that the dream encourages. Sociologist Robert Merton's comments on strain theory, or anomie, are helpful in considering this phenomenon. Borrowing the term "anomie" from Durkheim, Merton describes the decline of community and social order in society as a whole, and its replacement by disorder and alienation. Individuals who feel cut off from society may still strive for common goals, but they are more likely to take uncommon paths to reach them.[32] As Yvonne Jewkes notes, "Anomie usually describes a situation where a society places strong emphasis on a particular goal, but far less emphasis on the appropriate means of achieving that goal."[33] Messner and Rosenfeld say that the combination of "strong pressures to succeed monetarily and weak restraints on the selection of means" is intrinsic to the concept of the American Dream, which they also argue "contributes to crime directly by encouraging people to employ illegal means to achieve goals that are culturally approved."[34] It is Nancy's desire to hold on to her piece of the American Dream that leads her to engage in criminal activities but at the same time makes her a relatable heroine.

Nancy embodies many aspects of the standard American Dream narrative. As the series begins, she is staring down a list of emotional and financial challenges. She just lost her husband, she is broke, and she has spent the past seventeen years or so raising her sons, and therefore does not have the skills necessary to land the kind of job that would pay enough for her to afford her comfortable lifestyle. But she is perky, charming, and determined to overcome her obstacles. She is the classic underdog figure, practically obliging the audience to root for her. Her hard work, ingenuity, and determination are qualities that are admirable in our society, and which also make her good at what she does. As Messner and Rosenfeld note, these traits are common to both "the archetypal American hero and the archetypal American villain."[35] In another context (such as the crime drama of *Close to Home*) Nancy could easily be positioned as a villain. However, in *Weeds*, there is no doubt that Nancy is the story's heroine.

Nancy has much in common with the heroes of gangster films, who also embody the American Dream but use criminal methods to achieve it. Thomas Schatz argues that gangsters and businessmen have similar values, but the gangster takes things too far, turning into a "somewhat misguided self-made American man."[36] Jack Shadoian sees gangster films as allegories of business in which overachievers are punished for striving a bit too much.[37] In other words, hard work is good, but not if it is taken too far. Traditional gangster films end with the punishment—usually death—of the heroes, reminding the audience of the consequences of uncontrolled ambition, but not before allowing them to celebrate the success of the hero along the way. Nancy does not meet the same demise that most gangster heroes do, but she does face increasingly serious consequences, including the murder of her boyfriend, physical threats to her immediate family, prison time, and a gunshot wound to the head.

Like gangster films and heist films, *Weeds* devotes a great deal of attention to the careful planning and work involved in the hero's attempts at success. The series depicts Nancy going through many of the same experiences faced by any small business owner. For example, Nancy quickly realizes that she cannot do everything herself and begins to build a business pyramid, with herself at the top and employees beneath her. She must deal with the hassles of getting utility service and insurance for the bakery that initially serves as her cover operation. After deciding to become a grower, she attends a marijuana convention, where individuals have booths set up to display their latest offerings. Like any other entrepreneur, Nancy uses this opportunity to size up the competition, do some networking, and learn the tricks of the trade. By depicting Nancy's business in this way, *Weeds* suggests that, aside from its illegality, selling drugs is about the same as selling anything else in an open market.[38] Nancy is portrayed as an everywoman, working very hard to support her family and earning the admiration of viewers. Although she follows a path that most of us would likely avoid, Nancy's hard work and determination lead her to economic success, allowing her to embody the American Dream.

Weeds presents a complicated view of moral boundaries, with the difference between right and wrong not always as clear-cut as we might like it to be. For Nancy, providing for her family (generally viewed as the right thing for a mother to do) is accomplished through illegal activity (seen as wrong). The moral uncertainty of the series sets it apart from traditional crime films and crime series that clearly establish good guys and bad guys, right and wrong. *Weeds* has been generally promoted (by Showtime and the series producers) as a comedy, not a crime show. As Thomas Leitch argues in his discussion of comic crime films, crime comedies "are more often classified as comedies (films people laugh at) that happen to be about crime . . . because comedy is a stronger, more broadly recognized genre."[39] But classifying *Weeds* as a comedy does not change the fact that criminal activity is central to the series' concept.

Seen as a comedic crime series, *Weeds* has more in common with what Nicole Rafter identifies as "films of moral ambiguity." She notes that in this type of film, as opposed to more traditional crime films, "the standards for judgments about guilt and innocence are difficult to discern," and "the crimes are likely to be committed by ordinary people."[40] Films like *Mystic River* (2003) and *Monster* (2003), for example, feature protagonists who commit acts that society has deemed wrong (including murder), but at least partially defend these acts by portraying the criminals as victims themselves. The characters are left with few, if any, viable options, and thus the line between right and wrong becomes less clear. Nancy Botwin may not be a murderer (though in the fifth season she does attempt to order a hit on one of her enemies), but the boundary between right and wrong is constantly blurred by the fact that she uses socially unacceptable means to achieve socially encouraged goals. In this regard, *Weeds* is certainly not unique, but rather part of a larger trend in recent television programming that John Sumser identifies as a "transition from moral certainty to moral ambiguity."[41] In recent decades, programs like *Homicide: Life on the Street* (1993–1999), *NYPD Blue* (1993–2005), *The Shield* (2002–2008), *24* (2001–2010), and *Dexter* (2006–2013) have offered characters who sometimes bend or break the rules in their search for truth and justice. In its own unique style, *Weeds* continues this trend by challenging ideas of moral certainty in two basic ways: through the treatment of the series protagonist, Nancy, and through flawed characters like Celia and Peter (Martin Donovan), who supposedly represent the voice of moral authority.

With Nancy, it is a case of the ends justifying the means—at least partly. Unlike crime narratives that focus on the efforts of police and prosecutors, and pay little attention to the criminal's motivation, *Weeds* spends a considerable amount of narrative time exploring the reasons behind Nancy's behavior. The first season's episode "Free Goat," for example, focuses on Nancy's financial troubles and her efforts to provide for her family. When she picks up her son Shane (Alexander Gould) from his martial arts lessons, she finds out that her check to pay for the lessons bounced. Her utilities start getting shut off because of non-payment. She has to leave her car and wedding ring with Heylia as collateral, because she spends all her cash to have Shane's broken arm treated. Throughout all this, Nancy's sons are dealing with emotional stress caused by the loss of their father and, in Silas's (Hunter Parrish) case, the loss of a girlfriend. To shield them from any more stress, Nancy hides her financial situation, making excuses for the disconnected utilities and promising Shane a new video camera that she knows she cannot afford. The needs of her sons are presented as a legitimate motivation, making her criminal behavior seem more justified.

While Nancy's actions blur moral boundaries by suggesting that criminal behavior may be justifiable in certain situations, the voices of moral authority in the series offer no help in terms of clarifying such boundaries. First there is Celia, who is elected to the city council and immediately launches an anti-drug campaign with the moralistic slogan "Drugs are wrong!" Meanwhile, she regularly drinks herself into a stupor, commits adultery, accepts bribes from a local businessman, and slips laxatives into her daughter's candy to make her lose weight. Then there is Peter, Nancy's boyfriend who happens to be a DEA agent. Despite representing the nation's ultimate voice of authority, the federal government, Peter overlooks Nancy's drug dealing and even goes so far as to target a cartel that is competing with Nancy, thus clearing a path for her success.

The morally dubious behavior of Celia and Peter, the two characters seemingly in positions of moral authority within the community, helps to develop some of the themes of *Weeds* while making it even harder to condemn Nancy for her criminal activities. Since the series does not feature any characters with unquestionable moral standards, it is easier to read Nancy as generally good. Or, as Mary-Louise Parker described her character at the 2007 Emmy Awards, "An enterprising single mother who makes unusual choices to provide for her children."

Celia and Peter also contribute to *Weeds'* critique of our imperfect system of governance and authority. Whether elected by the people (as Celia is) or hired/appointed by a government body (as Peter is), government officials are just as flawed as the people they represent, serve, and protect. In an era filled with heavily publicized government scandals, *Weeds* merely reflects the reality that mainstream America (represented by the middle-class suburban community of Agrestic) is coming to terms with. By not providing the audience with even the option of identifying with a character on a higher moral plane, *Weeds* suggests that no one should stand in moral judgment of others when they have their own flaws to reckon with. Rather than pointing accusatory fingers at individuals or small groups, *Weeds* calls into question the American Dream itself, implicating everyone who believes in it, and showing the potential harm that it can cause.

Crime and Suburbia

The basic comedic concept of *Weeds* depends on the perceived mismatch between Nancy's illegal activities and her suburban surroundings. The joke does not work without the generally held belief that there is little if any crime in suburbia. This belief also provides the dramatic springboard for *Close to Home*, which explores suburban crime from a very different angle. *Close to Home* is a legal drama that focuses on a young, aggressive prosecutor named Annabeth Chase (Jennifer Finnigan) as she investigates and tries cases that take place in suburban Indianapolis, where she is also a resident. In the pilot episode, the crime in question is committed less than a mile from Annabeth's house, and many episodes emphasize that Annabeth is part of the broader suburban community in which she works. Playing on fears of crime in our own back yard, an ad for the series announced that "Prosecutor Annabeth Chase has discovered crime has a new address." While serious crime plays a role in many contemporary suburban narratives, *Close to Home* is the only one that focuses on fighting that crime in an attempt to protect suburban life.

The basic concept of *Close to Home* relies on the mythic image of a crime-free suburbia, which can be traced to the earliest suburban developments, particularly the promotions for those developments. Suburbs were pitched as spaces where families could move to get away from the various ills of the city, not the least of which was crime. Writing in 1914, housing reformer Carol Aronovici supported her argument for increased suburban development by noting that "statistics show us that density of population goes hand in hand with frequency of deaths, sickness, and crime."[42] Suburban planning was her solution to escaping those problems. This belief was widespread, and Jackson notes that early suburban developers "offered the exciting prospect that disorder, prostitution, and mayhem could be kept at a distance, far away in the festering metropolis."[43] Media texts over the years have reinforced the notion that crime is a phenomenon of the city and not suburbs. For example, crime and urban life go hand-in-hand in the tradition of film noir, while early family sitcoms presented a suburban utopia where the most serious crimes were missing curfew and lying to parents. The teen comedy *Adventures in Babysitting* (1987) offers a clear example of the contrast imagined by many Hollywood narratives. The film focuses on a teenage babysitter from a suburb of Chicago as she ventures into the city to pick up a friend who is stranded at a downtown bus station. Once in the city, she and the kids she is babysitting come face to face with teenage prostitutes, car thieves, gang violence, and other criminal

FIGURE 16. This ad for *Close to Home* plays on fears of crime creeping into suburbia. Author's personal collection. © CBS.

activities before finally "escaping" to the safety and tranquility of their suburban home.

The myth of a crime-free suburbia has become increasingly difficult to sustain, in part because of a trend in news coverage of criminal activity, which actually exaggerates the prevalence of suburban crime. In a study of local TV news coverage of crime in cities and suburbs, Danilo Yanich found that although actual crime rates remain higher in urban centers, the news coverage given to suburban crimes far outweighs that of urban crimes: "Many of the suburban crime stories articulated a consistent theme—the spread of crime and danger from the core city into the suburbs."[44] High-profile suburban murder and abduction cases, like those involving the Menendez brothers, Laci Peterson, Andrea Yates, JonBenet Ramsey, and the Columbine High School shootings have also contributed to a moral panic over the nationwide infiltration of crime into the suburbs. While *Weeds* uses suburban crime as a source of comedy, the anxieties associated with what Yanich refers to as "crime creep" are dramatized in a more serious fashion in films and series like *American Beauty*, *Happiness*, *Traffic*, *The Sopranos*, *The Riches*, *Breaking Bad*, and *Close to Home*.

Close to Home bucks the trend of moral ambiguity evident in most recent crime narratives by returning to a more traditional, conservative stance of moral certainty. While most recent suburban narratives (including *Weeds* and the others mentioned above) as well as contemporary legal dramas such as *The Practice* (1997–2004) and *Boston Legal* (2004–2008) often test the limits of morality by presenting protagonists who frequently blur moral boundaries, *Close to Home* is very clear about the differences between right and wrong. As a character, Annabeth embodies moral certainty and prevails in the courtroom almost all the time.

In many ways the legal drama is an ideal narrative setting for debating morality. After all, the American legal system, particularly criminal law, is inherently adversarial, with its plaintiffs versus defendants and, more important for most dramas, the prosecutors versus defense attorneys. This offers the perfect setup for a clash between right and wrong, good and evil. And as Steve Greenfield and Guy Osborn point out, there is often an additional clash between "the formal process of law . . . and what we might construe as justice."[45] Leitch notes that dramatized criminal cases are always about more than the case itself—whether someone did or did not commit a particular crime. He says that it is the business of all legal dramas "to explore conflicting views about morality and power,"[46] by using individual cases to raise questions about broader social debates. Given that legal dramas tend to end with a decision from the judge or jury, they offer the potential for a definitive answer to the moral questions that have been raised, sending a clear message about the distinction between right and wrong.

In the case of *Close to Home*, Annabeth and her associates are always depicted as being morally right and fighting for justice. Unlike series such as *The Practice*, which often feature attorneys "doing their job" by defending people that they know are guilty, *Close to Home* rarely presents a conflict between occupational and moral duties. Annabeth aggressively prosecutes criminals who are unquestionably bad, and her quest for justice results in successful convictions in all but one episode over the show's two-season run. The most common hurdle she faces is the legal process itself, which often gets in the way of an easy conviction.

Because of the challenges involved with working through the legal system, the drama often finds Annabeth negotiating the differences between morality and legality. For example, many of the criminals that Annabeth prosecutes are clearly guilty (in her mind, and because her viewpoint dominates the series, in the mind of the audience as well), but are able to use legal loopholes and technicalities to initially avoid charges or delay proceedings. These distractions frustrate Annabeth, extend the drama, and allow the series to identify flaws in the American legal system.

For example, in the episode "Suburban Prostitution," Annabeth arranges a sting operation to bust a woman who has been running a prostitution ring. After police seize the woman's computer and Annabeth tries to enter its contents (which all but prove the woman's guilt) as evidence, the defense attorney challenges the move, saying that the warrant covered only seizure of the computer, not its contents. From the standpoint of a legal system protecting the rights of its assumed-innocent citizens, blocking the contents' admission seems reasonable. From the standpoint of a prosecutor's office intent on establishing moral authority and social order by prosecuting criminals regardless of their rights, this is seen as an unnecessary obstacle. Given the framing of stories in *Close to Home*, regulations that protect alleged criminals are seen as flaws in the system. Commenting on similar situations in other legal dramas, Elayne Rapping notes that justice is often found only "when the actors are able to work around the system to force morality out of it by brute force."[47] In other words, the system may be flawed, but an individual with enough strength, moral character, and the ability to manipulate the legal system can bring about justice.

Annabeth is clearly presented as a voice of moral authority. She draws this authority from two sources—her role as an officer of the court and her role as a wife and mother. As a prosecuting attorney, she is granted official authority to act on behalf of the state in enforcing its laws, which codify legal definitions of right and wrong. Her status as a mother, however, is what defines her moral center. Mothers, for most people, provide the earliest definitions of right and wrong, and Annabeth constantly reminds co-workers and clients that she, too, is a mother and therefore understands how important it is to put criminals away. Even when legal technicalities get in the way, her role as a vigilant mother makes her keep fighting for justice, and it is her voice that fuses legality and morality within the narrative.

The idea of moral certainty in the face of legal ambiguity, as well as Annabeth's role in that debate, is displayed in an episode called "The Rapist Next Door." In this episode, a woman in Annabeth's neighborhood is raped, and many members of the community immediately blame a registered sex offender who has moved in nearby. Although the prosecutors do not have any evidence to suggest that this man committed the crime, the neighborhood is overtaken by panic, and before long vigilantes are threatening him and vandalizing his home.

This episode draws on a particularly significant suburban fear that has been dealt with in many recent suburban narratives—the fear of sex offenders (convicted or not) moving into the neighborhood. *Desperate Housewives* features a story arc in its third season involving a neighbor suspected of being a pedophile, which leads community members to picket outside his house. In the 2006 film *Little Children*, a convicted sex offender moves back into the community, causing one neighbor to stand in his front yard with a megaphone, warning everyone of the "pervert" living among them. The 1998 film *Happiness* features a suburban father who drugs and rapes two of his young son's classmates, causing neighbors to paint the words "Serial Rapist Pervert" on the front of his house. The documentary film *Capturing the Friedmans* (2003) tells the story of a Long Island family torn apart by accusations and eventually convictions related to child molestation in their home. And the controversial "To Catch a Predator" episodes of *Dateline NBC* (1992–) feature journalists and police officers conducting sting operations to expose and arrest potential child molesters and pedophiles, many of whom live in quiet suburban neighborhoods. While sex offenders are a concern for anyone, they strike a particular nerve within the suburban context, because such offenses threaten the ideals of family, childhood, and safety that are so embedded in the suburban dream. This episode of *Close to Home* adds yet another take on the recurrent suburban nightmare.

In this episode the law and morality are enforced in slightly different ways. The prosecutors eventually find and convict the man who actually committed the rape in question, and they also jail one of the vigilantes for threatening the man that neighbors suspected of committing the crime. The law, therefore, is enforced by punishing the individuals who, in this particular instance, committed crimes as defined by their local governing bodies.

The morality of the episode comes through in a different way. It is embodied by the vigilantes and the other residents who express outrage over the convicted rapist living among them. Even Annabeth's husband says that he would kill the sex offender if he ever came close to Annabeth. The convicted rapist may not be legally guilty in this particular case, but he is forever morally guilty by virtue of having raped someone in the past. His social punishment will continue long after he has served his state-ordered sentence. Although Annabeth and the other prosecutors officially condemn vigilante violence, Annabeth sympathizes with the man convicted of threatening the suspected rapist after she finds out that his daughter was raped and murdered years before. Claiming to understand his feelings of parental loss, Annabeth promises to ask the court to go easy on him. He will still be punished, because he broke a law. But because he was threatening a convicted rapist as a misplaced act of vengeance for his lost daughter, his crime is positioned as morally understandable. In legal terms, the vigilante is in jail and the convicted sex offender is free, but the episode makes it very clear that the vigilante's search for justice, albeit misplaced, is morally superior to any act of a known sex offender. It is the rapist, after all, that threatens "the family" and all the values associated with it, while the vigilante is working to protect those values, just as Annabeth and the other prosecutors are.

Because of its sense of moral certainty, and its clearly defined boundaries between right and wrong, Close to Home rarely spends time considering the motivation for the crimes committed. Whereas Weeds focuses on Nancy's needs and desires and how those lead her to engage in criminal behavior, the focus of Close to Home is on punishment, justice, and restoring order to the community. Gray Cavender and Sarah Deutsch note that CSI (2000–), another television crime drama from Close to Home's executive producer Jerry Bruckheimer, has a similar moral certainty. As a result, "criminals are typically selfish, venal, remorseless people, so no causal explanation of criminality is needed."[48] While this is generally true for Close to Home, the series presents a notable exception that simultaneously clarifies and complicates its moral position. While the primary criminal (the one brought to justice at the end of a given episode) is portrayed as inherently bad, thus deserving no explanation of motivation, there are often lesser criminals along the way.

One such example is the vigilante from the episode described above. He does commit a crime by threatening someone with a gun, but his behavior is explained as the angry response of a man upset over the loss of his daughter. Another example is from the episode "Suburban Prostitution," in which Annabeth prosecutes a local madam who has been exploiting and blackmailing suburban women to force them into prostitution in order to make herself rich. The lesser criminal in the episode is the woman originally busted for turning tricks. The episode reveals that she only did so because her husband lost his job, and she was desperate to earn enough money to hang onto the house and feed her kids. When she tried to quit, she was blackmailed into continuing. A third example comes from the episode "Land of Opportunity," in which the primary criminal is one who has used threats and violence to coerce appraisers into inflating the value of homes built by his company, so that he can make millions of dollars while causing homeowners to go broke when they end up selling their homes for half of what they paid. The lesser criminal in this case is the man who drives his truck into the front window of the appraiser's office after losing his life savings, his retirement money, and his children's college funds.

In these and other examples, *Close to Home* presents a clear distinction between criminals who are morally corrupt and regular people who happen to get caught up in terrible situations—usually as a result of the primary criminal's acts. The behavior of the "regular people" is explained with a dose of sympathy and understanding, and their downfalls are often used as proof of the primary criminal's wicked ways. In addition to the crimes for which they are prosecuted, the rapist leads a reasonable man to become a violent vigilante, the madam forces vulnerable mothers into prostitution, and the real estate mogul turns regular homeowners into truck-wielding assailants. They are not just breaking the law—they are destroying the suburban American Dream, and clearly must be punished.

While the behavior of the lesser criminals is explained, it is not condoned, and therefore does not threaten the series' moral certainty about the distinction between right and wrong. The vigilante and disgruntled homeowner are both sentenced to jail time, and the prostitute commits suicide to avoid facing public humiliation. Motivated or not, crime in *Close to Home* is not tolerated, and anyone who disturbs the suburban ideals of safety, family, and stability, regardless of their reasons, will be punished. This is in many ways the anti-*Weeds*, providing a more conservative, moral hard line in the face of *Weeds*' moral ambiguity. Although the two series take very different approaches, they both look beyond the façade of the suburban American Dream to reveal some of the hard work—both legal and illegal—that goes into preserving it.

Suburban Motherhood

In addition to using Annabeth's parental status as a source of moral guidance, *Close to Home* uses it as a way of raising the issue of women in the workplace. In the pilot episode, Annabeth is returning to her office after her maternity leave, and many scenes revolve around the adjustments she (and others) must make. Her boss initially refuses her request for a small refrigerator in which to store her breast milk, but he quickly realizes that this option is better than letting Annabeth store breast milk in the break room. Annabeth expresses anger over the fact that another prosecutor, Maureen (Kimberly Elise), got a promotion instead of her, arguing that the choice was made based on Annabeth's leave, thus constituting discrimination. Maureen, now Annabeth's supervisor, makes a few condescending remarks about Annabeth's taking time off, and perhaps not being emotionally ready to work because of her post-pregnancy hormonal changes. Maureen is framed as a career woman who is, as she says, "married to [her] job" instead of being married to a husband.

Initially, the antagonistic relationship between Annabeth and Maureen suggests a conflict between two types of women: those who dedicate their lives to their careers, and those who try to balance career and family. However, this conflict quickly dissipates as Annabeth and Maureen bury the hatchet, and the true relationship between work and motherhood becomes apparent. As the series progresses, motherhood is no longer seen as being in conflict with Annabeth's job. Quite the contrary, it is the driving force, and in fact Annabeth's work as a prosecutor becomes an extension of her work as a mother. In this way, Close to Home has much in common with Weeds. Despite their many differences, the most obvious being their opposing takes on morality and legality, both Weeds and Close to Home present motherhood as the most important job of all.

Of the many ways in which these two series differ from the majority of crime narratives in both film and television, one of the most significant is in their focus on women. Historically, crime stories, whether they deal with criminals, police, attorneys, or some combination of the three, have tended to revolve around men. From hard-boiled detective novels, the classic gangster films of James Cagney, and To Kill a Mockingbird (1962) to The Godfather saga (1972, 1974, 1990), Matlock (1986–1995), and NYPD Blue (1993–2005), men have dominated crime narratives. Women are commonly present as girlfriends or victims, but rarely do they take center stage. Weeds and Close to Home are part of a recent trend toward emphasizing women within such narratives. Other prominent examples include films like *The Brave One* (2007) and *Chicago* (2002), and television series including *The Closer* (2005–2012), *Damages* (2007–2012), and *Rizzoli & Isles* (2010–).

In some cases, the fact that a lead character is a woman does not have much of an impact on the narrative. In other words, female detectives, criminals, and lawyers often carry out their roles just as a man would, and gender seems not to be an issue. Nancy and Annabeth, however, clearly carry the burden of motherhood (particularly society's expectations of what a mother should be) with them into their work. In his analysis of the crime films of Michael Mann, Jonathan Rayner notes that even when a family or domestic situation is present, alternative systems of value (as defined by work, crime, justice, etc.) end up dominating, and professionalism trumps domesticity.[49] For Nancy and Annabeth, their status as mothers is always present and comes to bear on every decision they make, in or out of the workplace. J. A. Lindstrom notes that in most crime narratives, both criminals and detectives are generally "free of attachments," because they need to be flexible enough to either chase criminals or flee from the law.[50] This is clearly not the case with suburban crime narratives, where familial attachments are a defining element of characters' lives, whether they are men or women. In *The Sopranos*, for example, dramatic conflict is just as likely to come from Tony's (James Gandolfini) family as it is from his involvement with the mafia. In *Breaking Bad*, Walter (Bryan Cranston) is driven to criminal activity by what he sees as his obligation to provide for his family financially, even after his death.

In both *Weeds* and *Close to Home*, motherhood serves as the primary motivation, and in Nancy's case justification, for the actions of the lead characters.[51] Each series spends a significant amount of screen time setting up the importance that each woman places on her children, and the threat of losing or failing their children provides a constant drive within the narratives. Lindstrom notes that heist films often feature domestic scenes to demonstrate the lives that the criminals really want: "These domestic scenes are about the anticipated material rewards of criminal activity."[52] Similarly, *Weeds* uses moments of family togetherness (sometimes through reminiscing about the days before Nancy's husband died) to remind the audience exactly what is at stake, and why

Nancy is doing what she's doing. For example, Nancy's younger son, Shane, has a difficult time dealing with the loss of his father. He begins lashing out at school, writing gangsta-style raps about shooting other kids, and eventually making a mock-terrorist video where he cuts off a classmate's head. Nancy realizes that she must shield him from any more trauma and change, and thus tries even harder to provide him with a normal life, paying for it with the money she earns while dealing.

In *Close to Home*, domestic scenes act as a demonstration of what Annabeth is trying to protect through her work, and what is threatened by her failure to successfully prosecute criminals. In the episode "The Rapist Next Door," Annabeth's husband asks her how they are supposed to protect their daughter when there are rapists on the street. Annabeth says, "We look out for her. We lock our doors and teach her to do the same. And then I go to work tomorrow and try to put the bad guys away." As this statement makes clear, Annabeth's job as a prosecutor is an extension of her role as a mother. She sees "putting the bad guys away" as another way of protecting her daughter.

Despite the emphasis on motherhood as a driving force in these series, Nancy and Annabeth both employ other women to carry out some of the roles traditionally associated with motherhood, such as keeping up the house and looking after the children. Nancy employs a woman named Lupita (Renee Victor), a live-in housekeeper who tends to laundry and cleaning, and often knows more about what is happening with Shane and Silas than Nancy does. Annabeth leaves her daughter at a daycare center and with a variety of babysitters as she works her long hours at the office.

Hiring domestic help is an increasingly common phenomenon among working parents. Parents focus on providing their children with opportunities for their own economic success, often at the expense of spending time with them. Messner and Rosenfeld argue that "the lack of emphasis on *parenting* in the American Dream has contributed to the outsourcing of childcare as parents try to balance the competing demands of work and family."[53] The obvious irony is that for women striving for the American Dream, including Nancy and Annabeth, being a good mother is partially defined as achieving enough financial success to be able to pay someone else to take care of your children.

Both Annabeth and Nancy are positioned as sympathetic protagonists within their respective series based largely on their performance as mothers. While neither is a perfect mother (though Annabeth comes much closer than Nancy), they are both clearly invested in what they perceive as their motherly duties, and because they are striving to be better mothers, they are framed within their respective series as heroic figures. Annabeth's courtroom battles are made to seem admirable because they extend her motherly protectiveness to incorporate the entire community. And Nancy's illegal activities are portrayed as forgivable because they are motivated by her motherly instincts. These series reflect an idea verbalized in another suburban narrative, *Desperate Housewives.* In the episode "My Husband, the Pig," Edie (Nicolette Sheridan) laments, "No matter what else she does, if a woman isn't a good mother, she's a failure." Through their focus on motherhood, *Weeds* and *Close to Home* reveal the paid and unpaid work that women and mothers have always done to maintain the suburban way of life, while simultaneously reifying this role as an expectation of successful motherhood.

Working for the Dream

In chapter 4 I referred to Robert Ray's argument that individual Hollywood films often contain competing ideological messages, thereby allowing audiences to "have things both ways." Rather than committing to one point of view or another, the competing messages create a certain ambiguity in any given film, and Ray argues that this approach enables viewers to confirm their own predispositions about the ideas presented.[54] The same can be said for *Weeds* and *Close to Home*, which contain seemingly contradictory messages about the American Dream and about appropriate roles for women in our society.

For example, both series manage to balance conflicted views on the relationship between crime and the consumer-oriented, success-driven ethos of the American Dream. *Weeds* critiques conspicuous and excessive consumption every chance it gets, and it makes very clear that Nancy's criminal behavior is the direct result of her desire to maintain her lifestyle. Yet financial success continues to be Nancy's primary goal, and the series celebrates her achievement of that success when she does attain it. *Close to Home* places the blame for crime on bad people and their inherently immoral behavior, suggesting that these villains are threatening the assumed stability of middle-class values for everyone else in their neighborhood. But even as the series shifts the ultimate blame to the "bad guys," it hints at systemic problems as well, given that the "lesser criminals" discussed above often commit their smaller crimes in a desperate attempt to keep up with their neighbors. So while the middle-class American Dream is what Annabeth tries so hard to protect, the series also hints that this dream can act as a root cause of social problems.

Both series also display the tension between two views that have dominated discourses on gender since the 1970s feminist movement. On one hand is the conservative view that women belong in the home, tending to their husband's needs and raising children. Feminists have advocated freedom from these limitations, encouraging women to move beyond the domestic sphere and into the workplace. Nancy and Annabeth manage to embody both these views. Despite her offbeat business choice, Nancy is a successful entrepreneur, quickly turning a small-paying hobby into a lucrative enterprise. Annabeth is quickly climbing the ladder of the very competitive legal profession. Yet the labor of both of these women is primarily contained within the domestic sphere of suburbia. Nancy sells to her neighbors and Annabeth prosecutes her neighbors, but as the title of one series makes clear, the women remain remarkably close to home, and the emphasis on motherhood as the driving force behind their careers keeps them from being disconnected from their expected motherly duties. So both women manage to break out of the traditional homemaker role while still remaining tied to the home.

On the surface, *Weeds* and *Close to Home* are about crime. One woman commits crimes while the other fights crimes. And both series emphasize the importance of motherhood in defining the success or failure of a woman in our society. But in the end, *Weeds* and *Close to Home* are stories about work—why we work, how we work, and the rewards and consequences of that work. Specifically, these programs are about the paid and unpaid labor that goes into protecting and maintaining the suburban American Dream. While earlier programs such as *Father Knows Best* and *Leave It to Beaver* assumed and eventually normalized suburban middle-class status and values, *Weeds* and *Close to Home* reveal just how much effort is required to sustain that lifestyle. In *Weeds* the focus is on preserving a particular level of economic status, as demonstrated by the ability to purchase consumer goods with the money one earns. In *Close to Home* the focus is on protecting suburban middle-class values, like safety and family, for the entire community. Both series suggest that one of the biggest threats to the American Dream is other people who are also trying to achieve that dream. Left to their own devices in a free market economy, they turn to criminal or ethically questionable activities to reach their goals and end up hurting other people in the process. Dramatizing national anxieties about the shrinking middle class and rising crime rates, both series remind us that no matter how "normal" the suburban middle-class lifestyle may seem, the American Dream comes with no guarantees, and the American way of life is a privilege that can be taken away at any moment. Moreover, both *Weeds* and *Close to Home* show how people's desperate attempts to protect the American Dream can sometimes lead to its destruction.

Conclusion

There Goes the Neighborhood

I began this book with descriptions of the opening moments from two prominent suburban narratives: *American Beauty* and *Desperate Housewives*. These two examples, along with the other films and television programs discussed throughout the book, have much in common with respect to their depiction of suburbia. They all offer images of tasteful single-family homes in visually appealing neighborhoods with tree-lined streets. The sizes of the homes, as well as their interior and exterior designs, suggest comfortable middle-class status. While these neighborhoods might be an economic step up from the reality of most viewers, they are still within the realm of possibility for those who believe in the American Dream. These are also exclusively residential communities. Aside from a few drug dealers and real estate agents who work within their own neighborhoods, most of the characters with paying jobs commute somewhere else to work, because they live in spaces that are separated from industrial, corporate, and retail districts. This image of a purely residential, middle-class community is very common in popular media, but it is clearly not the only image of suburbia in circulation.

The 1999 film *Office Space* offers a very different vision of suburbia. The film opens with a shot of a freeway interchange. There are clusters of midsize office buildings on either side of the road and an overpass taking cars across the freeway from one cluster to the other. The sizes and arrangements of the buildings, along with their placement straddling the freeway just off the overpass, suggest that this is a development that has sprung up along the outerbelt freeway of a larger city. Traffic on the multilane freeway is bumper-to-bumper and barely moving. Characters from the film are shown sitting in the stalled traffic or jockeying for position in an attempt to find a lane where the cars are actually moving. Their eventual destination is the office of Initech, a generic technology company housed in a large flat building that spreads outward rather than rising upward. Adding to the sprawling feel of the building are the large parking lot and vast green lawn that expand the company's geographic footprint and indicate the presence of cheap real estate.

The Bravo reality series *The Real Housewives of Orange County* (2006–) offers another, very different picture of suburbia. The first episode opens with a montage of images that immediately suggest wealth: enormous houses, country clubs, expensive cars, and fancy jewelry. The images are accompanied by a series of voiceover comments from the titular housewives like "Life is different in a gated community," "The land here is a million an acre," "When you're not behind the gates, you don't know what you're missing," and "It isn't just a place to live, it's a lifestyle." This is followed by the opening title sequence, which begins with a shot of the sun rising (or perhaps setting) over the horizon, along with onscreen text announcing that "7 million families live in gated communities." The next shot is a pan of hundreds of rooftops in a vast residential development. The program's title is introduced in the third shot, appearing in between the two opening halves of an enormous wrought-iron gate. The rest of the title sequence uses a montage of images to introduce the various housewives that are featured on the series. The women are shown engaging in a variety of activities such as driving sports cars, riding horses, shopping for jewelry, and receiving Botox injections. As the title sequence ends, there is a shot of the enormous gate sliding shut, followed by a final shot of the five women smiling at the camera.

The opening sequences of *Office Space* and *The Real Housewives of Orange County* are quite different from the images analyzed in most of this book. The world of *Office Space* is dominated by traffic-filled highways, office parks, chain restaurants, and apartment complexes instead

FIGURE 17. Unlike the quaint, tree-lined streets of most suburban narratives, *Office Space* presents a suburban landscape dominated by office parks and congested freeways. Frame enlargement.

of single-family homes. And unlike the deliberately typical families that populate most onscreen suburbs, the "real" housewives are exceptional in many ways. Their comments and activities suggest that their gated community is elite, exclusive, and populated by extremely affluent families. These examples serve as a reminder that, despite the familiarity of middle-class residential neighborhoods, suburbia can take a variety of forms, both onscreen and off. Dolores Hayden lays out a typology of suburban forms that have been popular in the United States over the years, including "picturesque enclaves," "streetcar buildouts," "sitcom suburbs," and "rural fringes."[1] These variations demonstrate the range and complexity of real suburban developments, though fictional treatments rarely approach that level of complexity. Additionally, storytellers who choose to explore suburbia can and do take a variety of approaches to the subject. Examining some of these contrasting views helps to demonstrate the range of possibilities for storytellers, and helps to explain why one version of suburbia appears onscreen more often than any other.

Alternative Approaches

The discussion so far in this book has been focused on two basic types of suburban representations: the fully fictional Hollywood narrative that presents suburbia as a middle-class residential enclave, and the promotional image created by those who are trying to sell properties in specific suburban communities. While the former tends to present a vision of perfection that breaks down under scrutiny, the latter ignores all imperfections in the interest of making the sale. But there are additional images outside these categories that also contribute to the intertextual construction of suburbia. Documentary films and reality television programs, for example, are less likely to rely on the fantasies offered by fictional and promotional texts. And within the realm of fictional narratives, there are storytellers that imagine suburbs as something other than middle-class bedroom communities and those that take suburbia as their setting without making it a focal point of their story.

While the creators of fictional suburban narratives may choose to make their characters and situations realistic as a way of making stories relatable for viewers, they do not generally present their stories as factual. Documentary filmmakers make a different claim. Despite the fact that editorial choices made by the filmmaker will always shape the presentation of events and characters, documentaries are—in the minds of both filmmakers and viewers—rooted in facts. In other words, while most suburban narratives involve at least some layer of fantasy to enhance whatever realism they may include, documentaries about suburbia claim to tell stories that have actually happened or are currently happening. As a result, their approach to suburbia often differs from that of scripted narratives.

The 2004 documentary *The End of Suburbia: Oil Depletion and the Collapse of the American Dream* raises concerns about the sustainability of the suburban way of life. Relying heavily on interviews with scholars and policymakers, the film argues that the consumption patterns associated with suburban living, especially the dependence on automobiles, cannot be maintained as the earth's supply of fossil fuels begins to dwindle. Given this argument, the film's treatment of suburbia is, not surprisingly, quite different from that of most Hollywood narratives. *The End of Suburbia* opens with excerpts from "In the Suburbs," the short film produced in 1957 by *Redbook* magazine as a tool for attracting potential advertisers. "In the Suburbs" depicts *Redbook* readers as upwardly mobile young adults with new homes in the suburbs, and in turn presents suburbia as a space of happiness, family values, convenience, and free-wheeling consumption. After these excerpts, *The End of Suburbia* moves to a rapidly edited montage that blends images of early suburbs with images of contemporary suburbs as the narrator raises concerns about suburbia's sustainability and asks, "Does the suburban dream have a future?" Following this introduction, the film cuts to an interview with James Howard Kunstler, the author of numerous critiques of suburban sprawl, who says, "The whole suburban project I think can be summarized pretty succinctly as the greatest misallocation of resources in the history of the world." He goes on to answer the narrator's previous question by noting that the United States invested the majority of its post–World War II wealth in "a living arrangement that has no future." The rest of the film builds on this idea, relying heavily on interviews with scholars and policymakers who warn of the Earth's impending oil depletion and our need to plan ahead.

The End of Suburbia is somewhat similar to many Hollywood narratives in that it begins with a positive image of suburbia and immediately undercuts that image. In this case, the positive image of suburbia is presented as a relic of the past—a misguided fantasy that has led to a present crisis with even more serious consequences for our future. The film sends a very clear message that holding onto the suburban dream is dangerous, and urges viewers to take appropriate steps to solve the problem. One solution offered by some of the film's talking heads is a shift to New Urbanist development, which they argue will decrease the dependence on fossil fuels by minimizing the need for cars. This invocation of New Urbanism offers a striking contrast to the promotional materials examined in chapter I. Most of the communities included in that discussion would be considered examples of New Urbanism, yet their approach to the concept is very different from that used in *The End of Suburbia*. Instead of focusing on the environmental benefits of New Urbanism, the promotions emphasize ideals like tradition, family, and community. They present their developments as the epitome of the suburban American Dream, while *The End of Suburbia* presents New Urbanism as a necessary alternative to that same dream. While the promotional materials reinforce a fantasy in order to sell property, the documentary urges people to change that fantasy in order to avoid disaster.

Radiant City (2006) offers a similarly bleak view of suburbia but takes a slightly different approach. Moving beyond the environmental argument, *Radiant City* also includes critiques of some of the social problems caused by suburban development, including the drawbacks of single-use residential models, the lack of public gathering spaces, and the resulting loss of human interaction. The film incorporates a variety of perspectives on suburban life, including comments from scholars, designers, and suburban residents. In the end, they all point to the same concerns about isolation, lack of engagement, and over-dependence on the automobile. Like *The End of Suburbia, Radiant City* suggests that suburban life is neither environmentally nor socially sustainable, and it stresses the need for viable alternatives.

Documentaries like *Capturing the Friedmans* (2003) and *Farmingville* (2004) focus on topics other than suburbia but use the suburb as a setting and crucial element of the stories that they present. *Capturing the Friedmans* investigates a case of child molestation and the convicted men who may or may not have been guilty, while *Farmingville* examines a conflict between undocumented workers and the neighbors who want to see them kicked out. Both take place in the suburbs of Long Island, and they offer real world cases that echo the situations dramatized by many fictional suburban narratives. Unlike *The End of Suburbia*, these films do not blame suburban development for the problems at hand, but they demonstrate that suburbs are not immune to the problems of society.

Like documentaries, reality television programs purport to offer access to real people and real situations. Scholars, critics, and viewers have all raised questions about just how "real" such programming is, but the shows do have distinct qualities that set them apart from traditional comedies and dramas. In general, most of the programs are built around individuals who are not professional actors, and while they may be placed in rather contrived situations, their behavior in those situations is generally unscripted. As such, reality programs set in the suburbs have the potential to offer views of suburbia that are very different from those that come from the imagination of a writer or director. As it turns out, the suburbs of reality TV have much in common with their fictional counterparts.

The short-lived reality competition program *There Goes the Neighborhood* (CBS, 2009) features eight suburban families whose neighborhood is temporarily enclosed by a twenty-foot wall. They compete in a variety of challenges and competitions in an attempt to outlast the other families and win a cash prize. The focus on the competition does not leave a lot of airtime for the program to explore social issues, but the families' actions and on-camera interviews raise many of the same concerns that are dramatized in more depth by other suburban narratives. For example, assumed norms about family structures, racial homogeneity, and heteronormativity are challenged by the makeup of the families in the competition, which include a single mother as well as interracial and lesbian couples. One man worries out loud that he has failed as a father and masculine role model when he loses a challenge to another contestant. Another family confides that if they do not win the competition, they may lose their home to foreclosure. Although these issues are subordinated to the game, their presence does subtly echo the plotlines of other suburban stories.

The Real Housewives of Orange County premiered during the second season of *Desperate Housewives* and was clearly designed to capitalize on the success of its predecessor. By announcing itself as a real-life alternative to the women of Wisteria Lane, *The Real Housewives* suggests that is has already removed the façade of scripted drama, thus offering previously unavailable insights into suburban life. Adding to the connection suggested by the title, the opening credit sequence features a shot of the five housewives holding oranges in their hands as they look at the camera—a clear reference to the title sequence of *Desperate Housewives*, which features its main characters in a similar pose, but holding apples. As I noted above, this series is set in an exclusive gated community and features women who are extremely wealthy. So while this lifestyle may be closer to reality than *Desperate Housewives*, it is a reality that only exists for an elite few. While the program initially focuses on a variety of aspects of life in the community of Coto de Caza, the show's emphasis on wealth and catfights eventually overshadows everything else. This has become the template for the long list of similar programs set in other locations, including *The Real Housewives of Atlanta* (2008–), *The Real Housewives of New Jersey* (2009–), and *The Real Housewives of Beverly Hills* (2010–). In between feuds, screaming matches, and all-out brawls (particularly in the New Jersey edition), episodes have featured the wealthy housewives going on shopping sprees and vacations, showing off their new cars, boats, and Rolex watches, and throwing extravagant birthday parties, bridal showers, housewarming parties, and million-dollar weddings. The show's producers help to draw attention to the extravagance by including dialogue that mentions the cost of various items, close-up shots of cash registers tabulating purchases, and onscreen text announcing the value of items being displayed.

While the extreme wealth of the Real Housewives sets them apart from the families of most suburban narratives (not to mention the majority of viewers), one aspect of their financial situation is very familiar: its vulnerability. As discussed in chapter 5, many contemporary suburban narratives, including *Weeds, Breaking Bad,* and *Fun with Dick and Jane,* emphasize the financial struggles that people face as they attempt to hold onto their piece of the suburban American Dream. These stories echo nationwide concerns in an era dominated by recession, unemployment, and foreclosures, and the Real Housewives have not been immune. During the fifth season of the Orange County edition, the national financial crisis takes its toll on some of the housewives, many of whom earned their fortunes in either real estate or construction. Tamra and her husband are forced to sell the dream home they helped design because they owe more than it is worth and fear losing everything. Lynn and her family downsize from their original home in an attempt to save money, but they still end up being evicted from their smaller home when they cannot keep up with their payments. Jeana describes having to sell off many of her possessions to stay afloat, noting that her income is down by two-thirds as a result of the collapsing real estate market. She eventually announces that she is leaving the show, in part to focus on rebuilding her sputtering career.

These programs demonstrate that while the lavish lifestyles of the wealthy suburban elite may be enviable, they are also vulnerable, and even a wrought-iron gate cannot protect people from financial collapse. In general, although the storytelling formats of reality television programs like *There Goes the Neighborhood* and the various *Real House-wives* programs differ from those of comedies and dramas, they still tend to unearth the tensions that lie beneath the tranquil image of suburban life.

As the elite gated community featured in *The Real Housewives of Orange County* suggests, not all suburbs look alike. And although scripted narratives tend to favor a particular version of suburbia, there are some films and series that take different approaches. The previously mentioned *Office Space* is one such example. The film's depiction of a world defined by office parks, apartment complexes, and chain restaurants looks nothing like the familiar suburbs of *Leave It to Beaver.* It is so different from most cinematic and televisual constructions of suburbia that some viewers may not initially recognize it as suburban. But in reality, the environments depicted in *Office Space* are a more accurate portrayal of America's evolving suburban landscape.

The suburban configuration dramatized in this film has been given various names, including "edge city,"[2] "technoburb,"[3] "edgeless city,"[4] and "edge node,"[5] and it has altered the relationship between city and suburb. While the "bedroom community" model of suburbia suggests that people leave the suburbs to go into the city for work, shopping, and entertainment, the reality is that postwar suburbanization was not solely about residential spaces. In addition to pushing housing outside city limits, suburban growth has led to the decentralization of manu-facturing, commerce, and professional services. As a result, in most metropolitan areas individuals are more likely to commute from one suburb to another than from a suburb to the city.[6] Unlike the carefully planned, pedestrian-friendly, mixed-use neighborhoods that define New Urbanism, much of the contemporary suburban landscape is "a hopeless jumble of housing, industry, commerce, and even agricultural uses," all of which is "absolutely dependent on its road system."[7]

Office Space emphasizes the frustrations that are generated by this type of suburban development, playing them largely for comedic effect. For example, the car-oriented environment causes irritation beyond the traffic mess that opens the film. To get from their cars to the build-ing, Peter (Ron Livingston) and his co-workers have to navigate a sea of parking spaces broken up by drainage ditches and retention ponds.

And while characters in most suburban narratives live with their families in nicely built detached houses, *Office Space* is populated largely by single men who live in enormous, generic apartment complexes with paper-thin walls. The film also mocks the endless array of interchangeable chain restaurants that are clustered together near the Initech office. One day while getting coffee at one of the restaurants—a TGI Friday's clone called Chotckie's—Peter notices an attractive waitress named Joanna (Jennifer Aniston). When he asks her to have lunch with him at the restaurant next door, Joanna responds by asking, "When you say next door, do you mean Chili's or Flinger's?" When Joanna eventually joins Peter at Flinger's, she comments about how nice the restaurant is, but aside from different color tablecloths, it is virtually indistinguishable from the restaurant she just left.

The blandly corporate feel of the entire environment in *Office Space* is quite unlike the environments examined throughout this book. But as Shaun Huston points out, despite its different visual portrayal of suburban space, the film deals with some of the dramatic themes that are common to suburban narratives set in bedroom communities, including "the alienation, ennui, and emptiness of suburban existence."[8] Much like Lester Burnham in *American Beauty* or Frank Wheeler in *Revolutionary Road*, Peter is frustrated by his boring and repetitive corporate job. And like many fictional suburban men, Peter feels oppressed by his surroundings at work and at home, and he begins to find happiness only after dumping his overbearing girlfriend and finding a construction job that involves "making bucks, getting exercise, working outside." Despite these similarities, *Office Space* differs from most suburban narratives in a crucial way: it never presents a façade of happiness or beauty. The suburban world of this film is frustrating and unpleasant from the very first shot, and it never improves. While job changes may provide some small satisfaction, the characters are unable to escape or significantly improve their situations—the best they can hope for is to learn to accept their lives and make the best of them.

Despite the foregrounding of suburbia in many recent Hollywood narratives, there are still some that use the suburb as a setting without turning it into a prominent thematic element. For example, the central family in the film *The Kids Are All Right* (2010) and the characters in the

ABC comedy *Modern Family* (2009–) clearly reside in suburban neighborhoods. Instead of focusing on the particular behaviors, mores, and values generally associated with suburbia, these texts emphasize the tense conflicts and humorous predicaments that their characters face, with suburbia serving as a largely unremarkable background. However, this is not to say that the suburban setting is unimportant. After all, *The Kids Are All Right* focuses on a lesbian couple, their teenaged children, and the man who provided the sperm to inseminate the two mothers. *Modern Family* features a gay couple raising an adopted baby from Vietnam, as well as a middle-aged white man married to a much younger Colombian woman. Although these texts do not draw attention to suburban norms by making them the focus of their stories, each of them quietly challenges assumptions about the social identities and family structures of suburban residents.

Clearly the visual representation of suburbia can take a variety of forms. This can involve different approaches, like scripted fiction, persuasive advertising, documentaries, and reality television. Regardless of the format used, the types of suburbs depicted can also vary, just as they do offscreen, from middle-class bedroom communities to high-end gated communities to ethnic enclaves to environments where office buildings outnumber houses. The various configurations of suburbia that exist in the United States are all represented at least to some degree in contemporary popular culture, but despite the range of options available, storytellers tend to return to one particular version of suburbia more than any other. As a result, the image of the suburb as a middle-class bedroom community continues to dominate our cultural imagination, even as the reality of suburban life becomes increasingly difficult to define.

Storytelling in Suburbia

By and large, the films and television series examined in this book are so heavily influenced by their suburban settings that they are inseparable from them. Moving these narratives out of the suburbs would radically alter them, in some cases beyond recognition. So why are so many contemporary cultural producers making suburbia such a crucial component of their stories? And why do they so frequently return to a specific version of suburbia? What does this space allow them to do that they could not do elsewhere? To answer these questions, we must consider the position that suburbia occupies in our nation's collective cultural imagination.[9]

First, suburban spaces are in many ways seen as interchangeable. As Silverstone notes, suburbia is "instantly recognizable though never entirely familiar,"[10] creating valuable possibilities for cultural producers. Unlike many cities that have distinct identities (New York vs. Miami, for example), most suburban communities onscreen are simultaneously everyplace and no place. The unidentified suburb in *American Beauty*, for example, or the fictional Wisteria Lane of *Desperate Housewives* resemble but do not duplicate communities across the country.[11] Even the suburbs that are given specific locations still have the look and feel of similar suburbs nationwide. *Big Love*'s Henrickson family, for example, lives in Sandy, Utah, a real suburb of Salt Lake City. Describing the fictionalized version of Sandy, Will Scheffer notes that he and his series co-creator Mark Olsen "wanted it to be a suburbia that transcended a specific geographic location," because they knew they were working with large themes that were not limited to one community.[12] This approach allows one suburb to stand in for all suburbs, suggesting a universal nature in the stories that are told there.

Additionally, suburbia is seen as the space of the mainstream. The fact that suburbia is now home to the majority of the U.S. population helps to reinforce the image of suburbia as the space of everyday Americans—the space where typical families lead typical lives. While there are plenty of Americans living outside the suburbs, and not all suburbanites live or act the same way, Wayne Brekhus argues that suburbia has developed an image as a place where people play up their "averageness."[13] Because they are located in between urban and rural spaces (both physically and culturally) suburbs combine elements from both ends of the rural/urban continuum to find a space somewhere in the middle, avoiding the extremes. And although real-life suburbs can be very poor or very rich, the narrative focus on middle-class suburbs allows storytellers to avoid economic extremes as well, thereby enhancing the sense of "averageness." This offers viewers a sense of familiarity, which many find comforting and enticing.

With suburbia established as the space of the mainstream—of "typical," "normal," or "average" families—it becomes the ideal setting to explore questions of difference and otherness. This may be, in part, what has attracted so many cultural creators who are themselves othered in our society to produce stories set in the suburbs. *American Beauty, Big Love, The Pacifier, Far from Heaven, Desperate Housewives*, and *The Hours* all feature writers, directors, or producers who are openly gay. The bulk of suburban narratives emphasize individuals who, in one way or another, do not fit the apparent norm. It may be because of their race, ethnicity, sexual orientation, religious beliefs, political leanings, or just their unusual behavior, but characters who are different stand out in ways that they might not in another setting.

The timing of the recent wave of suburban narratives may have something to do with the increased political weight of American suburbs. Given the growth of the suburban population throughout the twentieth century, it is not surprising that by 1992, a majority of U.S. voters were living in the suburbs. This made suburban voters a powerful constituency, leading political commentator William Schneider to refer to the 1992 election as the dawn of the "suburban century" in politics.[14] Although suburban voting records from the 1950s through the 1980s indicate a strong preference for Republican candidates, there was a surge in suburban support for Democrats during the 1990s, turning suburbs into political battlegrounds during nationwide elections.[15] By the turn of the millennium, the suburbs were both politically powerful and ideologically contested, making them a great place for cultural producers to locate stories that deal with politically charged social issues and themes such as the family, citizenship, and class struggles.

Jim Leonard, creator of *Close to Home*, recognizes the politically charged nature of suburbia in noting that within our country's collective imagination there is both a "Republican suburb and a Democratic suburb. . . . One side celebrates the mother, the family, the church . . . sort of a 'Rockwellian' normalcy. And yet the reality is that in nineteen out of twenty houses, both parents work, and between them they're scraping together what Dad used to make twenty-five years ago, and the kids are in daycare."[16] The conflict between, among other things, differing expectations for families and parents establishes suburbia as the ideal location for *Close to Home*, the idea for which was driven, in part, by Leonard's desire to create a series that could explore the challenges faced by working mothers.

Similarly, Gary Ross, writer/director of *Pleasantville*, says that his film was partially inspired by the "values war" that has been fought by liberal and conservative groups in recent years. He notes that his story examines "the clash between that thing we say we long for—that we miss—versus where we are right now," and he suggests that *Pleasantville* ends up advocating a third option, which is "an open society and an open culture—and an open mind."[17] Will Scheffer says that when he and partner Mark Olsen were developing the idea for *Big Love*, "it was right around the time that the Christian conservative movement was defining family for the country."[18] As a gay couple that had been together for over ten years at that point, their personal and creative response was to say, "We get to define what a family is," which led them to envision *Big Love* primarily as a show about marriage.[19] Most contemporary suburban narratives are not produced by writers or directors who set out to tell stories about suburbia, but given that political debates about family, traditions, gender, and class play out in a very real way in suburban America, this space becomes a logical setting for stories that explore such conflicts, and suburbia then becomes a vital component of the stories that unfold there. As real-life suburbs evolve and residents reject the false images fed to them in previous decades, storytellers are providing more challenging images that reflect the turbulent nature of suburban life.

In addition to engaging with the contemporary political climate, the recent surge in suburban narratives is also likely a generational phenomenon. After all, the men and women responsible for most of the texts examined in this book are in roughly the same age group and part of a generation of Americans who grew up living in the suburbs and/or watching the early sitcoms that initially glorified the suburbs. As writers, directors, and producers, they are reflecting on their own experiences to shape their storytelling. Speaking as one of these storytellers,

Jim Leonard notes that "we grew up in [suburbia] and we write what we know about. It's a pervasive place that most of us have come from. Whether it's Long Island suburbia or the Midwest or the South, most of us grew up in developments."[20] Will Scheffer comments on the significance of the experiences that he and Mark Olsen had growing up gay in suburbia and watching TV programs like *The Donna Reed Show* and *Father Knows Best*: "Suburban identity was so much a part of our history—personally and as a generation—that suburbia and what we had been fed on television growing up and how we experienced our own discomfort with that" shaped the development of *Big Love*.[21] In particular, Scheffer and Olsen saw *Big Love* as a chance to subvert the image of suburban fatherhood popularized by early sitcoms, and to explore what it means to hide your identity and feel like an outsider in your own community.

Other creators have translated their experiences more directly into their stories. Marc Cherry, for example, grew up in Orange County and has often talked about how *Desperate Housewives*' Van de Kamp family (particularly the relationship between Bree and Andrew) is based on his own family.[22] Emily Kapnek says that the inspiration for *Suburgatory* came from her experience being transplanted from Manhattan to the suburbs of Westchester County when she was a teenager.[23] Sam Mendes says that although he grew up in England, he was raised in the suburbs there, which made the space feel like familiar territory as he was directing *American Beauty* and *Revolutionary Road*.[24]

Regardless of their personal connections to suburbia or their motivations for setting stories there, most creators draw on a similar vision of suburbia as the location for their stories: the middle-class bedroom community with white picket fences and well-manicured lawns. This image is especially useful in suburban narratives because it represents a plausible fantasy for many people. Although they may dream about the wealth and opulence displayed by the Real Housewives, that kind of lifestyle is way out of reach for most Americans. And the depressingly generic and corporatized world of *Office Space* is a reality for many but probably not something that anyone would wish for. The suburbs on display in most of the films and series discussed in this book are the kinds of neighborhoods that are both desirable and recognizable to most people. They are nice without being too fancy, and those who do not live in similar neighborhoods have probably at least driven through them.

But while the neighborhoods may resemble existing suburbs, their exaggerated reality pushes them into the realm of fantasy—a conscious decision on the part of many creators. Todd Haynes, for example, favored artifice over realism in the design of *Far from Heaven*. Although many of the film's scenes were shot on location, he says that "the entire film was basically an attempt to make locations look like sets."[25] The creators of *Big Love* aimed for an image that was closer to reality but still slightly exaggerated, settling on a neighborhood that "looks like your normal suburb—but the colors are a little bit brighter."[26] Jim Leonard notes that the vision of suburban Indianapolis used in *Close to Home* was influenced by "pictures of suburbia that were high gloss and high resolution, where the grass feels almost too green and the sky is almost too blue—pictures that become almost surreally perfect."[27] Creators often use this approach to present an appealing environment before revealing what's really going on with the characters. Describing the look and feel of Wisteria Lane, Marc Cherry says, "We were so hoping to at least entice the audience in this lovely, lovely world—to make it all so palatable so that it was easier for them to take the dark stuff we were serving up as the main course."[28] The difference that Cherry refers to between the appealing exterior and the darker realities of suburbia is a central preoccupation of contemporary suburban narratives, and this is where many writers and directors draw on the idea of the suburban façade.

Different narratives employ different ways of separating the illusory surface from the reality that it conceals. Some take this idea very literally, revealing that there is, in fact, something hidden beneath the surface of suburbia. For example, in *The Pacifier*, the seemingly typical suburban family home conceals an underground vault that protects top-secret information about national security. In *Mr. & Mrs. Smith*, John hides his weapons underneath the tool shed while Jane hides hers in a secret compartment inside the oven. In *Disturbia*, the home of a mysterious neighbor hides a deep pit that serves as a dumping ground for the bodies of murder victims. In all these cases, there is something physically hidden beneath the suburban surface.

In other cases, the distinction between the false surface and the underlying truth is handled with a bit more subtlety. Many characters, for instance, lead double lives, working to maintain a behavioral façade that conceals secrets about their true actions or identity. For many, the secret is adultery or illicit sexual activity. Central characters in *The Ice Storm*, *American Beauty*, *Little Children*, *Happiness*, *Far from Heaven*, *Revolutionary Road*, *Desperate Housewives*, *Weeds*, *Swingtown*, and *Mad Men* engage in sexual activities outside the bounds of their marriages and try very hard to keep these activities hidden from their spouses.

Other characters maintain distinct secret identities. For John and Jane Smith, the entire suburban life is a cover, intended to conceal their true identities as highly trained assassins. Similarly, the family in *The Incredibles* struggles to lead a quiet suburban life in order to hide the fact that they are superheroes with super powers. The central family in *The Riches* assumes the identity of a wealthy deceased couple and has to conceal the fact that they are actually con artists who travel the country living hand to mouth. The family in *The Joneses* is secretly a group of salespeople, playing the role of the happy family as a way of showcasing the products they are trying to sell. In *Pleasantville*, David and Jennifer pretend to be Bud and Mary Sue in order to blend into their new surroundings. And in *The Truman Show*, every person that Truman interacts with is an actor playing a role in order to develop Truman's story.

Even the stories that do not feature characters who are professional actors emphasize the level of performance that goes into maintaining a particular façade in everyday life. The Henrickson family of *Big Love* performs the role of three separate families to hide their polygamist lifestyle. Laura Brown in *The Hours* and Frank Whitaker in *Far from Heaven* perform the roles of contented wife and husband in order to mask the queer desires that threaten to destroy their families. In *The Gates*, vampires, werewolves, and witches try to conceal their differences by blending in as members of a typical community. And in *Weeds*, Nancy tries desperately to play the role of the typical suburban mom, even as she slides deeper and deeper into the violent and dangerous world of drug trafficking. Whether they are concealing secret identities, affairs, desires, relationships, or activities, the majority of the characters in suburban narratives essentially lead double lives, and the narratives go to great lengths to reveal this.

Breaking through the façade of suburban life is clearly a central concern for these films and series, so it is important to consider what the stories reveal in the process. Taken as a group, the narratives examined in this book emphasize the tensions and contradictions that are embedded in and concealed by the myth of suburban perfection. Some texts demonstrate how a nostalgic attachment to the version of suburbia depicted in postwar sitcoms is generally at odds with the need for positive social change. Others suggest that the privileged position of the nuclear family is not the result of its inherent merits, but of laws and customs that systematically marginalize alternative family structures. Some stories focus on the damages that can result from efforts to build a homogenous community out of very different individuals. Others point to the impossibility of living up to the gendered expectations placed on men and women, especially when the idealized versions of masculinity or femininity are at odds with the necessities of domestic life. Additionally, many of the stories reveal that the American Dream is not only a goal that many people strive for, but also the root of many of society's problems—problems that may eventually destroy any hope of actually achieving that dream.

These are tensions and contradictions that are so deeply embedded in the suburban fabric that it is very difficult for cultural producers working within this space to avoid them. Each of the films and series touches on a number of these conflicts, but individual texts handle them in different ways. For example, in some cases, the contradictions are miraculously (and impossibly) resolved by the end of the story— usually in order to facilitate a happy ending. *The Pacifier* identifies the contradiction between violent, heroic masculinity and domestic life, drawing on this mismatch as a source of comedy. By the end of the film, however, the contradiction is conveniently suppressed in favor of a happy ending, as the violently masculine hero decides to settle into the domestic space that his presence initially disrupted.

Both *The Truman Show* and *Pleasantville* go to great lengths to demonstrate the artificial, constructed nature of our media-saturated, consumer-oriented society, suggesting that this is a world from which we can never escape. And yet each film's ending features its hero leaving the confines of a television series to enter the "real world," celebrating the transition as a triumph for both Truman and David. By releasing the men from the artificial worlds they have inhabited, the films' conclusions suggest that reality and truth can, in fact, be separated from artifice and performance. This conclusion conveniently ignores the constant tension between reality and artifice that dominates both films.

Other texts offer a less simplified response to the contradictions. Instead of suppressing the tensions to facilitate the illusion of closure, many suburban narratives bring them to the surface and leave them unresolved, encouraging further discussion and exploration. For the television series, this is partially due to the serial nature of the form. For example, *Big Love, Desperate Housewives*, and *Weeds* all use the contradiction between public image and private behaviors as a constant source of both comedy and drama. While individual story arcs may reach a point of closure, the ongoing tensions help to sustain the long-term development of the series. In *Close to Home*, the primary contradiction lies in the fact that while Annabeth prosecutes criminals in order to protect the suburban American Dream, it is that same dream that drives most of the criminals to commit their crimes. And while Annabeth successfully puts individual criminals behind bars at the end of each episode, the fact that there is always another criminal turning the American Dream against itself proves that the contradiction can never be fully resolved.

Many of the films also leave contradictions unresolved. *Far from Heaven* identifies the irreconcilable difference between mainstream values as determined by a community and the desires of individuals within that community. The film ends with Cathy, Frank, and Raymond picking up the pieces after their lives are thrown into complete disarray. *American Beauty* emphasizes the conflicts between the demands of the family unit, the wants and needs of individual family members, and the expectations of the outside world. By the end, both the Burnham family and the Fitts family are left in ruins, with one father dead, the other father a murderer, both mothers far from mentally stable, and children who want nothing more than to escape. *The Ice Storm* also focuses on conflicts between the needs of the family and the desires of individuals. Although the Hood family is together at the end of the film, the final scene depicts the father weeping uncontrollably as the rest of the family looks on in stunned silence. Rather than offering convenient closure by suppressing the tensions they have raised, these films allow the contradictions to linger, drawing attention to similar contradictions embedded in American life.

Although they offer varying degrees of resolution, all the texts examined in this book draw attention to contradictions that the myth of suburban perfection actively conceals. Preservation of this myth involves a process of overlooking, eliminating, ignoring, and intentionally forgetting anything that disturbs the fantasy image. For example, taking a nostalgic view of suburban life involves a willful misremembering of the past, highlighting the positives and eliminating the negatives. Emphasizing the privacy of detached homes allows people to hide flawed families behind closed doors. A focus on community can encourage people to play up their similarities while overlooking important differences. To maintain rigidly defined notions of appropriate masculinity and femininity, one must often ignore how poorly suited such notions are to the realities of contemporary everyday life. And faith in the American Dream requires us to ignore the fact that in a competitive capitalist society, one person's success often leads to another person's failure. By conveniently omitting certain viewpoints and the tensions that they cause, the suburban myth reinforces a variety of conservative ideologies, including an emphasis on tradition and clear gender roles, the privileging of nuclear families and homogenous communities, and the belief that hard work trumps all adversity in the pursuit of the American Dream. By refusing to ignore the contradictions embedded in the suburban myth, contemporary suburban narratives actively engage in the cultural debates currently playing out in American suburbia, challenging the conservative values that the myth reinforces.

It would, however, be an oversimplification to say that all these films and series are strictly anti-conservative. In addition to exposing tensions within the suburban ideal, the use of the façade as a narrative device introduces a certain amount of ambiguity to the narratives in which it appears. Even if they seem to favor one interpretation over another, texts employing the façade do offer two versions of suburbia simultaneously: the perfect and the flawed. Most stories suggest that the flawed version is the real one, but the perfect version is still present at some level. For those viewers who dislike suburbia, the perfect image can be dismissed as an illusion, with the trials and tribulations of the characters confirming beliefs about the negative aspects of suburban life. For those who embrace suburbia and the values it represents, the perfect image remains available as a goal that might still be attainable for some, even when it doesn't work out for the specific characters involved. This may partially explain why the *Office Space* version of suburbia is less common in contemporary media. After all, this version is frustrating and unpleasant from start to finish, never offering even a glimmer of hope that this space could provide happiness or satisfaction.

If suburban settings are used to establish characters as typical or ordinary, and then the removal of the façade reveals that there is more to these characters than meets the eye, what becomes of the sense of ordinariness when the façade is removed? Does it break down along with the façade? If so, this would suggest that the conflicts revealed in these stories are anomalies, and that the characters involved are not, in fact, as ordinary as they initially seemed. Or perhaps it is the breakdown of the façade that finally reveals the true definition of ordinary. In this view, the problems explored in these stories are universal, and the image of suburban bliss merely hides the truth. Again, one's interpretation is likely to be shaped by preexisting opinions about suburbia. For those who embrace and strive for the ideal of suburban perfection, the characters in these narratives are the exception to the rule—individuals who fail to achieve the potential offered by the suburban dream. For those who doubt the suburban ideal, these characters dramatize the results of the failed promises embodied by that ideal. For the vast numbers of Americans who fall somewhere in the middle, the ambiguity of these narratives reflects and reinforces the complexities of their love/hate relationship with suburbia.

The use of the façade thus enables and even encourages multiple interpretations, allowing narratives to simultaneously critique and celebrate suburbia, which may, in turn, help these stories appeal to a broader audience. This is hardly surprising, given the profit-driven nature of Hollywood. A film or series that offers an all-out attack on suburban values risks alienating a large portion of its potential audience, given how many viewers live in the suburbs. The executives who finance these productions are not likely to take such a risk. As a result, the most unequivocal critiques of suburban life are left to the independently produced and distributed documentaries, for which box office success is not always the number one goal. While the ambiguity introduced by the façade may soften Hollywood narratives' critique of conservative suburban values, it does not negate it. Even when these stories leave room to imagine that the suburban ideal might be realized, they still reveal irreparable cracks in its foundation.

Suburbia may seem to be a rather mundane world, but the conflicts and tensions that play out in the everyday spaces of the suburbs echo similar conflicts and tensions that are woven into American society as a whole. By exploring the quotidian world of suburbia, cultural producers are able to reveal and work through the complexities that shape the day-to-day existence of the American people. Using the suburb as a metaphorical stand-in for the nation, contemporary suburban narratives invite us to reexamine the values embodied by the American Dream, the American people, and America itself.

NOTES

INTRODUCTION

1. Dolores Hayden, *Building Suburbia: Green Fields and Urban Growth, 1820–2000* (New York: Vintage Books, 2003), 3. See also Bruce Katz and Robert E. Lang, eds., *Redefining Urban and Suburban America: Evidence from Census 2000* (Washington, D.C.: Brookings Institution, 2003).

2. Robert Fishman, *Bourgeois Utopias: The Rise and Fall of Suburbia* (New York: Basic Books, 1987), 4.

3. John Archer offers an in-depth discussion of this connection in his *Architecture and Suburbia: From English Villa to American Dream House, 1690–2000* (Minneapolis: University of Minnesota Press, 2005).

4. Fishman, *Bourgeois Utopias*, 107–116.

5. Kenneth T. Jackson, *Crabgrass Frontier: The Suburbanization of the United States* (New York: Oxford University Press, 1985), 7–11.

6. Ibid., 33.

7. Jackson refers to these developments as "romantic suburbs" (ibid., 73–86), while Hayden calls them "picturesque enclaves" (*Building Suburbia*, 45–70).

8. Sam Bass Warner, *Streetcar Suburbs: The Process of Growth in Boston, 1870–1900* (Cambridge, Mass.: Harvard University Press, 1962).

9. Jackson, *Crabgrass Frontier*, 124–128.

10. Ibid., 234–238.

11. Frank Hobbs and Nicole Stoops, *Demographic Trends in the 20th Century* (Washington, D.C.: U.S. Census Bureau, 2002), 33.

12. See chapter 3 for a more detailed discussion of racial exclusion in suburbia.

13. Robert Beuka, *SuburbiaNation: Reading Suburban Landscape in Twentieth-Century American Film and Fiction* (New York: Palgrave Macmillan, 2004), 7.

14. Archer, *Architecture and Suburbia*, 180.

15. Hayden, *Building Suburbia*, 10.

16. Roger Silverstone, "Introduction," in *Visions of Suburbia*, ed. Roger Silverstone (London: Routledge, 1997), 4.

17. Fishman, *Bourgeois Utopias*, 4.

18. Lynn Spigel, *Welcome to the Dreamhouse: Popular Media and Postwar Suburbs* (Durham, N.C.: Duke University Press, 2001), 32.

19. Beuka, *SuburbiaNation*, 4; Margaret Marsh, *Suburban Lives* (New Brunswick, N.J.: Rutgers University Press, 1990), xii; Silverstone, "Introduction," 13.

20. Catherine Jurca, *White Diaspora: The Suburb and the Twentieth-Century American Novel* (Princeton, N.J.: Princeton University Press, 2001), 13.

21. Jeff Hopkins, "Mapping of Cinematic Places: Icons, Ideology, and the Power of (Mis)representation," in *Place, Power, Situation, and Spectacle: A Geography of Film*, ed. Stuart C. Aitken and Leo E. Zonn (Lanham, Md.: Rowman & Littlefield, 1994), 47.

22. For historical accounts, see Gwendolyn Wright, *Building the Dream: A Social History of Housing in America* (New York: Pantheon Books, 1981); Jackson, *Crabgrass Frontier*; Fishman, *Bourgeois Utopias*; Marsh, *Suburban Lives*; Lizabeth Cohen, *A Consumer's Republic: The Politics of Mass Consumption in Postwar America* (New York: Vintage Books, 2003); Ann Forsyth, *Re-forming Suburbia: The Planned Communities of Irvine, Columbia, and the Woodlands* (Berkeley: University of California Press, 2005); and Robert Lewis, ed., *Manufacturing Suburbs: Building Work and Home on the Metropolitan Fringe* (Philadelphia: Temple University Press, 2004). Sociology: Wayne H. Brekhus, *Peacocks, Chameleons, Centaurs: Gay Suburbia and the Grammar of Social Identity* (Chicago: University of Chicago Press, 2003). Anthropology: Constance Perin, *Belonging in America: Reading between the Lines* (Madison: University of Wisconsin Press, 1988); John D. Dorst, *The Written Suburb: An American Site, and Ethnographic Dilemma* (Philadelphia: University of Pennsylvania Press, 1989); and Setha Low, *Behind the Gates: Life, Security, and the Pursuit of Happiness in Fortress America* (New York: Routledge, 2003). Political science: Valerie C. Johnson, *Black Power in the Suburbs: The Myth or Reality of African American Suburban Political Incorporation* (Albany: State University of New York Press, 2002). Geography: James Duncan and Nancy Duncan, *Landscapes of Privilege: The Politics of the Aesthetic in an American Suburb* (New York: Routledge, 2004); and Linda McDowell, *Gender, Identity & Place: Understanding Feminist Geographies* (Minneapolis: University of Minnesota Press, 1999). Architecture: Dolores Hayden, *Redesigning the American Dream: Gender, Housing, and Family Life*, revised and expanded ed. (New York: W. W. Norton, 2002); Hayden, *Building Suburbia*; and Dolores Hayden, *A Field Guide to Sprawl* (New York: W. W. Norton, 2004). Urban planning and design: Edward J. Blakely and Mary Gail Snyder, *Fortress American: Gated Communities in the United States* (Washington, D.C.: Brookings Institution Press, 1997); and Andres Duany, Elizabeth Plater-Zyberk, and Jeff Speck, *Suburban Nation: The Rise of Sprawl and the Decline of the American Dream* (New York: North Point Press, 2000). Literature: Jurca, *White Diaspora*; and Martin Dines, *Gay Suburban Narratives in American and British Culture: Homecoming Queens* (New York: Palgrave Macmillan, 2010).

Media and cultural studies: Archer, *Architecture and Suburbia*; Spigel, *Welcome to the Dreamhouse*; Beuka, *SuburbiaNation;* and Nina Liebman, *Living Room Lectures: The Fifties Family in Film and Television* (Austin: University of Texas Press, 1995).

23. Kelvinator, "Home, Home at Last" (advertisement), *American Home*, December 1944, 55. Reproduced in *The Suburb Reader*, ed. Becky M. Nicolaides and Andrew Wiese (New York: Routledge, 2006), 260.

24. Spigel, *Welcome to the Dreamhouse*, 107–135.

25. Mary Beth Haralovich, "Sitcoms and Suburbs: Positioning the 1950s Homemaker," *Quarterly Review of Film & Video* 11 (1989): 74.

26. Liebman, *Living Room Lectures*, 171; William Douglas, *Television Families: Is Something Wrong in Suburbia?* (Mahwah, N.J.: Lawrence Erlbaum Associates, 2003), 141.

27. Gerard Jones, *Honey, I'm Home! Sitcoms: Selling the American Dream* (New York: St. Martin's Press, 1992), 97; Haralovich, "Sitcoms and Suburbs," 77 and 80; Liebman, *Living Room Lectures*, 125 and 175.

28. Pamela Robertson Wojcik, *The Apartment Plot: Urban Living in American Film and Popular Culture, 1945–1975* (Durham, N.C.: Duke University Press, 2010), 5.

29. Merrill Schleier, *Skyscraper Cinema: Architecture and Gender in American Film* (Minneapolis: University of Minnesota Press, 2009), vii.

30. Ibid., 193.

31. Wojcik, *The Apartment Plot*, 19.

32. Despite the simple distinctions provided by mainstream media narratives, in reality the line between urban and suburban is rarely so clear. Many low-density, residential neighborhoods that appear suburban are actually situated within city limits. Aesthetically, they seem suburban, but legally and politically they are considered urban. Fictional treatments tend to avoid such distinctions, and since visual media relies more on aesthetic impressions than legal definitions, my identification of suburban spaces in this book is based on how neighborhoods look and feel onscreen rather than any concern for the precise location of legal boundaries.

33. Steve Macek, *Urban Nightmares: The Media, the Right, and the Moral Panic over the City* (Minneapolis: University of Minnesota Press, 2006), xix.

34. Martin Lefebvre, "Between Setting and Landscape in the Cinema," in *Landscape and Film*, ed. Martin Lefebvre (London: Routledge, 2006), 23.

35. Owen Gleiberman, "Revolutionary Road," *Entertainment Weekly*, 9 January 2009, 48.

36. Scott Simmon, *The Invention of the Western Film: A Cultural History of the Genre's First Half-Century* (Cambridge: Cambridge University Press, 2003), xiii.

37. Edward Dimendberg, *Film Noir and the Spaces of Modernity* (Cambridge, Mass.: Harvard University Press, 2004), 13–14.

38. John Fiske, *Television Culture* (New York: Methuen & Co., 1987), 108. See also Jonathan Gray, *Watching with The Simpsons: Television, Parody, and Intertextuality* (New York: Routledge, 2006).

39. Macek, *Urban Nightmares*, xvii–xix.

40. Chris Healy, "Introduction," in *Beasts of Suburbia: Reinterpreting Cultures in Australian Suburbs*, ed. Sarah Ferber, Chris Healy, and Chris McAuliffe (Melbourne: Melbourne University Press, 1994), xvii.

CHAPTER 1   TRADITIONAL VALUES

1. For the remainder of the discussion, I distinguish between titles of films and the television series that exist within the films through the use of punctuation. *The Truman Show* and *Pleasantville* thus refer to the films, while "The Truman Show" and "Pleasantville" refer to the series. The name of the town of Pleasantville appears without special punctuation.

2. Fredric Jameson, "Postmodernism, or the Cultural Logic of Late Capitalism," in *Media and Cultural Studies: Keyworks*, ed. Meenakshi Gigi Durham and Douglas M. Kellner (Oxford: Blackwell, 2001), 562, 563.

3. Although Seaside is technically a resort town, and not a suburb of a larger city, many of Seaside's design elements have been adopted for use in suburban communities across the country.

4. Lloyd W. Bookout, "Neotraditional Town Planning: A New Vision for the Suburbs?" *Urban Land* 51, no. 1 (1992): 23.

5. Dolores Hayden, *A Field Guide to Sprawl* (New York: W. W. Norton, 2004), 7.

6. Andres Duany, Elizabeth Plater-Zyberk, and Jeff Speck, *Suburban Nation: The Rise of Sprawl and the Decline of the American Dream* (New York: North Point Press, 2000), 4.

7. Congress for the New Urbanism, "Charter of the Congress for the New Urbanism, 1996," in *The Suburb Reader*, ed. Becky M. Nicolaides and Andrew Wiese (New York: Routledge, 2001), 485.

8. Alex Krieger, "Arguing the "Against" Position: New Urbanism as a Means of Building and Rebuilding Our Cities," in *The Seaside Debates: A Critique of the New Urbanism*, ed. Todd W. Bressi (New York: Rizzoli International Publications, 2002), 51–52.

9. Julie Campoli and Alex S. MacLean, *Visualizing Density* (Cambridge, Mass.: Lincoln Institute of Land Policy, 2007), 8–10.

10. Bruce Podobnik, "Assessing the Social and Environmental Achievements of New Urbanism: Evidence from Portland, Oregon," *Journal of Urbanism* 4, no. 2 (2011): 105–126; Ryan Falconer, Peter Newman, and Billie Giles-Corti, "Is Practice Aligned with the Principles? Implementing New Urbanism in Perth, Western Australia," *Transport Policy* 17, no. 5 (2010): 287–294.

11. Michael Sorkin, "The End(S) of Urban Design," in *Urban Design*, ed. Alex Krieger and William S. Saunders (Minneapolis: University of Minnesota Press, 2009), 179–180; Sheila Crowley, "Hope VI: What Went Wrong," in *From Despair to Hope: Hope VI and the New Promise of Public Housing in America's Cities*, ed. Henry G. Cisneros and Lora Engdahl (Washington, D.C.: Brookings Institution Press, 2009), 229–247.

12. See, for example, John Rothchild, "A Mouse in the House," *Time*, 4 December 1995, 23; Russ Rymer, "Back to the Future: Disney Reinvents the Company Town," *Harper's*, October 1996, 65–76; Douglas Frantz, "Living in a Disney Town, with Big Brother at Bay," *New York Times*, 4 October 1998, 31.

13. Andrew Ross, *The Celebration Chronicles: Life, Liberty, and the Pursuit of Property Value in Disney's New Town* (New York: Ballantine Books, 1999), 30, 36.

14. Keally D. McBride, *Collective Dreams: Political Imagination & Community* (University Park: Pennsylvania State University Press, 2005), 91–92.

15. Bookout, "Neotraditional Town Planning," 25.

16. As Greg Dickinson discusses in his analysis of Old Pasadena, reliance on nostalgia is also common in many urban renewal projects. Greg Dickinson, "Memories for Sale: Nostalgia and the Construction of Identity in Old Pasadena," *Quarterly Journal of Speech* 83 (1997): 1–27.

17. Janelle L. Wilson, *Nostalgia: Sanctuary of Meaning* (Lewisburg, Pa.: Bucknell University Press, 2005), 21. See also Andreea Deciu Ritivoi, *Yesterday's Self: Nostalgia and the Immigrant Identity* (Lanham, Md.: Rowman & Littlefield, 2002), 17.

18. Svetlana Boym, *The Future of Nostalgia* (New York: Basic Books, 2001), 16.

19. David Lowenthal, *The Past Is a Foreign Country* (Cambridge: Cambridge University Press, 1985), 6.

20. Fred Davis, *Yearning for Yesterday: A Sociology of Nostalgia* (London: Free Press, 1979), 123.

21. Ibid., 122.

22. Michael Kammen, *Mystic Chords of Memory* (New York: Vintage, 1991), 688.

23. Lowenthal, *The Past Is a Foreign Country*, 8.

24. Bookout, "Neotraditional Town Planning," 25.

25. Jason Miller, "Holding Patterns: Some TNDs Struggle to Get Off the Ground," *The Town Paper* 4, no. 2 (2002).

26. Boym, *The Future of Nostalgia*, xiv.

27. Given the nature of advertising, the promotional materials discussed in this chapter are more ephemeral than the films. Brochures are printed in limited quantities and websites are updated to provide new information or visual variety. The materials examined here were collected between 2005 and 2010, and they represent a snapshot of the images and language dominating suburban promotions during that time.

28. The film *Far from Heaven*, discussed in detail in chapter 3, takes a similar approach, as it is set not in the actual 1950s but in the version of the 1950s imagined by melodramas of that era.

29. Wilson, *Nostalgia: Sanctuary of Meaning*, 68.

30. Lowenthal, *The Past Is a Foreign Country*, 8.

31. Ibid., 206.

32. George Lipsitz, *Time Passages: Collective Memory and American Popular Culture* (Minneapolis: University of Minnesota Press, 1990), 5.

33. Arjun Appadurai, *Modernity at Large* (Minneapolis: University of Minnesota Press, 1996), 78.

34. Henry Glassie, "Tradition," *Journal of American Folklore* 108 (1995): 398.

35. Eric Hobsbawm, "Introduction: Inventing Traditions," in *The Invention of Tradition*, ed. Eric Hobsbawm and Terrence Ranger (Cambridge: Cambridge University Press, 1983), 1.

36. Lipsitz, *Time Passages*, 5.

37. Lowenthal, *The Past Is a Foreign Country*, 206.

38. Ibid., 210, 214–219.

39. K. Till, "Neotraditional Towns and Urban Villages: The Cultural Production of a Geography of 'Otherness,'" *Environment and Planning D: Society and Space* 11 (1993): 713, 717.

40. Ibid., 718.

41. Davis, *Yearning for Yesterday*, 57.

42. Wilson, *Nostalgia: Sanctuary of Meaning*, 8.

43. The Seaside Institute, "The Seaside Institute—About Us," 2008, http://www.theseasideinstitute.org/core/item/page.aspx?s=8621.0.0.7801 (25 March 2008).

44. Scott Doyon, "Selling the New Urbanism," *The Town Paper* 5, no. 3 (2003), 1.

45. Ibid.

46. Jean Baudrillard, *Simulacra and Simulation*, trans. Sheila Faria Glaser (Ann Arbor: University of Michigan Press, 1994), 1.

47. Nezar AlSayyad, *Cinematic Urbanism: A History of the Modern from Reel to Real* (New York: Routledge, 2006), 226.

48. Robert Stam, *Reflexivity in Film and Literature: From Don Quixote to Jean-Luc Godard* (Ann Arbor, Mich.: UMI Research Press, 1985), 1.

49. Ibid.

CHAPTER 2   BACK YARD FENCES

1. While this particular case deals with fictional characters in scripted scenarios, the chance to look inside the private lives of other people offered

by this film is very similar to the pleasures offered by contemporary reality TV programs, documentaries, and news stories that make similarly private situations available for public consumption.

2. *HBO: Big Love*, 2007, http://www.hbo.com/biglove/ (18 April 2007).

3. Larry Lyon and Robyn Driskell, *The Community in Urban Society*, 2nd ed. (Long Grove, Ill.: Waveland Press, 2012), 6.

4. Ibid.

5. Ferdinand Tönnies, *Community and Civil Society*, trans. Jose Harris and Margaret Hollis (Cambridge: Cambridge University Press, 2001).

6. This argument would later reappear as a central component of the New Urbanist movement, as discussed in chapter 1.

7. Olmsted, Vaux and Co., "Preliminary Report upon the Proposed Suburban Village of Riverside, near Chicago" (New York, 1868), reprinted in *Civilizing American Cities: A Selection of Frederick Law Olmsted's Writings on City Landscapes*, ed. S. B. Sutton (Cambridge, Mass.: MIT Press, 1971), 295.

8. Jane Jacobs, *The Death and Life of Great American Cities* (New York: Random House, 1961), 55.

9. Lynn Spigel, *Make Room for TV: Television and the Family Ideal in Postwar America* (Chicago: University of Chicago Press, 1992), 128.

10. Dianne Harris, "Race, Class, and Privacy in the Ordinary Postwar House, 1945–1960," in *Landscape and Race in the United States*, ed. Richard H Schein (New York: Routledge, 2006), 128.

11. Brenwick Development Company, Inc., *A Commitment to Quality—Brenwick Development*, 2006, http://www.brenwick.com/brenwick_standards.aspx (19 August 2010). Emphasis in original.

12. For more discussion of the tension between public and private in suburban spaces, see Barbara M. Kelly, *Expanding the American Dream: Building and Rebuilding Levittown* (Albany: State University of New York Press, 1993), 69; Lynn Spigel, *Welcome to the Dreamhouse: Popular Media and Postwar Suburbs* (Durham, N.C.: Duke University Press, 2001), 32; and Kenneth T. Jackson, *Crabgrass Frontier: The Suburbanization of the United States* (New York: Oxford University Press, 1985), 47–61.

13. Robert Fishman, *Bourgeois Utopias: The Rise and Fall of Suburbia* (New York: Basic Books, 1987), 34.

14. Jackson, *Crabgrass Frontier*, 61–66.

15. Laura J. Miller argues that the suburban designs intended to encourage family togetherness end up cutting people off from the outside in such a way that it increases the strain on family members, thus making it impossible for them to live up to the ideal of familial perfection. Laura J. Miller, "Family Togetherness and the Suburban Ideal," *Sociological Forum* 10, no. 3 (1995): 393–418.

16. Many scholars have discussed the long and complicated relationship between the family and suburbia. See, for example, Margaret Marsh, *Suburban Lives* (New Brunswick, N.J.: Rutgers University Press, 1990), 21–56; Gwendolyn Wright, *Building the Dream: A Social History of Housing in America* (New York: Pantheon Books, 1981), 96–113; Constance Perin, *Belonging in America: Reading between the Lines* (Madison: University of Wisconsin Press, 1988); and Spigel, *Make Room for TV*, 11–35.

17. Lawrence M. Friedman, *Private Lives: Families, Individuals, and the Law* (Cambridge, Mass.: Harvard University Press, 2004), 189.

18. Jacqueline Klosek, *The War on Privacy* (Westport, Conn.: Praeger, 2007), 35.

19. Michael J. Shapiro, *For Moral Ambiguity: National Culture and the Politics of the Family* (Minneapolis: University of Minnesota Press, 2001), 1.

20. Robert Wuthnow, "The Family as Contested Terrain," in *Family Transformed: Religion, Values, and Society in American Life*, ed. Steven M. Tipton and John Witte Jr. (Washington, D.C.: Georgetown University Press, 2005), 73.

21. Sarah Harwood, *Family Fictions: Representations of the Family in 1980s Hollywood Cinema* (London: Macmillan, 1997), 38, 55.

22. Jeff Weintraub, "The Theory and Politics of the Public/Private Distinction," in *Public and Private in Thought and Practice: Perspectives on a Grand Dichotomy*, ed. Jeff Weintraub and Krishan Kumar (Chicago: University of Chicago Press, 1997), 7.

23. Although critics have noted that Habermas's public sphere excluded many individuals, like women and racial minorities, in its ideal form it would allow for rational discussion and the democratic exchange of ideas, encouraging civic involvement and potentially leading to positive social change. While Habermas leaves the private as a largely unexplored remainder category, Arendt offers more insights into the relationship between public and private spheres. She argues that the private sphere provides the foundation for the public sphere, because it is in the private realm that we establish the morals and values that are necessary for ethical and meaningful participation in the public realm. Jürgen Habermas, "The Public Sphere," in *Rethinking Popular Culture: Contemporary Perspectives in Cultural Studies*, ed. Chandra Mukerji and Michael Schudson (Berkeley: University of California Press, 1991), 398–404; Hannah Arendt, *The Human Condition* (Chicago: University of Chicago Press, 1958).

24. Philippe Ariès, *Centuries of Childhood: A Social History of Family Life* (New York: Vintage, 1962).

25. Weintraub, "Theory and Politics," 18.

26. Beate Rossler, *The Value of Privacy* (Cambridge: Polity Press, 2005), 5.

27. Ferdinand David Schoeman, *Privacy and Social Freedom* (Cambridge: Cambridge University Press, 1992), 1.

28. See, for example, Catharine MacKinnon, "Feminism Unmodified: Discourse on Life and Law," in *Privacy: Cases and Materials*, ed. Richard C. Turkington, George B. Trubow, and Anita L. Allen (Houston: John Marshall Publishing Company, 1992), 11–13.

29. Schoeman, *Privacy and Social Freedom*, 193.

30. Arendt, *The Human Condition*, 50, 72.

31. Shapiro, *For Moral Ambiguity*, 76.

32. Harris, "Race, Class, and Privacy," 138–148.

33. Perin, *Belonging in America*, 26.

34. Rossler, *The Value of Privacy*, 151.

35. While the Martins' proximity is initially just a threat to the Henricksons' privacy, the threat is elevated when a financially devastated Carl turns violent and takes out his rage on Bill, shooting him in the street in front of their houses.

36. Laud Humphreys, *Tearoom Trade: Impersonal Sex in Public Places*, enlarged ed. (New York: Aldine, 1975), 159, quoted in Phillip Bryan Harper, *Private Affairs: Critical Ventures in the Culture of Social Relations* (New York: New York University Press, 1999), 74.

37. Erving Goffman, *The Presentation of Self in Everyday Life* (Garden City, N.Y.: Doubleday Anchor Books, 1959), 112.

38. Rossler, *The Value of Privacy*, 149, 147.

39. Schoeman, *Privacy and Social Freedom*, 19.

40. Paul Fairfield, *Public/Private* (Lanham, Md.: Rowman & Littlefield, 2005), 20.

41. MacKinnon, "Feminism Unmodified," 12.

42. Harper, *Private Affairs*, x.

43. Stephanie Coontz, *The Way We Never Were: American Families and the Nostalgia Trap* (New York: Basic Books, 1992), 9.

44. Coontz notes, for example, that while American colonial families were very disciplined, they were highly unstable, largely due to high mortality rates. Additionally, men and women during this period shared the provider role as they worked together on family farms or in small household businesses. When wage labor outside the home replaced household production during the mid-nineteenth century, men took on the breadwinner label and women's roles (in middle-class white families) shifted to focus on domesticity. Increased industrialization during the last third of the nineteenth century brought a rise in child labor, and by the early twentieth century children made up a large part of the workforce in mines, factories, and textile mills. See Coontz, *The Way We Never Were*, 9–13; and Stephanie Coontz, *The Way We Really Are: Coming to Terms with America's Changing Families* (New York: HarperCollins, 1997), 55.

45. Coontz, *The Way We Never Were*, 25.

46. Coontz, *The Way We Really Are*, 37.

47. Coontz, *The Way We Never Were*, 31–35.

48. Coontz, *The Way We Really Are*, 161–170.

49. Ibid., 157.

CHAPTER 3   SUBURBAN CITIZENSHIP

1. Keally D. McBride, *Collective Dreams: Political Imagination and Community* (University Park: Pennsylvania State University Press, 2005), 88.

2. Graham Day, *Community and Everyday Life* (London: Routledge, 2006), 1.

3. Gerald W. Creed, "Reconsidering Community," in *The Seductions of Community: Emancipations, Oppressions, Quandaries*, ed. Gerald Creed (Santa Fe, N.M.: School of American Research Press, 2006), 7.

4. James C. Davis, *Fear, Myth and History: The Ranters and the Historians* (Cambridge: Cambridge University Press, 1986), 95. Emphasis in original.

5. Benedict Anderson, *Imagined Communities* (London: Verso, 1983).

6. Linda Bosniak, *The Citizen and the Alien: Dilemmas of Contemporary Membership* (Princeton, N.J.: Princeton University Press, 2006), 1.

7. Ken Plummer, *Intimate Citizenship: Private Decisions and Public Dialogues* (Seattle: University of Washington Press, 2003), 50.

8. Robert Fishman, *Bourgeois Utopias: The Rise and Fall of Suburbia* (New York: Basic Books, 1987), 4.

9. James W. Loewen, *Sundown Towns: A Hidden Dimension of American Racism* (New York: New Press, 2005), 90–115.

10. George Lipsitz, *The Possessive Investment in Whiteness: How White People Profit from Identity Politics*, revised and expanded ed. (Philadelphia: Temple University Press, 2006), 26.

11. Robert M. Fogelson, *Bourgeois Nightmares: Suburbia, 1870–1930* (New Haven, Conn.: Yale University Press, 2005), 95.

12. For a detailed discussion of HOLC and FHA practices and their effects on racial segregation, see Lizabeth Cohen, *A Consumer's Republic: The Politics of Mass Consumption in Postwar America* (New York: Vintage Books, 2003); George Lipsitz, *The Possessive Investment in Whiteness*; Kenneth T. Jackson, *Crabgrass Frontier: The Suburbanization of the United States* (New York: Oxford University Press, 1985).

13. Lipsitz, *Possessive Investment*, 27. See also "Real Estate: 'Exclusive . . . Restricted,'" *U.S. News & World Report*, 14 May 1948, 22–23.

14. Douglas S. Massey and Nancy A. Denton, *American Apartheid: Segregation and the Making of the Underclass* (Cambridge, Mass.: Harvard University Press, 1993), 8.

15. William J. Sadler, "The Suburban and the City Child," *Suburban Life*, February 1910, 66.

16. Constance Perin, *Belonging in America: Reading between the Lines* (Madison: University of Wisconsin Press, 1988), 37.

17. Nancy Larson, "Gay Families, Keep Out!" *The Advocate*, 18 July 2006, 34–35.

18. Wayne H. Brekhus, *Peacocks, Chameleons, Centaurs: Gay Suburbia and the Grammar of Social Identity* (Chicago: University of Chicago Press, 2003); Becky M. Nicolaides, *My Blue Heaven: Life and Politics in the Working-Class Suburbs of Los Angeles, 1920–1965* (Chicago: University of Chicago Press, 2002); Andrew Wiese, *Places of Their Own: African American Suburbanization in the Twentieth Century* (Chicago: University of Chicago Press, 2004).

19. William H. Frey, "Melting Pot Suburbs: A Study of Suburban Diversity," in *Redefining Urban and Suburban America: Evidence from Census 2000*, ed. Bruce Katz and Robert E. Lang (Washington, D.C.: Brookings Institution Press, 2003), 155–179; William H. Frey and Alan Berube, "City Families and Suburban Singles: An Emerging Household Story," in *Redefining Urban and Suburban America: Evidence from Census 2000*, ed. Bruce Katz and Robert E. Lang (Washington, D.C.: Brookings Institution Press, 2003), 257–289.

20. See, for example, Paul Willeman, "Distanciation and Douglas Sirk," *Screen* 12, no. 2 (1971): 63–67; Paul Willeman, "Towards an Analysis of the Sirkian System," *Screen* 12, no. 4 (1972/73): 128–133; Laura Mulvey, "Notes on Sirk and Melodrama," in *Home Is Where the Heart Is: Studies in Melodrama and the Woman's Film*, ed. Christine Gledhill (London: BFI, 1987), 75–79; and Barbara Klinger, *Melodrama and Meaning: History, Culture, and the Films of Douglas Sirk* (Bloomington: Indiana University Press, 1994).

21. Willemen, "Towards an Analysis," 132.

22. Ibid., 131.

23. Niall Richardson, "*Poison* in the Sirkian System: The Political Agenda of Todd Haynes's *Far from Heaven*," *Scope: An Online Journal of Film Studies*, no. 6 (2006): n.p.

24. Ibid.

25. Scott Higgins, "Orange and Blue, Desire and Loss: The Colour Score in *Far from Heaven*," in *The Cinema of Todd Haynes: All That Heaven Allows*, ed. James Morrison (London: Wallflower Press, 2007), 107.

26. Todd McGowan, "Relocating Our Enjoyment of the 1950s: The Politics of Fantasy in *Far from Heaven*," in *The Cinema of Todd Haynes: All That Heaven Allows*, ed. James Morrison (London: Wallflower Press, 2007), 115.

27. Making the scene even more ridiculous is the fact that the car pulling out of the Solis family driveway (presumably Carlos leaving for work) is heading toward the closed end of the cul-de-sac. Given that this is the opening scene of the pilot, viewers are not likely to know the geography of the street yet, but a knowledgeable viewer will realize that either the car was intended to

add action to the scene, or Carlos doesn't know how to get out of his own neighborhood.

28. The opening shot is re-created in reverse (the crane pulls up and out instead of pushing down and in) as the final shot of the episode, and it is even less believable the second time. At its widest, the shot reveals the space in front of six houses on Wisteria Lane, and within this relatively small space there are no fewer than twenty-two people visible. In the absence of a block party, this level of activity is clearly far-fetched.

29. Niall Richardson, "As Kamp as Bree: The Politics of Camp Reconsidered by *Desperate Housewives*," *Feminist Media Studies* 6, no. 2 (2006): 161.

30. See, for example, Susan Sontag, "Notes on Camp," in *A Susan Sontag Reader*, ed. Susan Sontag (London: Penguin, 1982), 105–119. This essay offers an early attempt to provide a definition and theorization of camp, and while it has been disputed and updated by various scholars, it remains a solid beginning for any discussion of the topic.

31. Brett Farmer, *Spectacular Passions: Cinema, Fantasy, Gay Male Spectatorships* (Durham, N.C.: Duke University Press, 2000), 113.

32. See Pamela Robertson, *Guilty Pleasures: Feminist Camp from Mae West to Madonna* (London: I. B. Tauris, 1996), and Richardson, "As Kamp as Bree."

33. Michel S. Laguerre, *Minoritized Space: An Inquiry into the Spatial Order of Things* (Berkeley: Institute of Governmental Studies Press, 1999), 9.

34. Alexander Doty, *Making Things Perfectly Queer: Interpreting Mass Culture* (Minneapolis: University of Minnesota Press, 1993), xv.

35. Aaron Betsky, *Queer Space: Architecture and Same-Sex Desire* (New York: William Morrow and Company, 1997), 5.

36. Ibid., 142.

37. Ibid., 159.

38. Dereka Rushbrook, "Cities, Queer Space, and the Cosmopolitan Tourist," *GLQ* 8, nos. 1–2 (2002): 190.

39. Sharon Willis, "The Politics of Disappointment: Todd Haynes Rewrites Douglas Sirk," *Camera Obscura* 18, no. 3 (2003): 152. Emphasis in original.

40. Gill Valentine, "Renegotiating the 'Heterosexual Street': Lesbian Productions of Space," in *Bodyspace: Destabilizing Geographies of Gender and Sexuality*, ed. Nancy Duncan (London: Routledge, 1996), 150.

41. Lauren Berlant, *The Queen of America Goes to Washington City: Essays on Sex and Citizenship* (Durham, N.C.: Duke University Press, 1997), 160.

42. Martin Dines, "Sacrilege in the Sitting Room: Contesting Suburban Domesticity in Contemporary Gay Literature," *Home Cultures* 2, no. 2 (2005): 180.

43. Richard Sennett, *The Uses of Disorder: Personal Identity and City Life* (New York: Vintage Books, 1971).

44. James Duncan and Nancy Duncan, *Landscapes of Privilege: The Politics of the Aesthetic in an American Suburb* (New York: Routledge, 2004), 5.

45. James Duncan and Nancy Duncan, "Aesthetics, Abjection, and White Privilege in Suburban New York," in *Landscape and Race in the United States*, ed. Richard H. Schein (New York: Routledge, 2006), 167.

46. Ibid., 217.

47. Brekhus, *Peacocks, Chameleons, Centaurs*, 28, 49.

48. Diane Richardson, "Sexuality and Citizenship," *Sociology* 32, no. 1 (1998): 89.

49. Ruth Lister, "Sexual Citizenship," in *Handbook of Citizenship Studies*, ed. Engin F. Isin and Bryan S. Turner (London: Sage, 2002), 192.

50. David Bell and Jon Binnie, *The Sexual Citizen: Queer Politics and Beyond* (Cambridge: Polity, 2000), 141.

51. Jeff R. Crump, "Producing and Enforcing the Geography of Hate: Race, Housing Segregation, and Housing-Related Hate Crimes in the United States," in *Spaces of Hate: Geographies of Discrimination and Intolerance in the U.S.A.*, ed. Colin Flint (New York: Routledge, 2004), 229.

52. Lipsitz, *Possessive Investment*, 7.

53. Ibid., viii.

54. Day, *Community and Everyday Life*, 163.

55. David Sibley, *Geographies of Exclusion: Society and Difference in the West* (London: Routledge, 1995), 112.

CHAPTER 4   DESPERATE HUSBANDS

1. Daphne Spain, *Gendered Spaces* (Chapel Hill: University of North Carolina Press, 1992).

2. Linda McDowell, *Gender, Identity, and Place: Understanding Feminist Geographies* (Minneapolis: University of Minnesota Press, 1999), 75. Other scholars have made similar arguments about the gendering of the domestic and professional spheres. See Jane Rendell, *The Pursuit of Pleasure: Gender, Space, and Architecture in Regency London* (New Brunswick, N.J.: Rutgers University Press, 2002), 131; Witold Rybczynski, *Home: A Short History of an Idea* (New York: Viking, 1986), 70.

3. See, for example, the recent films involving Spider-Man (2002, 2004, 2007, 2012), Batman (2005, 2008, 2012), or the X-Men (2000, 2003, 2006, 2009, 2011); the *Pirates of the Caribbean* films (2003, 2006, 2007, 2011); the Jason Bourne films (2002, 2004, 2007, 2012); and the *Mission: Impossible* series (1996, 2000, 2006, 2011).

4. R. W. Connell, *Masculinities*, 2nd ed. (Berkeley: University of California Press, 2005), 77.

5. Ibid., 79.

6. Ibid., 78.

7. Ibid., 80.

8. See, for example, Demetrakis Z. Demetriou, "Connell's Concept of Hegemonic Masculinity: A Critique," *Theory and Society* 30 (2001): 337–361; and Tony Coles, "Negotiating the Field of Masculinity: The Production and Reproduction of Multiple Dominant Masculinities," *Men and Masculinities* 12, no. 1 (2009): 30–44.

9. Michael S. Kimmel, *Manhood in America: A Cultural History*, 2nd ed. (New York: Oxford University Press, 2006), 4.

10. Ibid., 5.

11. See also Tim Edwards, *Cultures of Masculinity* (London: Routledge, 2006); Richard Howson, *Challenging Hegemonic Masculinity* (London: Routledge, 2006); Harvey C. Mansfield, *Manliness* (New Haven, Conn.: Yale University Press, 2006); Angus McLaren, *The Trials of Masculinity: Policing Sexual Boundaries, 1870–1930* (Chicago: University of Chicago Press, 1997); George L. Mosse, *The Image of Man: The Creation of Modern Masculinity* (New York: Oxford University Press, 1996).

12. Susan Faludi, *Backlash: The Undeclared War against Women* (New York: Anchor Books, 1992); Susan Faludi, *Stiffed: The Betrayal of the American Man* (New York: William Morrow, 1999); Susan Faludi, *The Terror Dream: Fear and Fantasy in Post-9/11 America* (New York: Metropolitan Books, 2007).

13. Kenneth MacKinnon, *Representing Men: Maleness and Masculinity in the Media* (New York: Arnold, 2003), 19.

14. Kimmel, *Manhood in America*, 223.

15. Stacy Takacs, "Jessica Lynch and the Regeneration of American Identity and Power Post-9/11," *Feminist Media Studies* 5, no. 3 (2005): 299.

16. Laura J. Shepherd, "Veiled References: Constructions of Gender in the Bush Administration Discourse on the Attacks on Afghanistan Post-9/11," *International Feminist Journal of Politics* 8, no. 1 (2006): 21–23.

17. Rebecca A. Adelman, "Sold(i)ering Masculinity: Photographing the Coalition's Male Soldiers," *Men and Masculinities* 11, no. 3 (2009): 261.

18. Patricia Leigh Brown, "Heavy Lifting Required: The Return of Manly Men," *New York Times*, 28 October 2001, sec. 4; Julie Drew, "Identity Crisis: Gender, Public Discourse, and 9/11," *Women and Language* 27, no. 2 (2004): 71–73; Takacs, "Jessica Lynch," 300–301; Shepherd, "Veiled References," 25–28.

19. Takacs, "Jessica Lynch," 307.

20. Drew, "Identity Crisis," 76.

21. Steven Cohan, *Masked Men: Masculinity and the Movies in the Fifties* (Bloomington: Indiana University Press, 1997), 38.

22. Susan Jeffords, *Hard Bodies: Hollywood Masculinity in the Reagan Era* (New Brunswick, N.J.: Rutgers University Press, 1994), 166.

23. Faludi, *The Terror Dream*.

24. George W. Bush, "The Fifth Anniversary of September 11, 2001," *Vital Speeches of the Day* 72, no. 24 (2006): 659.

25. Faludi, *The Terror Dream*, 8, 23.

26. Paul Smith, *Clint Eastwood: A Cultural Production* (Minneapolis: University of Minnesota Press, 1993), 156.

27. Mark Gallagher, *Action Figures: Men, Action Films, and Contemporary Adventure Narratives* (New York: Palgrave Macmillan, 2006), 67.

28. The story of *The Sound of Music* offers an interesting parallel to *The Pacifier* in that both Maria and Shane fill in for an absent mother and try to bring discipline to a bunch of unruly children. This is emphasized by the fact that the mother in *The Pacifier* is named Julie Plummer, a name that combines the names of Julie Andrews and Christopher Plummer, the stars of the big-screen version of *The Sound of Music* (1965). Thanks to Eric Schramm for bringing this to my attention.

29. Connell, *Masculinities*, 78.

30. Ibid., 119.

31. *American Beauty* offers an example of what can happen when a military man's violent tendencies are not contained successfully. Colonel Fitts, whose violent streak is ignited by the reappearance of repressed homosexual desires, beats his son and murders his neighbor in fits of rage.

32. Susan Jeffords, *The Remasculinization of America: Gender and the Vietnam War* (Bloomington: Indiana University Press, 1989), xiv.

33. Tania Modleski makes a similar argument about the men in *Three Men and a Baby*. Tania Modleski, *Feminism without Women* (New York: Routledge, 1991), 88.

34. Peter Kramer, "Would You Take Your Child to See This Film? The Cultural and Social Work of the Family-Adventure Movie," in *Contemporary Hollywood Cinema*, ed. Steve Neale and Murray Smith (London: Routledge, 1998), 294.

35. Peter Brooks, *The Melodramatic Imagination: Balzac, Henry James, Melodrama, and the Mode of Excess* (New Haven, Conn.: Yale University Press, 1976); Thomas Elsaesser, "Tales of Sound and Fury: Observations on the Family Melodrama," in *Home Is Where the Heart Is: Studies in Melodrama and the Woman's Film*, ed. Christine Gledhill (London: BFI, 1987), 43–69; see also Barbara Klinger, *Melodrama and Meaning: History, Culture, and the Films of Douglas Sirk* (Bloomington: Indiana University Press, 1994); Nina Liebman, *Living Room Lectures: The Fifties Family in Film and Television* (Austin: University of Texas Press, 1995), 15–21.

36. Liebman, *Living Room Lectures*, 6.

37. Elsaesser, *"Tales of Sound and Fury,"* 61–62.

38. Ibid., 55–56.

39. Gallagher, *Action Figures*, 60–66; Linda Williams, "Melodrama Revised," in *Refiguring American Film Genres*, ed. Nick Browne (Berkeley: University of California Press, 1998), 42–88.

40. See Jeffords, *Hard Bodies*; Yvonne Tasker, *Spectacular Bodies: Gender, Genre, and the Action Cinema* (New York: Routledge, 1993); Chris Holmlund, "Masculinity as Multiple Masquerade: The 'Mature' Stallone and the Stallone Clone," in *Screening the Male: Exploring Masculinities in Hollywood Cinema*, ed. Steven Cohan and Ina Rae Hark (London: Routledge, 1993), 213–229.

41. See Jeffords, *Hard Bodies.*

42. Ben Singer, *Melodrama and Modernity: Early Sensational Cinema and Its Contexts* (New York: Columbia University Press, 2001), 222.

43. Tasker, *Spectacular Bodies*, 149.

44. Liebman, *Living Room Lectures*, 218.

45. Christine Gledhill, "Rethinking Genre," in *Reinventing Film Studies*, ed. Christine Gledhill and Linda Williams (New York: Oxford University Press, 2000), 225.

46. Connell, *Masculinities*, 78–80.

47. See the episode of *Mission: Impossible* entitled "The Carriers" (1966); *The Man from U.N.C.L.E.* episode entitled "The Suburbia Affair" (1967); *The X-Files* episode "Arcadia" (1999); and the *Alias* episode "Welcome to Liberty Village" (2005).

48. This is echoed in the 2010 news reports about the Russian spies living in the United States. After the spies were discovered, many news stories emphasized how they had hidden themselves in the suburbs so that they could go unnoticed. See, for example, Peter Applebome, "Suburban Life, Secret or Open, Is Complicated," *New York Times*, 1 July 2010, A23; Manny Fernandez and Fernanda Santos, "Dogs, Children, Gardening: Couples Accused as Spies Were Suburbs Personified," *New York Times*, 30 June 2010, A10.

49. Holmlund, "Masculinity as Multiple Masquerade," 214.

50. Judith Halberstam, *Female Masculinity* (Durham, N.C.: Duke University Press, 1998), 2.

51. Elsaesser, "Tales of Sound and Fury," 47.

52. Laura Mulvey, "Notes on Sirk and Melodrama," in *Home Is Where the Heart Is: Studies in Melodrama and the Woman's Film*, ed. Christine Gledhill (London: BFI, 1987), 76.

53. Gallagher, *Action Figures*, 67.

54. Ibid., 69.

55. Robert Ray, *A Certain Tendency of the Hollywood Cinema, 1930–1980* (Princeton, N.J.: Princeton University Press, 1985), 312.

56. Ibid., 326.

CHAPTER 5   PROTECTING THE SUBURBAN LIFESTYLE

1. Mary Beth Haralovich, "Sitcoms and Suburbs: Positioning the 1950s Homemaker," *Quarterly Review of Film & Video* 11 (1989): 74.

2. After Nancy and her family move away from Agrestic, the focus on suburban life ceases to be a primary concern for the series, and therefore my comments focus primarily on the first three seasons.

3. Dolores Hayden, *Redesigning the American Dream: Gender, Housing, and Family Life*, revised and expanded ed. (New York: W. W. Norton, 2002), 50.

4. Lizabeth Cohen, *A Consumer's Republic: The Politics of Mass Consumption in Postwar America* (New York: Vintage Books, 2003), 195. For further discussion of the suburban home as a commodity and a space for consumption, see Jackson Lears, *Fables of Abundance: A Cultural History of Advertising in America* (New York: Basic Books, 1994), 124–126; and Gary Cross, *An All-Consuming Century: Why Commercialism Won in Modern America* (New York: Columbia University Press, 2000), 86–87.

5. Hayden, *Redesigning the American Dream*, 50.

6. Betty Friedan, *The Feminine Mystique*, 5th ed. (New York: W. W. Norton, 2001), 206. Emphasis in original.

7. Ibid., 209–211.

8. Nina Leibman, *Living Room Lectures: The Fifties Family in Film and Television* (Austin: University of Texas Press, 1995), 61.

9. Ibid., 109.

10. Gerard Jones, *Honey, I'm Home! Sitcoms: Selling the American Dream* (New York: St. Martin's Press, 1992), 95.

11. George Lipsitz, *Time Passages: Collective Memory and American Popular Culture* (Minneapolis: University of Minnesota Press, 1990), 39.

12. Barbara Ehrenreich, *Fear of Falling: The Inner Life of the Middle Class* (New York: Pantheon Books, 1989), 3.

13. Jeffrey M. Hornstein, *A Nation of Realtors: A Cultural History of the Twentieth-Century American Middle Class* (Durham, N.C.: Duke University Press, 2005), 35.

14. Ibid., 202.

15. Robert H. Frank, *Falling Behind: How Rising Inequality Harms the Middle Class* (Berkeley: University of California Press, 2007), 8–9.

16. Ibid., 43.

17. Alladi Venkatesh, "Changing Consumption Patterns," in *Postsuburban California: The Transformation of Orange County Since World War II*, ed. Rob Kling, Spencer Olin, and Mark Poster (Berkeley: University of California Press, 1995), 159.

18. Ehrenreich, *Fear of Falling*, 15.

19. Diana Kendall, *Framing Class: Media Representations of Wealth and Poverty in America* (Lanham, Md.: Rowman & Littlefield, 2005), 206.

20. Department of Housing and Urban Development, Office of Policy Development and Research, "Report to Congress on the Root Causes of the Foreclosure Crisis" (Washington, D.C.: Government Printing Office, 2010), 3.

21. Administrative Office of the United States Courts, "2010 Report of Statistics Required by the Bankruptcy Abuse Prevention and Consumer Protection Act of 2005" (Washington, D.C.: Government Printing Office, 2011), 5; Administrative Office of the United States Courts, "2009 Report of Statistics Required by the Bankruptcy Abuse Prevention and Consumer Protection Act of 2005" (Washington, D.C.: Government Printing Office, 2010), 5.

22. Catherine Rampell, "Report Details Woes of Student Loan Debt," *New York Times*, 20 July 2012, B7.

23. Tamar Lewin, "Student Loan Default Rates Rise Sharply in Past Year," *New York Times*, 13 September 2011, A14.

24. U.S. Census Bureau, "Income, Poverty and Health Insurance Coverage in the United States: 2010," 2011, http://www.census.gov/hhes/www/poverty/data/incpovhlth/2010/index.html (20 October 2011).

25. See, for example, Newt Gingrich's book *To Save America: Stopping Obama's Secular-Socialist Machine* (Washington, D.C.: Regnery Publishing, 2011).

26. Tea Party Patriots, Inc., "Tea Party Patriots Mission Statement and Core Values," 2010, teapartypatriots.org/Mission.aspx (20 October 2011).

27. Elizabeth Kneebone and Emily Garr, "The Suburbanization of Poverty: Trends in Metropolitan America, 2000–2008" (Washington, D.C.: Brookings Institution, 2010), 1.

28. Keith J. Hayward, *City Limits: Crime, Consumer Culture and the Urban Experience* (London: Glasshouse Press, 2004), 161. Emphasis in original.

29. John Archer, *Architecture and Suburbia: From English Villa to American Dream House, 1690–2000* (Minneapolis: University of Minnesota Press, 2005), 250.

30. Messner and Rosenfeld, *Crime and the American Dream*, x.

31. Hornstein, *A Nation of Realtors*, 7.

32. Robert K. Merton, "Social Structure and Anomie," *American Sociological Review* 3 (1938): 672–682.

33. Yvonne Jewkes, *Media and Crime* (London: Sage, 2004), 14.

34. Messner and Rosenfeld, *Crime and the American Dream*, x.

35. Ibid., 3.

36. Thomas Schatz, *Hollywood Genres* (Philadelphia: Temple University Press, 1981), 84.

37. Jack Shadoian, *Dreams and Dead Ends: The American Gangster/Crime Film* (Cambridge, Mass.: MIT Press, 1977), 5.

38. Messner and Rosenfeld make a similar argument about the drug trade. See *Crime and the American Dream*, 92.

39. Thomas Leitch, *Crime Films* (New York: Cambridge University Press, 2002), 265.

40. Nicole Rafter, *Shots in the Mirror: Crime Films and Society*, 2nd ed. (New York: Oxford University Press, 2006), 214.

41. John Sumser, *Morality and Social Order in the Television Crime Drama* (London: McFarland & Company, 1996), 161.

42. Carol Aronovici, "Suburban Development," *Annals of the American Academy of Political and Social Science* 51 (1914): 237.

43. Kenneth T. Jackson, *Crabgrass Frontier: The Suburbanization of the United States* (New York: Oxford University Press, 1985), 70.

44. Danilo Yanich, "Crime Creep: Urban and Suburban Crime on Local TV News," *Journal of Urban Affairs* 26, no. 5 (2004): 547.

45. Steve Greenfield and Guy Osborn, "Film Lawyers: Above and Beyond the Law," in *Criminal Visions: Media Representations of Crime and Justice*, ed. Paul Mason (Portland, Ore.: Willan, 2003), 241.

46. Leitch, *Crime Films*, 248.

47. Elayne Rapping, *Law and Justice as Seen on TV* (New York: New York University Press, 2003), 47.

48. Gray Cavender and Sarah K. Deutsch, "*CSI* and Moral Authority: The Police and Science," *Crime Media Culture* 3, no. 1 (2007): 78.

49. Jonathan Rayner, "Masculinity, Morality, and Action: Michael Mann and the Heist Movie," in Mason, *Criminal Visions*, 87.

50. J. A. Lindstrom, "Work and Genre: *Heat*," *Jump Cut* 43 (2000): 23.

51. Ironically, Nancy's previous willingness to throw herself completely into motherhood is what ultimately led to her criminal acts. As a young wife, she left college just short of completing her degree so that she could devote herself full-time to raising her sons. But being the model wife and mother left her with no marketable skills, leading her to find alternative means of providing for her family after her husband's death. In this way, Nancy's criminal status can be seen as the result of her efforts to live up to traditional ideals of what a good mother should be.

52. Lindstrom, "Work and Genre," 25.

53. Messner and Rosenfeld, *Crime and the American Dream*, 8. Emphasis in original.

54. Robert Ray, *A Certain Tendency of the Hollywood Cinema, 1930–1980* (Princeton, N.J.: Princeton University Press, 1985), 312, 326.

CONCLUSION

1. Dolores Hayden, *Building Suburbia: Green Fields and Urban Growth, 1820–2000* (New York: Vintage Books, 2003).

2. Joel Garreau, *Edge City: Life on the New Frontier* (New York: Anchor Books, 1992).

3. Robert Fishman, *Bourgeois Utopias: The Rise and Fall of Suburbia* (New York: Basic Books, 1987).

4. Robert E. Lang, *Edgeless Cities: Exploring the Elusive Metropolis* (Washington, D.C.: Brookings Institution Press, 2003).

5. Hayden, *Building Suburbia*.

6. Kenneth T. Jackson, *Crabgrass Frontier: The Suburbanization of the United States* (New York: Oxford University Press, 1985), 267.

7. Fishman, *Bourgeois Utopias*, 190.

8. Shaun Huston, "Filming Postbourgeois Suburbia: *Office Space* and the New American Suburb," *Journal of Popular Culture* 42, no. 3 (2009): 498.

9. For additional assistance with such questions, I turn also to comments made by the creators of some of these texts. These statements, offered primarily in interviews and DVD commentary tracks, offer insights into the motivations and thought processes involved in the development of many recent suburban narratives. I do not mean to suggest that the creators' intentions provide a definitive interpretation of the texts being examined, but rather I offer them as one element among many that come together to shape the negotiated meanings of the narratives being examined.

10. Roger Silverstone, "Introduction," in *Visions of Suburbia*, ed. Roger Silverstone (London: Routledge, 1997), 4.

11. While the climate and foliage of Wisteria Lane clearly suggest Southern California, the license plates on all vehicles identify them as being from the Eagle State, thus avoiding location specificity.

12. Will Scheffer, phone interview with the author, 27 July 2012.

13. Wayne H. Brekhus, *Peacocks, Chameleons, Centaurs: Gay Suburbia and the Grammar of Social Identity* (Chicago: University of Chicago Press, 2003), 6.

14. William Schneider, "The Suburban Century Begins," *Atlantic*, July 1992, 33–44.

15. Seth C. McKee and Daron R. Shaw, "Suburban Voting in Presidential Elections," *Presidential Studies Quarterly* 33, no. 1 (2003): 125–144.

16. Jim Leonard, phone interview with the author, 24 July 2012.

17. Gary Ross, director's commentary, *Pleasantville* DVD.

18. Will Scheffer, phone interview.

19. Ibid.

20. Jim Leonard, phone interview.

21. Will Scheffer, phone interview.

22. Michael Fleeman, "The Original Desperate Housewife," *People*, October 2005, 60–62.

23. "Q&A," *Marie Claire*, November 2011, 150.

24. Sam Mendes, director's commentary, *Revolutionary Road* DVD.

25. Todd Haynes, director's commentary, *Far from Heaven* DVD.

26. Will Scheffer, phone interview.

27. Jim Leonard, phone interview.

28. Marc Cherry, interviewed in "Dressing Wisteria Lane" (bonus feature), *Desperate Housewives* DVD, season 1, disc 3.

INDEX

action films, 20; and masculinity, 27, 142–143, 175; and *Mr. & Mrs. Smith*, 163–164, 165, 169–170, 172–173, 177, 178; and *The Pacifier*, 142, 154, 177, 178
Addams Family, The (1964–1966), 12
adultery, 14; in *American Beauty*, 72, 89, 95; in *Far from Heaven*, 32, 121; and suburban façade, 228; in *Weeds*, 197
Adventures in Babysitting (1987), 198–199
Adventures of Ozzie and Harriet, The (1952–1966), 2, 12, 33, 113, 168, 184
advertising, 12, 13, 20, 21, 25, 182, 183. *See also* promotional materials
Afghanistan War, 147
African Americans, 8, 59; in *Desperate Housewives*, 26, 133, 135–136, 138; in *Far from Heaven*, 26, 119, 122–123, 129–130, 135, 138
Alabama, 108
Alias (2001–2006), 166, 170–171
Aliens (1986), 165
Ali: Fear Eats the Soul (1974), 115
Allen, Joan, 48–49, 71
All That Heaven Allows (1955), 13, 115, 168
AlSayyad, Nezar, 67
Amelia Park, Fla., 45
American Beauty (1999), 17, 32–33, 164, 200, 221, 223, 224, 226; adultery in, 72, 89; death in, 95, 97; families in, 18–19, 26, 71–72, 78–81, 89–90, 94, 100; front vs. back stages in, 89–90, 92, 93, 95; homosexuality in, 95, 114, 249n31; and Lowe's advertising, 24; marriage in, 95, 97; masculinity in, 142; and *Mr. & Mrs. Smith*, 170, 173; murder in, 2, 72; neighbors in, 85–86, 87–88; opening scene of, 1, 2; promotional materials, 73; public and private in, 26, 69–70, 71–72, 78–81, 83, 94–95, 97, 98, 100, 102; secrecy in, 95, 97, 100; sexuality in, 69, 228; suburban façade in, 18–19, 90, 100, 118; and suburban images, 73; and suburban intertext, 21; and suburbs, 102, 212; unresolved contradictions of, 230; visibility in, 85–86, 94; women in, 173

American Dream, 181, 186; and capitalism, 231; in *Close to Home*, 27, 209, 210, 230; contradictory messages about, 209; and crime, 193, 230; and exclusion vs. inclusion, 26; and financial struggles, 219; as goal and problem, 229; and homes, 4, 193; and Lowe's advertising, 24; meanings of, 192–193; and parenting, 208; and suburban façade, 205; and suburban intertext, 23; and suburbs, 212; in *Weeds*, 27–28, 182, 187, 192, 193–194, 195, 209; and work, 193, 210, 231
American Home (magazine), 12
Anderson, Benedict, 107
Andrews, Julie, 249n28
Aniston, Jennifer, 221
apartment complexes, 213, 220
apartment plots, 13–14, 15
Appadurai, Arjun, 52
Archer, John, 192
Arendt, Hannah, 78, 84, 242n23
Ariès, Philippe, 78–79
Arizona, 108
Aronovici, Carol, 198
Arrested Development (2003–2006), 180, 192
Asian Americans, 26, 190
Asian immigrants, 58, 138
assimilation, 132–136, 138
automobiles, 214; and development of suburbs, 6, 7; in *The End of Suburbia*, 215, 216; in *Office Space*, 212, 213, 220–221; and public and private, 95; in *Radiant City*, 217
autonomy, 92–93, 94, 97

Bachelor in Paradise (1961), 13
Bachmann, Michele, 23, 67
Back to the Future (1985), 113
Baker, Dylan, 71
Baudrillard, Jean, 67
Beauty and the Beast (1991), 149
Beck, Glenn, 67
bedroom communities, 220, 222, 226
Beecher, Catharine, 75, 111–112

Bening, Annette, 72
Bentley, Wes, 69
Berlant, Lauren, 125
Betsky, Aaron, 120, 121
Beuka, Robert, 21
Bewitched (1964–1972), 12
Big Daddy (1999), 152, 155
Big Love (2006–2011), 3, 17, 72, 223, 224; and Christian conservative movement, 225; and early sitcoms, 226; family in, 26, 71–72, 78, 81–83, 94, 95–97, 101, 225, 228; as fantasy, 227; front vs. back stages in, 90–91, 92–93; homosexuals in, 114; lack of closure in, 230; masculinity in, 142; murder in, 102; neighbors in, 85, 86, 87–88; promotional materials, 73; public and private in, 26, 71–72, 78, 81–83, 94, 95–97, 98, 101–102, 230; suburban façade in, 90–91, 118; and suburban images, 73; visibility in, 85, 86–87, 94
Birch, Thora, 69
Birther Movement, 108
Bookout, Lloyd, 38, 41
Bosniak, Linda, 107
Boston Legal (2004–2008), 200
Boym, Svetlana, 39, 41
Boys N the Hood (1991), 16
Brady Bunch, The (1969–1974), 180
Brave One, The (2007), 207
Breaking Bad (2008–2013), 3, 142, 180, 192, 200, 207, 219
Brekhus, Wayne, 131, 223
Brenwick homes, 75
Brookings Institution, 187
Brooks, Peter, 164
Bruckheimer, Jerry, 204
Buffy the Vampire Slayer (1997–2003), 166
'Burbs, The (1989), 113
Bush, George W., 107, 147, 150, 162
Bush administration, 156–157, 160, 177, 178
business, 185; in *Close to Home*, 179; in *Desperate Housewives*, 134; in *Far from Heaven*, 130; and gangsters, 194; and neotraditional town planners, 41; in *Weeds*, 182, 190, 191–192, 194–195, 210. *See also* work/labor

Cagney, James, 206
Calthorpe Associates, 65
Campoli, Julie, 37
camp sensibility, 117, 125, 127–128
capitalism, 186, 187, 231
Capturing the Friedmans (2003), 203, 217
Carrey, Jim, 33
Cat on a Hot Tin Roof (1958), 164
Cavender, Gray, 204
Celebration, Fla., 37–38
Chan, Jackie, 165, 170
Charlie's Angels (2000), 166
Charlie's Angels: Full Throttle (2003), 166
Chavira, Ricardo Antonio, 105

Cheever, John, 13
Cherry, Marc, 125, 127, 226, 227
Chicago (2002), 207
children: in *Capturing the Friedmans*, 217; in *Close to Home*, 207, 208; and consumption, 184; in *Desperate Housewives*, 126; in domestic melodramas, 168; and fear of sex offenders, 202–203; in *The Kids Are All Right*, 222; and labor, 243n44; outsourcing of care for, 208; in *The Pacifier*, 152, 155, 156, 157–159, 161; suburbs as ideal for, 112; and utopian vision of suburbs, 11; in *Weeds*, 207–208; and West Clay promotional video, 30; and zoning laws, 112. *See also* families; fathers; mothers
Christianity, 53
Chronicles of Riddick, The (2004), 153
cities: complexities of, 13–15; crime in, 8, 11, 28, 198, 200; in *Desperate Housewives*, 123–124, 125; in film noir, 19, 20; flight to suburbs from, 109; and Gesellschaft, 74, 106; and homosexuals, 112; and Jacobs, 74; joy and excitement of, 16–17; and New Urbanism, 36, 37; non-whites in, 113; and nuclear family, 75; population of, 4, 8; and privacy, 84; problems of, 8, 11, 16, 28; suburbs as contrast to, 8, 11, 15–16, 28, 106, 198, 237n32; and transportation, 5–6
citizenship, 9, 137, 224; cultural, 108; debates over, 107–108; in *Far from Heaven* and *Desperate Housewives*, 27, 107, 137, 138, 139; and public sphere, 78; and suburban intertext, 23
civil rights movement, 111, 142
Clinton, Hillary, 23
Closer, The (2005–2012), 207
Close to Home (2005–2007), 3, 194, 224–225; American Dream in, 27, 209, 210, 230; crime in, 27–28, 179, 180–181, 198, 200, 201–205, 210, 211, 230; as fantasy, 227; homes in, 27, 179, 198, 199, 204–205, 210; "Land of Opportunity" episode, 179, 204–205; middle class in, 28, 180, 181, 210, 211; morality in, 181, 200, 201–205, 210, 211; mothers in, 202, 205–209, 210, 225; "The Rapist Next Door" episode, 202, 203–204, 205, 208; suburban façade in, 181; "Suburban Prostitution" episode, 201, 204, 205; women in, 181, 205–209, 210; work in, 181, 205–209, 210–211, 225
Cohan, Steven, 148, 150, 155; *Masked Men*, 149
Cohen, Lizabeth, 183
Cold War, 148, 149
Columbine High School, 200
comedy/humor, 20; in *Big Love*, 230; in *Desperate Housewives*, 118, 134, 230; in *Mr. Blandings Builds His Dream House*, 13; in *Mr. & Mrs. Smith*, 145, 169, 174, 177,

178; in *The Pacifier*, 145, 155, 156, 177, 178, 229; in *Weeds*, 181, 195, 200, 230

comic books, 16

communities, 10; actual lived vs. imagined national, 137; and apartment plots, 14; and Celebration, Fla., 38; and citizenship, 107–108; conceptions of, 105–107; in *Desperate Housewives*, 104, 137, 138–139; and differences, 231; and exclusion vs. inclusion, 26, 104, 106–107, 137; in *Far from Heaven*, 104, 137, 138–139; as flawless, 128; and Gemeinschaft, 74; homogeneous, 128, 137, 138, 229, 231; imagined, 107; as inherently positive, 106; interdependence in, 74; and Mount Laurel, Ala., 103, 137; and national identity, 107; neotraditional, 38, 39, 40, 41–45, 50, 51, 62, 63, 65, 67; and neotraditional town planners, 41; and New Urbanism, 35; and nostalgia, 103; and Olmsted, 74; park-like, 6; participation in, 26; private management of, 37; promotional materials, 103–104, 106, 137; purified, 128; small-scale, 107; and suburban intertext, 23; and suburban perfection, 4; utopian, 8, 12; and The Villages promotion, 44–45. *See also* neighbors

conformity, 9, 92, 104, 107, 160; in *American Beauty*, 100; in *Desperate Housewives*, 105; and dystopian vision of suburbs, 11; in *Weeds*, 188

Congress for the New Urbanism, 36, 65

Connell, R. W., 144–145, 146, 158

Connery, Sean, 165

conservatism, 29; and culture wars, 53; and family, 73, 77, 160; and nostalgia, 66–67; in *Pleasantville*, 225; and public and private, 73, 102; and suburban intertext, 23; and suburban myth, 231; and suburbs as utopia, 28

consumption: in *Close to Home*, 181; and credit, 185; in *The End of Suburbia*, 215; happiness through, 183; and Lowe's advertising, 25; and 1950s sitcoms, 183; right to, 191; and social class, 184; and suburbs, 182–183, 184; and television sitcoms, 183–184; and utopian vision of suburbs, 12; in *Weeds*, 180, 181, 182, 187–191, 209, 211; and women, 183

Cookout, The (2004), 2, 114

Coontz, Stephanie: *The Way We Never Were*, 99–100, 243n44; *The Way We Really Are*, 99–100, 243n44

Cooper, Chris, 70

Cosby Show, The (1984–1992), 113

Cranston, Bryan, 207

credit system, 185

Creed, Gerald, 106

crime, 109; and American Dream, 193, 230; in cities, 8, 11, 28, 198, 200; in *Close to Home*, 27–28, 179, 180–181, 198,

200, 201–205, 210, 211, 230; in *CSI*, 204; in *Desperate Housewives*, 123–124; in *Far from Heaven*, 135; and suburbia, 198, 200; in *Weeds*, 182, 187, 191–192, 193–197, 200, 204, 209, 210, 211, 253n51. *See also* law

crime comedies, 195

crime narratives, 195, 206, 207

Cross, Marcia, 105

Crump, Jeff, 132–133

CSI (2000–), 204

Culp, Steven, 124

Curtis, Jamie Lee, 163

Damages (2007–2012), 207

Dangerous Minds (1996), 16

Dateline NBC, "To Catch a Predator" series, 203

Davis, Fred, 40, 63

Davis, James, 106–107

Davis, Viola, 129

Day, Graham, 106, 137

Delany, Dana, 105

Democratic Party, 186, 224

Dennis the Menace (1959–1963), 12

Denton, Nancy, 111

Department of Housing and Urban Development (HUD), 37

Desk Set (1957), 14

Desperate Housewives (2004–2012), 3, 17, 32–33, 114, 190, 202, 223, 224; African Americans in, 26, 133, 135–136, 138; artificial present in, 117; assimilation in, 133–136; camp sensibility in, 117–118, 125, 127–128; Cherry on, 226; and citizenship, 107; "Come in Stranger" episode, 124; community in, 104, 137, 138–139; ethnicity in, 104–105, 134–135; exclusion vs. inclusion in, 26–27, 104, 109, 119, 123–128, 134, 137–138, 139–140; families in, 126, 127, 226; as fantasy, 227; and Gemeinschaft and Gesellschaft, 106; "Guilty" episode, 124; heteronormativity in, 105, 126, 127, 132; homosexuality in, 26, 127, 130, 131–132; immigrants in, 26; lack of closure in, 230; Latinos in, 26, 133–135, 138; and Lowe's advertising, 24; minority groups in, 26–27; "My Husband, the Pig" episode, 209; opening scenes of, 1–2, 116–117, 245–246n27, 246n28; promotional materials, 117; and public vs. private, 71, 230; and *The Real Housewives of Orange County*, 218; sexuality in, 228; style of, 116–118; suburban façade in, 18, 118, 125; and suburban intertext, 21; and suburbs, 212; suicide in, 2; visibility in, 128, 130, 131–132, 136, 138; wealthy class in, 124, 132, 133; women in, 117–118; "You Gotta Get a Gimmick" episode, 18, 133–134

detective dramas, 16

detective novels, 206

detective series, 170–171
Deutsch, Sarah, 204
Dexter (2006–2013), 171, 196
Dickinson, Greg, 239n16
Diesel, Vin, 143, 153, 165
Dimendberg, Edward, 20
Dines, Martin, 21, 126
directors, 224, 225–226
Disney World, 37–38
Disturbia (2007), 2–3, 71, 227
Dobbs, Lou, *War on the Middle Class*, 185–186
documentary films, 215
Dodgeball (2004), 174
domestic comedies, 15
domestic help, 208
domesticity, 150; and apartment plots, 14; in *Close to Home*, 27, 210; and masculinity, 27; in *Mr. & Mrs. Smith*, 170, 178; in *The Pacifier*, 151, 154–155, 156, 159, 160, 178, 229; and wage labor, 243n44; in *Weeds*, 210. *See also* homes
domestic melodrama. *See* family/domestic melodrama
Donna Reed Show, The (1958–1966), 12, 168, 179, 183, 226
Donovan, Martin, 196
Douglas, William, 12
Downing, Andrew Jackson, 75
Doyon, Scott, 65
DREAM (Development, Relief, and Education for Alien Minors) Act, 108
drugs, 212; in *American Beauty*, 70, 72, 80, 95, 100; and cities, 16, 28, 37; in *Close to Home*, 28; in *Happiness*, 71, 202; sexual performance, 147; in *Traffic*, 192; in *Weeds*, 28, 195, 196, 197, 228
Duany, Andres, 36
Duany Plater-Zyberk (DPZ), 35, 65
Duncan, James, 128, 129
Duncan, Nancy, 128, 129
Durkheim, Émile, 193
Dushku, Eliza, 163
dystopia vision, 8, 11–12, 13, 15, 17, 29

East of Eden (1955), 168
Eastwood, Clint, 165
economic diversity, 38
economic recession, 146, 186, 219
economic reform, 4
economic status, 181, 211. *See also* social class
economic success, 193, 195, 208
economy, 78, 145–146, 186–187. *See also* finances
Edward Scissorhands (1990), 3
Ehrenreich, Barbara, 184, 185
elections: of 1992, 224; of 2012, 108
Elise, Kimberly, 206
Elsaesser, Thomas, 164, 173
End of Suburbia, The (2004), 215–217
ethnicity, 8, 222; and apartment plots, 14; and assimilation, 132–133; in *Desperate Housewives*, 104–105, 134–135; and homogeneous community, 128; and 1950s sitcoms, 12; visibility of, 128; in *Weeds*, 190. *See also* race
Executive Suite (1954), 14
Extreme Makeover: Home Edition (2003–2012), 85

Fair Housing Act, 111
Faludi, Susan, 146, 150–151
families, 11, 69–102; in action films, 165; alternative, as marginalized, 229; in *American Beauty*, 18–19, 26, 71–72, 78–81, 89–90, 94, 100; in American culture, 73–78; and Ariès, 78–79; in *Big Love*, 26, 71–72, 78, 81–83, 94, 95–97, 101, 225, 228; in *Breaking Bad*, 207; and Celebration, Fla., 38; in *Close to Home*, 208, 211; colonial, 243n44; and conservatism, 160; and consumption, 184; continuity of, 59–60; and crime narratives, 207; in crisis vs. in transition, 77; in *Desperate Housewives*, 126, 127, 226; and development of suburbs, 8; differing expectations for, 225; in domestic melodramas, 168, 169; extended, 99; in *Far from Heaven*, 19, 129; and front vs. back stages, 93; and Gemeinschaft, 74; heterosexual, 111–112; house as retreat for, 75; ideal space for, 75–76; in *The Incredibles*, 228; isolation of, 26; isolation vs. togetherness of, 241n15; in *The Joneses*, 228; in *The Kids Are All Right*, 221–222; and Lowe's advertising, 23–24; and masculinity, 149; in *Modern Family*, 222; in *Mr. & Mrs. Smith*, 169; mythical vision of, 99; and neighbors, 85; in 1950s, 99; nontraditional, 101; nuclear, 3–4, 26, 28, 67, 71, 75–76, 99, 100, 101, 102, 112, 113, 126, 229, 231; and Olmsted, 74; in *The Pacifier*, 157, 160, 227; in *Pleasantville*, 33; political debates about, 225; in promotional materials, 44–45, 51, 52, 57, 58–59; and public vs. private, 26, 70–71, 94; and *The Real Housewives* programs, 214, 219; and reality TV, 84–85; in *The Riches*, 228; and sex offenders, 203; in state of flux, 100; and suburban intertext, 23; and suburban perfection, 3–4; and suburbs, 4, 11, 28, 111–112; in *There Goes the Neighborhood*, 218; traditional, 26; in *True Lies*, 163; typical, 223–224; utopian vision of, 11, 12, 28; and visibility, 84; vulnerability and intimacy in, 93, 94; in *Weeds*, 195, 196, 207–208. *See also* children; fathers; mothers; parents
family action films, 163
family comedies, 177, 178
family/domestic melodrama, 20, 97, 175; in *Mr. & Mrs. Smith*, 163, 164, 165, 168, 169, 173, 175. *See also* melodrama

family sitcoms, 2, 12–13, 18, 28–29, 33
Family Ties (1982–1989), 15, 113
family values, 26, 77, 98–99, 102
Far from Heaven (2002), 2, 114, 169, 190, 224; African Americans in, 26, 119, 122–123, 129–130, 135, 138; camp sensibility in, 127–128; citizenship in, 27, 107, 137, 138, 139; community in, 104, 137, 138–139; and earlier films, 115–116; exclusion vs. inclusion in, 26–27, 104, 109, 119–123, 127–128, 135, 137–138, 139–140; families in, 19, 129; as fantasy, 227; gay bars in, 119, 121, 123; and Gemeinschaft vs. Gesellschaft, 106; heteronormativity in, 105, 119, 120, 122, 125; heterosexuality in, 123; homophobia in, 104; homosexuality in, 26, 115, 119–122, 123, 125, 127, 130–131, 138, 139; masculinity in, 142; minoritized space in, 123; minority groups in, 26–27; mothers in, 122; and *Mr. & Mrs. Smith*, 170; nostalgia in, 32; past in, 116, 117; queerness in, 125, 127; queer spaces in, 119–122, 123; race in, 26, 32, 104, 105, 115; segregation in, 123; sexuality in, 32, 105, 228; style in, 114–116, 118; suburban façade in, 18–19, 118, 228; theater in, 119–120, 123, 125; unresolved contradictions of, 230; use of space in, 119; visibility in, 128, 129–131, 136, 138; whites in, 26, 105, 119, 122, 123, 129; women in, 122; work/labor in, 129
Farmer, Brett, 117
Farmingville (2004), 217
Fassbinder, Rainer Werner, 115
Fast and the Furious, The (2001), 153
Father Knows Best (1954–1963), 12, 21, 33, 113, 168, 179, 183, 211, 226
fathers: and *Big Love*, 226; and early sitcoms, 226; and masculinity, 149; in *The Pacifier*, 157, 158–159, 161, 162; in *There Goes the Neighborhood*, 218. *See also* families
Federal Housing Administration (FHA), 6–7, 8, 110
femininity, 141; and action films, 166; in domestic melodramas, 168; and domestic sphere, 146; impossible expectations of, 229; and Lynch, 148; in *Mr. & Mrs. Smith*, 166–168, 169–170, 171–172, 173, 176; in *The Pacifier*, 154, 158, 161, 162, 166, 176; rigidly defined notions of, 231; and September 11 attacks, 148. *See also* women
feminism, 142; and camp, 117; and domestic privacy laws, 80; and masculinity, 145, 146; and *Mr. & Mrs. Smith*, 173; and public and private, 97; and role of women, 210; and September 11 attacks, 151
Ferrera, America, 17
FHM (magazine), 146

film noir, 16, 19, 20, 198
finances, 219; and bankruptcies, 146, 186; in *Breaking Bad*, 219; and Home Owners Loan Corporation, 6; and *Mr. Blandings Builds His Dream House*, 13; in 1950s movies and TV series, 179–180; and *The Real Housewives* programs, 219; in *Weeds*, 193–194, 196, 209–210, 219. *See also* economy
Finnigan, Jennifer, 198
firefighters, 150, 176
Fishman, Robert, 4, 10, 75, 109
Fogelson, Robert, 110
Ford, Faith, 161
Fox, Matthew, 176
Frank, Robert, 185
Friedan, Betty, 13; *The Feminine Mystique*, 9, 183
Friedman, Lawrence, 76
Fun with Dick and Jane (2005), 2, 114, 192, 219

Gallagher, Mark, 177
Gandolfini, James, 207
gangster films, 194, 206
Gans, Herbert, *The Levittowners*, 9
Garden State (2004), 2
Garrett, Brad, 157
gated communities, 213, 214, 218, 220, 222
Gates, The (2010), 3, 228
gay bars, 119, 121, 123
gay rights, 67, 142
gays. *See* homosexuals/homosexuality
Gemeinschaft, 73–74, 106, 112
gender, 11; in action films and melodramas, 165; and crime stories, 206–207; in domestic melodramas, 168, 169; and homes, 27; and Lowe's advertising, 25; in *Mr. & Mrs. Smith*, 165, 170, 171–172, 175; and 1950s sitcoms, 12; performative nature of, 117; political debates about, 225; reversal of traditional, 152; and suburban intertext, 23; and suburban myth, 231; and suburban perfection, 4; and suburbs as utopia, 28
Gesellschaft, 73–74, 106, 112
GI Bill. *See* Servicemen's Readjustment Act (GI Bill)
Gibson, Mel, 165
Glassie, Henry, 53
Gledhill, Christine, 169
Gleiberman, Owen, 19
Godfather, The, series (1972, 1974, 1990), 206
Goffman, Erving, 88
Goldbergs, The (1949–1956), 184
Goodman, Paul, *Growing Up Absurd*, 9
Good Times (1974–1979), 113, 180
Goodwin, Ginnifer, 72
Gould, Alexander, 196
government, 6–7, 8, 41, 76, 110, 111, 185. *See also* law

Graduate, The (1967), 113
Great Depression, 6, 145
Greenfield, Steve, 200
Growing Pains (1985–1992), 15, 113, 180

Habermas, Jürgen, 78, 242n23
Habersham, S.C., 52–53
Halberstam, Judith, 172
Happiness (1998), 2, 71, 114, 169, 200, 202–203, 228
Happy Days (1974–1984), 15, 113, 180
Haralovich, Mary Beth, 12, 180
Harper, Phillip Bryan, 97–98
Harris, Dianne, 75
Harris, Ed, 47
Hartman, Thom, *Screwed*, 186
Harwood, Sarah, 77
Hatcher, Teri, 124
Haussmann, Eugène-Georges, 5
Hayden, Dolores, 9, 183, 214; *A Field Guide to Sprawl*, 35
Haynes, Todd, 26, 115–116, 127, 227
Haysbert, Dennis, 104
Hayward, Keith, 191
Healy, Chris, 29
heist films, 194, 207
heteronormativity, 113, 114; and culture wars, 53; in *Desperate Housewives*, 105, 126, 127, 132; in *Far from Heaven*, 105, 119, 120, 122, 125; and politics, 67; in promotional materials, 66; and queer theory, 125; spatial, 125; in *There Goes the Neighborhood*, 218
heterosexuality: in action films, 165; and exclusion vs. inclusion, 26; in *Far from Heaven*, 123; and promotional materials, 51, 52; and suburbs, 109; and utopian vision of suburbs, 15
Higgins, Scott, 115–116
Highgrove, Charlotte, N.C., 52
Hispanics, 190
history, 34; as consensual and subjective, 57; as fabricated, 60–61; masculinity in, 145, 146; and memory, 56; and neotraditional marketing, 42; and neotraditional town planners, 41; and New Urbanism, 39; and nostalgia, 40, 60; and past, 56–57; in promotional materials, 46, 56–61, 65–66; selective use of, 60, 61. *See also* memory; nostalgia; past; tradition
Hobsbawm, Eric, 53
Hofer, Johannes, 39
Hollywood, 233
Holmlund, Chris, 172
Home From the Hill (1960), 168
Home Improvement (1991–1999), 180
homeland security, 139, 150, 160, 177
home loans, 110
homeowners' associations, 56, 62–63
homeownership, 6, 25, 132–133, 184
Home Owners Loan Corporation (HOLC), 6, 8, 110

homes: in *American Beauty*, 69, 70, 71, 73, 79, 80, 85, 89, 92, 93, 95, 212; and American Dream, 4, 193; and apartment plots, 14; appraisal practices for, 110; in *Big Love*, 72, 73, 81, 82, 83, 86, 90–91, 93, 96; in *Close to Home*, 27, 179, 198, 199, 204–205, 210; and construction industry, 6, 7; and consumption, 12, 183; in *Desperate Housewives*, 116–117, 126, 127, 132, 133, 134, 135, 212; in domestic melodramas, 164, 166; exclusion from, 109–114; in *Far from Heaven*, 104, 122–123, 129, 131; and fear of sex offenders, 202–203; and front vs. back stages, 88–89; and gender roles, 27; and government, 6–7, 110, 111; in "In the Suburbs," 216; and Lowe's advertising, 23, 24, 25; and masculinity, 149, 150; and middle class, 4, 5, 184, 212; and mortgage crisis, 23, 186, 187; in *Mr. & Mrs. Smith*, 151, 162, 163, 169, 171, 172, 174, 177; and nostalgia, 39, 40, 43, 44–45, 51; in *Office Space*, 213–214, 221; ownership of, 51, 132–133, 184; in *The Pacifier*, 151, 155, 156, 157, 160, 161, 162, 177; in *Pleasantville*, 33, 62, 68; and privacy, 71, 75–76, 78, 79, 84, 97, 231; in promotional materials, 44–45, 51, 103; and race discrimination, 8, 113; and *The Real Housewives* programs, 213, 219; and reality TV, 85; and redlining, 110; and restrictive covenants, 8, 109–111; and September 11 attacks, 150; single-family, 4, 5, 84; and skyscraper films, 15; social interaction in, 78–79; and suburbia as utopian space, 2; in *The Truman Show*, 62, 68; and visibility, 84, 87; in *Weeds*, 182, 190, 192, 208, 210; and women, 97, 99, 111–112, 141, 183, 210; and zoning laws, 109, 112. *See also* domesticity
Homicide: Life on the Street (1993–1999), 196
homoeroticism, 172–173
homogeneity, 8, 9, 128, 136, 137, 218
homophobia, 26, 104
homosexuals/homosexuality, 66, 99; in *American Beauty*, 95, 98, 114, 249n31; in *Big Love*, 114; and camp, 117; and cities vs. suburbs, 112; and citizenship, 108; in *Desperate Housewives*, 26, 104, 105, 125–126, 127, 130, 131–132, 138, 139; and exclusion vs. inclusion, 26, 104, 111–114; in *Far from Heaven*, 26, 104, 115, 119–122, 123, 125, 127, 130–131, 138, 139; and homogeneous community, 128; and identity commuters, 131; in *The Kids Are All Right*, 222; and marriage, 4, 76, 77, 108, 139; and masculinity, 145; in *Modern Family*, 222; in *The Pacifier*, 158; in postwar period, 99; and privacy, 97–98; in *There Goes the Neighborhood*, 218; visibility of, 128; of writers, directors, and producers,

224, 226; and zoning laws, 112. *See also* heteronormativity
Honeymooners, The (1955–1956), 14
Hope VI initiative, 37
Hopkins, Jeff, 10
Hornstein, Jeffrey M., 184, 193
horror films, 16, 20
Hours, The (2002), 2, 32, 114, 224, 228
How I Met Your Mother (2005–), "I Heart NJ" episode, 16
Humphreys, Laud, 87
Hunt, Helen, 16
Hunter, Holly, 171
Hussein, Saddam, 147
Huston, Shaun, 221

Ice Storm, The (1997), 2, 32, 71, 142, 164, 170, 228, 230–231
I Love Lucy (1951–1957), 14, 113
Imitation of Life (1959), 115
immigrants/immigration, 4, 26, 67, 107–108, 139
Incredibles, The (2004), 2, 170, 171, 228
industrialization, 6, 145–146, 243n44
Interstate Highway Act, 7
intertextuality, 19–23, 20–21, 34, 52, 72–73. *See also* suburban intertext
Iraq War, 147–148, 150, 178
irony, 115–116, 117, 127–128, 208, 253n51

Jackson, Kenneth T., 198
Jacobs, Jane, 74
Jacott, Carlos, 86
Jameson, Fredric, 34
Janney, Allison, 72
Jefferson, Thomas, 9
Jeffersons, The (1975–1985), 113
Jeffords, Susan, 148, 150, 161; *Hard Bodies*, 149
Jewkes, Yvonne, 193
Jews, 133
Jolie, Angelina, 143, 166–168, 173
Jones, Gerard, 12, 183–184
Joneses, The (2010), 3, 228
Judgment Night (1993), 16
Jurca, Catherine, 10, 21

Kapnek, Emily, 226
Keats, John, *The Crack in the Picture Window*, 13
Kelvinator, 12
Kendall, Diana, 185
Kids Are All Right, The (2010), 221–222
Kimmel, Michael, 145–146
Kindergarten Cop (1990), 149
Kline, Kevin, 71
Krämer, Peter, 163
Krieger, Alex, 37
Kunstler, James Howard, 216

Laguerre, Michel, 119
Lakewood Terrace (2008), 3, 114
landownership, 57, 58–59, 145

Lara Croft: Tomb Raider (2001), 166
Lara Croft Tomb Raider: The Cradle of Life (2003), 166
Latinos, 26, 129, 133–135, 138
law, 97, 109, 201–202, 203. *See also* crime; government
Leave It to Beaver (1957–1963), 2, 12, 21, 113, 179, 183, 211, 220
Lebouf, Shia, 71
Lefebvre, Martin, 17
legal dramas, 200, 202
Leibman, Nina, 183
Leitch, Thomas, 195, 200–201
Leonard, Jim, 224, 226, 227
lesbians. *See* homosexuals/homosexuality
Lethal Weapon series (1987, 1989, 1992, 1998), 156, 177
Levitt, Abraham, 7
Levitt, Alfred, 7
Levitt, William, 7, 8
Levitt and Sons, 7
Levittowns, 7, 9
liberals, 23, 225
Liebman, Nina, 12, 168, 169
Lindstrom, J. A., 207
Linney, Laura, 46
Lipsitz, George, 51, 54, 111, 133, 134, 184
Little Children (2006), 2, 21, 114, 164, 202, 228
Little Shop of Horrors (1985), 16
Livingston, Ron, 220
Longoria, Eva, 105
Lost (2004–2010), 176
Lowenthal, David, 39, 50, 56, 57
Lowe's, advertising for, 23–25, 29
Lymelife (2008), 3
Lynch, Jessica, 148

Macek, Steve, 16, 28
MacKinnon, Catharine, 97
MacKinnon, Kenneth, 146
MacLean, Alex, 37
Mad about You (1992–1999), "Valentine's Day" episode, 16–17
Mad Men (2007–), 3, 32, 228
Maguire, Tobey, 33, 49, 71
Make Room for Daddy (1953–1965), 14
Malco, Romany, 190
Man Apart, A (2003), 153
Man from U.N.C.L.E., The (1964–1968), 170
Man in the Gray Flannel Suit, The (1956), 13, 113, 141, 149, 159, 179
Mann, Michael, 207
Man Show, The (1999–2004), 146
manufacturing, 12, 182, 183, 220
marriage, 11, 99; in *American Beauty*, 72, 90, 94–95, 97; in *Big Love*, 225; in *Close to Home*, 206; and conservatism, 67; in *Far from Heaven*, 26, 131; forced, 101; in *Mr. & Mrs. Smith*, 163, 164, 168; and rape, 97; in *Revolutionary Road*, 142; same-sex, 4, 76, 77, 108, 139; and zoning laws, 112. *See also* polygamy

masculinity, 144; in action-adventure films, 27, 142, 165, 175; in *American Beauty*, 142; in *Big Love*, 142; in *Breaking Bad*, 142; and Cold War, 148, 149; complicit, 144, 158, 170, 174; in culture, 145, 146; domestic, 149, 150, 152; and domesticity, 27; in domestic melodramas, 168, 175; expansion of, 161, 162; and family, 149; in *Far from Heaven*, 142; and fathering, 149; female, 172; and feminine traits, 152–153; hegemonic, 144–145, 147, 149, 152, 153, 158, 161–162, 166, 170, 174, 176–177, 178; heroic, 27, 142, 144, 150, 151, 152–162, 172, 174, 175, 176, 177, 178, 229; hierarchical nature of, 144, 145; in history, 146; and home, 149, 150; homosexual, 145; in *The Ice Storm*, 142; impossible expectations of, 229; marginalized, 144, 145; and media, 146–147; and military, 147–148, 150, 151, 152, 154, 155; in *Mr. & Mrs. Smith*, 27, 142, 143–144, 145, 146, 151, 162, 163, 166–168, 169–170, 171–172, 173, 174, 175, 176–178; in *The Pacifier*, 27, 142, 143–144, 145, 146, 151, 152–162, 166, 176–178, 229; patriotic, 150; as plural, 144; in *Revolutionary Road*, 142; rigidly defined notions of, 231; and September 11 attacks, 27, 147–148, 175–176, 178; and sexual performance drugs, 147; subordinate, 144, 145, 158; in *There Goes the Neighborhood*, 218; violent, 27, 144; weak, 151, 158; weaker versions of, 151; and World War II, 148–149
Massey, Douglas, 111
Matlock (1986–1995), 206
Maxim (magazine), 146
McBride, Keally, 38
McDowell, Linda, 141
McPartland, John, *No Down Payment*, 13
media, 21, 33–34, 40, 51, 54, 70, 146–147
melodrama, 164, 165, 169–170, 173, 175, 177; and *Far from Heaven*, 104, 114, 115, 127. *See also* family/domestic melodrama
memory: collective, 50–52, 53, 54; as faulty, 50, 54; and history, 56; and knowledge, 53, 54, 56; and mediated mass culture, 51, 54; and nostalgia, 40, 51; personal, 53; in *Pleasantville*, 50; in promotional materials, 42, 43, 44, 46, 50, 51–52, 65–66; selective, 60, 66; in *The Truman Show*, 50, 54. *See also* history; nostalgia; past; tradition
men: and action films, 165; in crime narratives, 206; in domestic melodramas, 168; dominant position of, 144; in *Far from Heaven*, 122; in *Office Space*, 221; separate spheres of, 141; and waged labor, 243n44. *See also* masculinity
Mendes, Sam, 226

Menendez brothers, 200
men's movement, 146
Merton, Robert, 193
Messner, Steven F., 192–193, 194, 208
Mexican Americans, 60, 107
middle class, 5, 29, 215, 222, 226; and averageness, 223–224; in *Close to Home*, 28, 180, 181, 210, 211; and culture wars, 53; and development of suburbs, 6; and exclusion vs. inclusion, 26; in *Far from Heaven*, 122; fears for, 185–186, 187; and homes, 4, 5, 184, 212; and income, 185; and Lowe's advertising, 25; and masculinity, 145; and 1950s movies and TV series, 12, 180; and post–World War II era, 149; in promotional materials, 52, 66; as social norm, 184; and suburbs, 4, 212; and utopian vision of suburbs, 15; and waged labor, 243n44; in *Weeds*, 180, 181, 182, 187, 190, 191, 197, 211; women's sphere in, 141
Milesbrand company, 65
military, 108, 147–148, 149, 150, 152, 154, 155, 178, 249n31
Miller, Laura J., 241n15
Minelli, Vincente, 115
minorities, 26–27, 60, 67, 119, 123
Mission: Impossible (1966–1973), 170
Modern Family (2009–), 222
Monster (2003), 195
Moore, Julianne, 104
morality: in *Close to Home*, 181, 200, 201–205, 210, 211; in *CSI*, 204; in legal dramas, 200–201; in *Weeds*, 187, 195–197, 205, 211
mortgage crisis, 23, 186
mortgages, 6–7, 110, 186
mothers: in *Close to Home*, 202, 205–209, 210, 225; in *Desperate Housewives*, 209; in *Far from Heaven*, 122; and Friedan, 9; in *The Pacifier*, 161, 162; in *There Goes the Neighborhood*, 218; in *Weeds*, 195, 196, 197, 206, 207, 209, 210, 228, 253n51; and West Clay promotional video, 30; working, 225. *See also* children; families
Mountain's Edge, Nev., 45, 57
Mount Laurel, Ala., 103, 137
Mr. Blandings Builds His Dream House (1948), 13, 141, 179
Mr. Mom (1983), 152, 155
Mr. & Mrs. Smith (2005), 2, 17, 162–175; and action films, 163–164, 165, 169–170, 172–173, 177, 178; and *American Beauty*, 170, 173; comedy/humor in, 145, 169, 174, 177, 178; domesticity in, 170, 178; family in, 169; and *Far from Heaven*, 170; femininity in, 166–168, 169–170, 171–172, 173, 176; gender in, 165, 170, 171–172, 175; and genre hybridity, 169–170; home in, 151, 162, 163, 169, 171, 172, 174, 177; marriage in, 163, 164, 168; masculinity

in, 27, 142, 143–144, 145, 146, 151, 162, 163, 166–168, 169–170, 171–172, 173, 174, 175, 176–178; melodrama in, 163, 164, 165, 168, 169, 173, 175; and September 11 attacks, 27, 144, 177; sexuality in, 166, 168; suburban façade in, 227, 228; therapy in, 168, 169; violence in, 162, 166, 168, 170; women in, 151, 162, 169, 173–174; work in, 171
Mulvey, Laura, 175
Munsters, The (1964–1966), 12
murder, 200; in *American Beauty*, 2, 72, 100, 230; in *Big Love*, 102, 249n31; in *Close to Home*, 203; in *Desperate Housewives*, 124, 135; in *Disturbia*, 71, 227; in *Judgment Night*, 16; in *The Pacifier*, 143; in *Weeds*, 192, 194, 195
Murphy Brown (1988–1998), 77
musical comedy, 16
Mystic River (2003), 195

Napoleon III, 5
National Association of Realtors, 103
Native Americans, 58, 66
neighbors, 74; in *American Beauty*, 85–86, 87–88; in *Big Love*, 85, 86, 87–88; and Celebration, Fla., 38; and public and private, 85, 102; and suburban perfection, 4; and utopian vision of suburbs, 11; and visibility, 85; in *Weeds*, 190. *See also* communities
Neighbors, The (2012–), 3
New Jack City (1991), 16
New Urbanism, 35–39, 41–42, 50, 65, 216
9/11 attacks. *See* September 11, 2001 attacks
No Down Payment (1957), 3, 13, 14, 113, 141, 168, 179
nostalgia, 23, 25, 229; and change, 63; as clashing with freedom, knowledge, and growth, 32; and community, 103; continuity through, 41, 63; and control, 63–64; ersatz or armchair, 52; in *Far from Heaven*, 32; and history, 58, 60; as inhibiting self-awareness, 56; and Lowe's advertising, 24; manipulative potential of, 40; and marketing of suburban developments, 31; and media, 32, 33–34; and memory, 51, 66, 231; nature of, 50; and neotraditional developers, 40, 41–42; and New Urbanism, 35, 39; in *Pleasantville*, 25, 32, 33–35, 40, 49–50, 63, 64; and politics, 66–67; and postmodernity, 34; private vs. collective, 40; in promotional materials, 25, 30, 43, 50, 65–67; social role of, 39–40; and suburban intertext, 23, 68; in *The Truman Show*, 25, 31–32, 33–35, 40, 49–50, 63, 64; and urban renewal, 239n16; utopian dimension of, 25, 41–42. *See also* history; memory; past

NYPD Blue (1993–2005), 196, 206

Obama, Barack, 108, 186
Obama administration, 108
office buildings, 14, 212, 222
office parks, 213, 214, 220
Office Space (1999), 212–214, 220–221, 226, 232
Old School (2003), 174
Olmsted, Frederick Law, 74
Olsen, Mark, 223, 225, 226
O'Neill family, 59–60
Ontiveros, Lupe, 134
Ophuls, Max, 115
Orlando, Fla., 31, 38
Osborn, Guy, 200
Over the Edge (1979), 3, 15
Over the Hedge (2006), 2

Pacifier, The (2005), 2, 152–162, 224; and action films, 142, 154, 177, 178; children in, 152, 155, 156, 157–159, 161; comedy/humor in, 145, 155, 156, 177, 178, 229; domesticity in, 151, 154–155, 156, 159, 160, 178, 229; family in, 157, 160, 227; fathers in, 157, 158–159, 161, 162; femininity in, 154, 158, 161, 162, 166, 176; happy ending of, 229; homes in, 151, 155, 156, 157, 160, 161, 162, 177; homosexuality in, 158; masculinity in, 27, 142, 143–144, 145, 146, 151, 152–162, 166, 176–178, 229; mothers in, 161, 162; murder in, 143; patriarchy in, 154, 156, 158; and September 11 attacks, 27, 144, 156, 160, 177; and *The Sound of Music*, 249n28; suburban façade in, 227; violence in, 156, 159, 160–162; women in, 161
Palin, Sarah, 23, 67
parents: and American Dream, 208; differing expectations for, 225; and West Clay promotional video, 30. *See also* children; families; fathers; mothers
Paris, France, 5
Parker, Mary-Louise, 181, 189, 197
Parrish, Hunter, 196
past: artificial construction of, 34; in *Far from Heaven*, 116, 117; and history, 56–57; imagined, 33; and New Urbanism, 38, 39; and nostalgia, 40; in *Pleasantville* and *The Truman Show*, 49–50; in promotional materials, 42–46, 50, 52, 65–66; as static, unchanging, 56; visualization of, 42–50. *See also* history; memory; nostalgia; tradition
pastoral, 8–9
Patano, Tonye, 190
patriarchy, 12, 144, 145, 146, 154, 156, 158. *See also* fathers
Patriot Act, 76
Patterns (1956), 14
Paxton, Bill, 72

pedestrians, 35, 37, 38, 41
Perils of Pauline, The (1914), 165
Perin, Constance, 85
Perkins, Elizabeth, 189, 190
Peterson, Laci, 200
Philadelphia, Pa., 7
Pillow Talk (1959), 14
Pitch Black (2000), 153
Pitfall (1948), 149
Pitt, Brad, 143, 166–168
Plater-Zyberk, Elizabeth, 36
Pleasantville (1998), 2, 17, 113–114;
appearance vs. truth in, 46; black and
white vs. color in, 48–49; change in, 56,
64; and conservatism, 225; control in,
61, 62–64; happy ending of, 229–230;
homes in, 33, 62, 68; and knowledge,
42, 53, 54–55; and liberal vs.
conservative groups, 225; memory in,
50; and neotraditional communities,
42, 67; and 1950s sitcoms, 48; nostalgia
in, 25, 32, 33–35, 40, 49–50, 63, 64;
promotional materials, 42, 52, 68;
reality vs. artifice in, 46, 48–50, 230;
self-reflexivity of, 49, 68; suburban
façade in, 118, 228; and suburban
intertext, 67–68; and tradition, 50
Plummer, Christopher, 249n28
police/courtroom procedural, 27
police officers, 147, 150, 178, 203, 206
polygamy, 72, 81–83, 86, 96, 98, 101–102,
228. *See also* marriage
poor people, 5, 36, 51, 124, 185, 187, 191
Practice, The (1997–2004), 200, 201
private sphere. *See* public and private
procedural drama, 20
producers, 224, 225–226
promotional materials, 25, 30–31, 34,
198, 215; and *American Beauty*, 73; and
Big Love, 73; and community, 103, 104,
106, 137; crime in, 198; and *Desperate
Housewives*, 117; and *The End of Suburbia*,
216–217; and families, 51, 52; and
family genealogies, 57, 58–59; and
heterosexuality, 51, 52; and history,
57–61, 65–66; and homes, 44–45, 51,
103; and memory, 43, 44, 46, 50, 51–52,
65–66; and middle class, 52, 66; and
natural history, 57–58; and nostalgia,
25, 30, 43, 50, 65–67; and past, 42–46,
50, 52, 56, 65–66; and *Pleasantville*,
42, 52, 68; and public/private tension,
75; and suburban intertext, 68; and
tradition, 46, 50, 52–53, 64; and *The
Truman Show*, 42, 52, 68; and visual
presentation, 42–45; and whites, 51, 52.
See also advertising
prostitution, 198, 201, 204, 205
public and private, 10, 11, 231; in *American
Beauty*, 26, 69–70, 71–72, 78–81, 83,
94–95, 97, 98, 100, 102; in American
culture, 73–78; and Arendt, 242n23;

and Ariès, 78–79; and automobiles,
95; and autonomy, 97; in *Big Love*, 26,
71–72, 78, 81–83, 94, 95–97, 98, 101–102,
230; and conservatism, 102; contextual
distinctions between, 82–83;
definitions of, 78–80; in *Desperate
Housewives*, 71, 230; and families, 26,
70–71, 94, 97–102; and front vs. back
stages, 88, 92–93, 94; and Habermas,
242n23; and heteronormativity, 125;
and homes, 71, 75–76, 78, 79, 84, 97,
231; and homosexuals, 97–98; and
Jacobs, 74; and law, 97; legal, 79–80;
liberal-economistic model of, 78; and
mass media, 70; and neighbors, 102;
onion model of, 79; and performance,
88–94; and promotional materials,
75; and residential design, 74–75; and
science and technology, 76; social
context for, 78–80; and suburbs, 70–71;
in *The Truman Show*, 71; and visibility,
78, 83–88, 87; in *Weeds*, 230. *See also*
secrecy; visibility
public housing, 37
Pyfrom, Shawn, 105

Quaid, Dennis, 104
Quayle, Dan, 77
Queer Nation, 125
queer theory, 125

race, 8, 10, 11; and apartment plots, 14;
and conservatism, 67; in *Desperate
Housewives*, 104–105; exclusion and
inclusion by, 8, 26, 104, 109–111,
113–114; in *Far from Heaven*, 26, 32, 104,
105, 115; and Habermas, 242n23; and
homogeneous community, 128; and
Lowe's advertising, 24; and masculinity,
145; and 1950s sitcoms, 12; in *There Goes
the Neighborhood*, 218; in *Weeds*, 190–191;
and zoning laws, 109. *See also* African
Americans; ethnicity
Radiant City (2006), 217
Radnor, Josh, 16
Rafter, Nicole, 195
Rahm, Kevin, 105
Rambo series (1982, 1985, 1988), 149
Ramsey, JonBenet, 200
Rancho Santa Margarita, Orange County,
Calif., 59–60
rape, 80, 97, 202, 203–204, 205
Rapping, Elayne, 202
Ray, Robert, 177, 209
Rayner, Jonathan, 207
Real Housewives, The (series), 218–220, 226
Real Housewives of Atlanta, The (2008–),
3, 219
Real Housewives of Beverly Hills, The
(2010–), 219
Real Housewives of New Jersey, The
(2009–), 3, 219

Real Housewives of Orange County, The (2006–), 3, 84–85, 180, 213, 218–219, 220

realism, 215, 227

reality television programs, 84–85, 215, 217–218

Rear Window (1954), 14

Rebel without a Cause (1955), 13, 164

Redbook (magazine), "In the Suburbs," 182, 215–216

Reign over Me (2007), 176

Reiser, Paul, 16

Republican Party, 186, 224

Rescue Me (2004–2011), 176

restrictive covenants. *See under* homes

Revolutionary Road (2008), 3, 13, 19, 32, 142, 169, 221, 226, 228

Reynolds, Malvina, "Little Boxes," 188

Ricci, Christina, 71

Richardson, Niall, 117

Riches, The (2007–2008), 3, 180, 192, 200, 228

Riesman, David, 13; *The Lonely Crowd*, 9

Rizzoli & Isles (2010–), 207

romantic comedies, 176

Roosevelt (FDR) administration, 6, 110

Roseanne (1988–1997), 180

Rosenfeld, Richard, 192–193, 194, 208

Ross, Andrew, 38

Ross, Gary, 225

Rössler, Beate, 79, 86–87, 92

Rushbrook, Dereka, 121

Salt (2010), 166

Sanford and Son (1972–1977), 113

Santorum, Rick, 67

Schatz, Thomas, 194

Scheffer, Will, 223, 225, 226

Schleier, Merrill, *Skyscraper Cinema*, 14–15

Schneider, William, 224

Schoeman, Ferdinand, 79, 83, 93

Schwarzenegger, Arnold, 153, 162–163, 165

science fiction, 16

Seaside, Fla., 35, 65

Seaside Institute, "Marketing New Urban and Smart Growth Communities" seminar, 65

secrecy, 83, 95, 96, 97, 100. *See also* public and private; visibility

Secure Fence Act of 2006, 107

segregation, 109–114, 119, 123

self-reflexivity, 34, 48, 49, 68

Sennett, Richard, 128

September 11, 2001 attacks, 76; and masculinity, 27, 144, 147–148, 150–151, 175–176, 177, 178; and *Mr. & Mrs. Smith*, 27, 144, 177; and *The Pacifier*, 27, 144, 156, 160, 177

Servicemen's Readjustment Act (GI Bill), 7, 13

Seven Year Itch, The (1955), 14, 149

Sevigny, Chloë, 72

sex offenders, 202–203

sexuality, 10, 11; in *American Beauty*, 69, 228; in *Desperate Housewives*, 104, 228; exclusion and inclusion by, 26; in *Far from Heaven*, 32, 105, 228; in *Happiness*, 228; in *The Ice Storm*, 228; in *Little Children*, 228; in *Mad Men*, 228; in *Mr. & Mrs. Smith*, 166, 168; performative nature of, 117; in *Revolutionary Road*, 228; and suburban façade, 228; in *Swingtown*, 228; in *Weeds*, 228

Shadoian, Jack, 194

Shapiro, Michael, 77, 84

Shelley v. Kraemer, 110–111

Sheridan, Nicolette, 209

Shield, The (2002–2008), 196

Sibley, David, 139

Silverstone, Roger, 9, 223

Simmon, Scott, *The Invention of the Western Film*, 19

Singer, Ben, 165

Sirk, Douglas, 115

situation comedies (sitcoms), 20; and consumption, 183–184; and *Desperate Housewives*, 125; early, 3, 225; in era after September 11 attacks, 176; family, 2, 12–13, 18, 28–29, 33; and neotraditional communities, 67; of 1950s and 1960s, 2, 12, 48, 67, 179–180, 183; postwar, 73; single-father, 161; and utopian vision of suburbs, 12–13

skyscraper films, 14

Snow, Brittany, 156

social class, 5, 6, 9, 10; and consumption, 184; exclusion and inclusion by, 26; and masculinity, 145; political debates about, 225; in *Weeds*, 190, 191. *See also* middle class; poor people; wealthy class

social problem films, 16

socioeconomic status, 180, 187

Soong, Lucille, 134

Sopranos, The (1999–2007), 114, 180, 192, 200, 207

Sound of Music, The (1965), 249n28

Spacey, Kevin, 69

Spain, Daphne, *Gendered Spaces*, 141

Speck, Jeff, 36

Spigel, Lynn, 10

Spike TV, 146

Splendor in the Grass (1961), 164

Springfield Fort Mill, S.C., 25, 31, 45, 58–59

Spy Next Door, The (2010), 170

spy series, 170–171

stages, front vs. back, 88–94

Stallone, Sylvester, 153

Stam, Robert, 68

Stepford Wives, The (1975), 3, 15, 21, 113

Stepford Wives, The (2004), 2

Strong, Brenda, 116

Stuff (magazine), 146

suburban façade, 24, 29; ambiguity introduced by, 231–233; in *American Beauty*, 18–19, 90, 100, 118; of American Dream, 205; in *Big Love*, 90–91, 118; in *Close to Home*, 181; in *Desperate Housewives*, 18, 118, 125; in *Disturbia*, 227; and double lives, 227–229; in *Far from Heaven*, 18–19, 118, 228; and front vs. back stages, 89; of homogeneity, 137; in *The Hours*, 228; in *Mr. & Mrs. Smith*, 227, 228; in *The Pacifier*, 227; in *Pleasantville*, 118, 228; preservation of, 181; sexuality in, 228; in *The Truman Show*, 118, 228; in *Weeds*, 181, 228; and work, 228
suburban intertext, 20–23, 67–68. *See also* intertextuality
Suburban Life (magazine), 112
Suburban Shootout (2006–2007), 3
suburban sprawl, 31, 35–36
suburbs, 67; city as contrast to, 8, 11, 15–16, 28, 106, 109, 198, 237n32; as cultural construct, 10–11, 139; development of, 5–8; different versions of, 212–222; population of, 4, 8, 9, 223, 224–225
Suburgatory (2011–), 3, 21, 22, 226
suicide, 2, 117, 205
Summer Place, A (1959), 164
superheroes, 144
Supreme Court, 109, 110–111, 112
Surviving Suburbia (2009), 3
Sutherland, Kiefer, 176
Suvari, Mena, 69
Swingtown (2008), 3, 32, 228

Takacs, Stacy, 147
Tasker, Yvonne, 165
Tea Party movement, 66, 186–187
teen comedy, 198
Terminator series (1984, 1991, 2003, 2009), 156
Terminator 2: Judgment Day (1991), 149, 165
There Goes the Neighborhood (2009), 3, 218, 220
Thieriot, Max, 155
Three Men and a Baby (1987), 152, 155
Till, K., 59–60, 61
To Kill a Mockingbird (1962), 206
Tönnies, Ferdinand, 73–74, 106
tradition, 25; and cultural construction, 53; and Gemeinschaft, 74; and knowledge, 53, 56; and *Pleasantville*, 50; political debates about, 225; in promotional materials, 46, 50, 52–53, 64; as selectively constructed, 50; and suburban intertext, 23; and suburban myth, 231; and suburban perfection, 3; and *The Truman Show*, 50. *See also* history; memory; past
Traditional Neighborhood Developments (TNDs). *See* communities: neotraditional
traditional values, 30, 64, 67

Traffic (2000), 2, 192, 200
Tripplehorn, Jeanne, 72
True Lies (1994), 162–163, 170
Truman Show, The (1998), 2, 17; appearance vs. truth in, 46–48, 49–50; change in, 64; control in, 61–62, 63–64; evolution over time in, 56; happy ending of, 229–230; homes in, 62, 68; and knowledge, 42, 53–55, 56; and memory, 50, 54; and neotraditional communities, 67, 68; nostalgia in, 25, 31–32, 33–35, 40, 63, 64; privacy in, 71; and promotional materials, 42, 52, 68; reality vs. artifice in, 46–48, 49–50, 230; self-reflexivity of, 68; suburban façade in, 118, 228; and suburban intertext, 67–68; and tradition, 50; as utopia, 63
Trump, Donald, 108
24 (2001–2010), 176
Tyagi, Amelia Warren, *The Two Income Trap*, 186

Ugly Betty (2006–2010), "Sisters on the Verge of a Nervous Breakdown" episode, 17
underdog figure, 194
Updike, John, 13
urban renewal, 8
U.S. Constitution, 66–67
utopia, 3–4, 8, 17, 23, 63, 231; and families, 11, 12, 28; and heterosexuality, 15; and homes, 2; and middle class, 15; and neighbors, 11; and nostalgia, 25, 41–42; and situation comedies, 12–13; and whites, 15; and World War II, 12

Valentine, Gill, 125
VA loans, 7
Vaughn, Vince, 173
Venkatesh, Alladi, 185
Victor, Renee, 208
Vietnam War, 149, 150
Vietnam War films, 161
Village of Belle Terre v. Boraas, 112
Village of West Clay, Indianapolis, Ind., 25, 30–31, 45, 51–52, 53
Villages, The, Fla., 42–46, 60–61
violence: in action-adventure film, 142; and masculinity at end of World War II, 149; in *Mr. & Mrs. Smith*, 162, 166, 168, 170; in *The Pacifier*, 156, 159, 160–162; against women, 97, 99, 101
Virgin Suicides, The (1999), 2, 32
visibility, 83–88, 136; in *American Beauty*, 85–86, 94; in *Big Love*, 85, 86–87, 94; in *Desperate Housewives*, 128, 130, 131–132, 136, 138; in *Far from Heaven*, 128, 129–131, 136, 138; and front vs. back stages, 89; physical and social, 87. *See also* public and private; secrecy

Walt Disney Company, 37–38
Wanted (2008), 166

Warner, Sam Bass, 6

War on Terror, 76, 147, 148, 150, 151, 155, 156–157

Warren, Elizabeth, *The Two Income Trap*, 186

Wasilewski, Audrey, 86

Watch, The (2012), 3

Watkins, Tuc, 105

wealthy class, 5, 6, 51, 185; in *Desperate Housewives*, 124, 132, 133; in *The Real Housewives* programs, 213, 214, 218–219; and *Weeds*, 182

Wedding Crashers (2005), 174

Weeds (2005–2012), 3, 114; adultery in, 197; American Dream in, 27–28, 182, 187, 192, 193–194, 195, 209; business in, 182, 190, 191–192, 194–195, 210; children in, 207–208; comedy/humor in, 181, 195, 200, 230; conformity in, 188; consumption in, 180, 181, 182, 187–191, 209, 211; crime in, 182, 187, 191–192, 193–197, 200, 204, 209, 210, 211, 253n51; domesticity in, 210; drugs in, 28, 195, 196, 197, 228; and economic status, 181; families in, 195, 196, 207–208; finances in, 193–194, 196, 209–210, 219; "Free Goat" episode, 196; homes in, 182, 190, 192, 208, 210; middle class in, 180, 181, 182, 187, 190, 191, 197, 211; morality in, 187, 195–197, 205, 211; mothers in, 195, 196, 197, 206, 207, 209, 210, 228, 253n51; and public vs. private, 230; race in, 190–191; sexuality in, 228; social class in, 190, 191; suburban façade in, 181, 228; and suburban intertext, 21; wealthy class in, 182; women in, 181, 209, 210; work in, 27–28, 181–182, 194, 195, 207, 208, 210–211; working class in, 190, 191

Weintraub, Jeff, 79

westerns, 19, 20

whites, 113, 114; and apartment plots, 14; in *Close to Home*, 28; and culture wars, 53; in *Desperate Housewives*, 105; and development of suburbs, 8; and exclusion vs. inclusion, 26; in *Far from Heaven*, 26, 105, 119, 122, 123, 129; and FHA, 110; and flight from central cities, 8; and Lowe's advertising, 24; and masculinity, 145; in *Modern Family*, 222; in promotional materials, 51, 52, 60, 66; and restrictive covenants, 109–110; and utopian vision of suburbs, 15

Who's the Boss? (1984–1992), 15

Whyte, William H., 13; *The Organization Man*, 9

Willemen, Paul, 115

Williams, Vanessa, 105

Willingboro, N.J., 7

Willis, Bruce, 165

Willis, Sharon, 123

Wilson, Janelle, 50, 63

Wilson, Sloan, *The Man in the Gray Flannel Suit*, 13

Witherspoon, Reese, 33

Wojcik, Pamela Robertson, *The Apartment Plot*, 13–14, 15

Woman's World (1954), 14

women: in action films, 165–166; in *American Beauty*, 173; and Beecher, 111–112; in *Close to Home*, 181, 205–209, 210; and consumption, 183; in crime narratives, 206–207; in *Desperate Housewives*, 117–118; in domestic melodramas, 168; empowerment of, 165; in *Far from Heaven*, 122; and feminism, 210; and Friedan, 9; and Habermas, 242n23; and homes, 97, 99, 111–112, 141, 183, 210; and Iraq War, 148; of Levittown, 9; and melodramas, 165; in *Mr. & Mrs. Smith*, 151, 162, 169, 173–174; in *The Pacifier*, 161; and privacy, 97; and Rancho Santa Margarita, 60; in *The Real Housewives* programs, 213, 218–219; separate spheres of, 141; as strong, 151; subordination of, 144; victimization of, 165; violence against, 97, 99, 101; in *Weeds*, 181, 209, 210; and work, 97, 99, 243n44. *See also* femininity

Woodard, Alfre, 105

working class, 5, 14, 180, 190, 191

work/labor, 4, 180, 212; and American Dream, 193, 210, 231; and children, 243n44; in *Close to Home*, 181, 205–209, 210–211, 225; corporate, 221; in *Desperate Housewives*, 134; in *Far from Heaven*, 129; in *Farmingville*, 217; and gender, 183; and Lowe's advertising, 24; and mortgage crisis, 23; and mothers, 225; in *Mr. & Mrs. Smith*, 171; and New Urbanism, 36; in *Office Space*, 220, 221; and Rancho Santa Margarita, 60; and skyscraper films, 15; and suburban façade, 228; in *True Lies*, 163; in *Weeds*, 27–28, 181–182, 194, 195, 207, 208, 210–211; and women, 97, 99, 243n44. *See also* business

World War I, 109

World War II, 6, 7, 99, 150; era following, 148–149, 152, 159–160, 182; and masculinity, 145; and utopian vision of suburbs, 12

writers, 224, 225–226

Written on the Wind (1956), 115, 164

Wuthnow, Robert, 77

Xena: Warrior Princess (1995–2001), 166

X-Files, The (1993–2002), 170

xXx (2002), 153

Yanich, Danilo, 200

Yates, Andrea, 200

Yates, Richard, *Revolutionary Road*, 13

Yeo, Gwendoline, 134

York, Morgan, 157

ABOUT THE AUTHOR

DAVID R. COON is an assistant professor of media studies at the University of Washington Tacoma. He teaches courses in film studies, television studies, and video production. He has published essays examining film, television, advertising, gender, sexuality, and space in the *Journal of Popular Film and Television*, *Feminist Media Studies*, the *Journal of Homosexuality*, and *Polymath: A Journal of Interdisciplinary Arts and Sciences*.